Also by Robert Garner

ANIMALS, POLITICS AND MORALITY

ANIMAL RIGHTS: The Changing Debate (*editor*)

BRITISH POLITICAL PARTIES TODAY (*with Richard Kelly*)

ENVIRONMENTAL POLITICS

Political Animals

Animal Protection Politics in Britain and the United States

Robert Garner
Lecturer in Politics
University of Leicester

First published in Great Britain 1998 by
MACMILLAN PRESS LTD
Houndmills, Basingstoke, Hampshire RG21 6XS and London
Companies and representatives throughout the world

A catalogue record for this book is available from the British Library.

ISBN 0–333–61581–6 hardcover
ISBN 0–333–73000–3 paperback

First published in the United States of America 1998 by
ST. MARTIN'S PRESS, INC.,
Scholarly and Reference Division,
175 Fifth Avenue, New York, N.Y. 10010

ISBN 0–312–21208–9

Library of Congress Cataloging-in-Publication Data
Garner, Robert, 1960–
Political animals : animal protection politics in Britain and the
United States / Robert Garner.
p.   cm.
Includes bibliographical references and index.
ISBN 0–312–21208–9 (cloth)
1. Animal welfare—Great Britain.   2. Animal welfare—United
States.   3. Animal welfare—Political aspects—Great Britain.
4. Animal welfare—Political aspects—United States.   I. Title.
HV4545.A4G37 1997
179'.3'0941—dc21   97–38262
                                                              CIP

This book is printed on paper suitable for recycling and made from fully managed and
sustained forest sources.

10 9 8   7   6   5   4   3   2   1
07 06 05 04 03 02 01 00 99 98

Printed in Great Britain by
The Ipswich Book Company Ltd
Ipswich, Suffolk

Contents

List of Tables   viii
List of Abbreviations   x
Acknowledgements   xiii

Introduction   1
Animal protection and mainstream public policy   2
Pluralism, policy networks and animal
    protection   5
A guide to the chapters   8
Pluralism, animal protection and research
    methodology   12

1   **The Institutional Framework of Animal
Protection**   16
Legislative support for animal protection   16
Sectorization and the structure of animal
    protection decision-making   21
Institutional structures and animal protection
    in Britain   22
Institutional structures and animal protection in
    the United States   29

2   **The Economics and Politics of Animal
Exploitation**   39
The political economy of wildlife and animal
    entertainment   40
The economic structure of intensive agriculture   43
The animal research community   47
The political organization of the animal-use lobby   50

3   **The Animal Protection Movement:
Recruitment, Ideology and Strategy**   68
Mancur Olson and membership recruitment   68
Rational choice and human interests   71
Group maintenance and the role of the
    entrepreneur   73

Animal rights and solidaristic collectivism –
  A post-Olsonian agenda   76
Animal rights and the 'new welfarism'   81

4 **Lobbying for Animals**   93
The development of the modern animal
  protection movement   93
Key political actors   95
Financial resources and political influence   100
Organizational alliances and policy
  sectorization   103

5 **Parliament and Animal Protection**   109
Parliament's limited role   109
Parliament and hunting   111
Legislation, scrutiny and agenda setting   114
The extent of animal advocacy in parliament   115
Profile of animal advocates in the House   116

6 **American Legislators and Animal Protection**   122
The scope of Congressional support   122
Conclusion   136

7 **The Politics of Farm Animal Welfare in the
United States**   139
Historical origins and development of the
  agricultural policy community   140
Congressional committees and farm animal
  welfare   141
Congress, USDA and farm animals   146
A brighter future for farm animal welfare?   149

8 **The Politics of Farm Animal Welfare in Britain** 151
The challenge of animal welfare   152
A damage limitation exercise?   153
A genuine attempt to balance interests?   162
A policy community under siege   169

9 **The Politics of Animal Research in Britain**   176
Origins of the animal research policy network   176
Littlewood to Mellor   177

1986 Animals (Scientific Procedures) Act 182
Ten Years on – have the animals benefited? 187
The three Rs 192
Enforcement 198

10 **The Politics of Animal Research in the
United States** 202
Public pressure and Congressional action 202
Laboratory Animal Welfare Act 1966 202
Improved Standards for Laboratory Animals
Act 1985 205
Pet Theft Act 1990 208
What has Congress achieved? 209
Executive agencies and animal testing 214
The issue network and regulatory obstruction 215
Enforcement failures 223

**Conclusion: Animal Protection and
Pluralist Politics** 229
The degree of policy sectorization 229
Power structures within networks 230
The relationship between structure and outcome 231
Explaining change 234

Appendix I: Database Design 238
Appendix II: Questionnaire Design 239
Notes 240
Bibliography 267
Index 278

List of Tables

1.1 Bills on animal protection introduced in the British Parliament, 1950–95   17

1.2 Bills and resolutions on animal protection and wildlife conservation introduced in the US Congress in selected years between 1955 and 1968   19

1.3 Animal protection and wildlife conservation bills and resolutions introduced in the US House of Representatives, 1985–94   20

1.4 Targets of Parliamentary questions on animal protection and wildlife conservation, 1985–95   22

2.1 Interested parties at selected Congressional Hearings on the Endangered Species Act, 1973–82   40

2.2 Politically active animal use organizations in Britain and the United States   52

2.3 Animal welfare bills in Britain and the United States used in questionnaire   60

4.1 Reputional survey of British and American animal protection and wildlife conservation groups   96

4.2 The budgets of the major animal protection and wildlife conservation organizations in the United States, 1996   99

5.1 The top 36 animal advocates in the House of Commons, 1987–92   117

5.2 Geographical profile of MPs interested in animal issues, 1987–92   119

5.3 Party labels of MPs interested in animal issues, 1987–92   120

5.4 Support for animal issues in the House of Commons by gender, 1987–92   121

6.1 Congressional supporters of animal protection and wildlife conservation initiatives, 1985–94   123

6.2 Intensity of support for animal protection and wildlife conservation measures in the House of Representatives, 1985–94   123

6.3   Representatives displaying the greatest interest in
      wildlife conservation and animal protection bills
      and resolutions in the House, 1985–94   125
6.4   Support for wildlife measures in the US House of
      Representatives, 1985–94   126
6.5   Support for animal protection measures in the US
      House of Representatives, 1985–94   126
6.6   Geographical profile of Representatives
      interested in Animal Issues, 1985–94   128
6.7   Rural and urban profile of Representatives
      interested in animal issues, 1985–94   129
6.8   Party strength in the House of Representatives,
      1985–94   130
6.9   Party labels of Representatives interested in
      animal issues, 1985–94   131
6.10 Women in the House of Representatives and
      animal issues, 1985–94   132
6.11 Female Representatives most interested in animal
      issues, 1985–94   133
6.12 The age profile of Representatives, 1985–92   134
6.13 Age profile of Representatives interested in animal
      issues, 1985–92   134
9.1   Animal Procedures Committee: membership as at
      31 December 1994   190
9.2   Scientific procedures, 1987–94   193
9.3   Animal suffering in UK scientific procedures,
      1987–93   195
9.4   Enforcement under the 1986 Animals (Scientific
      Procedures) Act, 1987–94   199

List of Abbreviations

AAMR	Association for the Advancement of Medicine by Research
ABPI	Association of the British Pharmaceutical Industry
ABR	Association for Biomedical Research
AFBF	American Farm Bureau Federation
AFIA	American Feed Industry Association
AHA	American Humane Association
AMA	American Medical Association
AMPI	Associated Milk Producers Inc.
AMRIC	Animals in Medicines Research Information Centre
APC	Animal Procedures Committee
APHIS	Animal and Plant Health Inspection Service
ASPCA	American Society for the Prevention of Cruelty to Animals
AVMA	American Veterinary Medical Association
AWD	Animal Welfare Division
AWI	Animal Welfare Institute
BMA	British Medical Association
BPF	British Poultry Federation
BSE	Bovine Spongiform Encephalopathy
BST	Bovine Somatotropin
BUAV	British Union for the Abolition of Vivisection
BVA	British Veterinary Association
CITES	Convention on the International Trade in Endangered Species
CIWF	Compassion in World Farming
CJD	Creutzfeldt Jakob Disease
COPA	Comité des Organizations Professionelles Agricoles
CRAE	Committee for the Reform of Animal Experimentation
CTFA	Cosmetic, Toiletry and Fragrance Association
DHSS	Department of Health and Social Security
ECVAM	European Centre for the Validation of Alternative Methods
EDM	Early Day Motion
EU	European Union

FARM	Farm Animal Reform Movement
FAWAC	Farm Animal Welfare Advisory Council
FAWC	Farm Animal Welfare Council
FDA	Food and Drug Administration
FRAME	Fund for the Replacement of Animals in Medical Experiments
GATT	General Agreement on Tariffs and Trade
GECCAP	General Election Coordinating Committee for Animal Protection
HHS	Department of Health and Human Services
HSUS	Humane Society of the United States
IACUC	Institutional Animal Care and Use Committee
IES	Investigative and Enforcement Services Unit
IFAW	International Fund for Animal Welfare
LACS	League Against Cruel Sports
MAFF	Ministry of Agriculture, Fisheries and Food
MP	Member of Parliament
NABR	National Association for Biomedical Research
NAVS	National Antivivisection Society
NFU	National Farmers Union
NIH	National Institutes of Health
NRA	National Rifle Association
NSMR	National Society for Medical Research
NWF	National Wildlife Federation
OECD	Organisation for Economic Cooperation and Development
OIRA	Office of Information and Regulatory Affairs
OMB	Office of Management and Budget
OPRR	Office for the Protection of Research Risks
PAC	Political Action Committee
PETA	People for the Ethical Treatment of Animals
PHS	Public Health Service
PMA	Pharmaceutical Manufacturers Association
PMB	Private Members Bill
RDS	Research Defence Society
REAC	Regulatory Enforcement and Animal Care
RSPB	Royal Society for the Protection of Birds
RSPCA	Royal Society for the Prevention of Cruelty to Animals
SVS	State Veterinary Service
USDA	United States Department of Agriculture

UFAW   Universities Federation for Animal Welfare
WSPA   World Society for the Protection of Animals
WWF   World Wide Fund for Nature

Acknowledgements

A research project stretching over three years necessarily incurs many debts. As a participant observer I have been very fortunate in being able to see the work of the animal protection movement at close hand. Some of those whom I met in the course of my research have become good friends too. The number of people who have gladly given up their time to answer questions and furnish me with information is far too numerous for me to mention all of them here. A list of those who completed questionnaires and/or submitted themselves to a formal interview is included in the bibliography. To all of them a big thank you.

I wish to thank the library staff at the following institutions: the British Library of Political and Economic Science, MAFF, the Library of Congress (particular thanks to Henry Cohen), the American Embassy, and the universities of Exeter and Leicester. I wish also to express my gratitude to the RSPCA who provided a grant which was used for travel, book purchases and replacement teaching costs.

Numerous individuals helped with my research. Conversations with Jim Jasper and Andrew Rowan were always illuminating and stimulating and I have learnt a great deal from them. Julie Barbara's computer expertise put at my disposal was priceless and her friendship is much valued. I am also indebted to Sonia Burgess, of the politics department at Exeter University, who did the time-consuming and necessary job of collecting information from Hansard. Equally important was the database work done by June Garner, John Garner, Rachel Heywood and Natasha Sampson.

Finally, I would like to put on record in particular my admiration for Richard Ryder, Adele Douglass, Kim Stallwood and Henry Spira. Thank you for your support, encouragement and friendship.

Leicester   ROBERT GARNER

Introduction

This book explores the character of animal welfare policy-making in Britain and the United States. Comparative public policy has been defined as the study of 'how, why, and to what extent different governments pursue particular courses of action or inaction'.[1] In the same tradition, this study seeks to ask who makes decisions impinging on the well-being of animals, who attempts to influence these decisions, why certain decisions are taken rather than others, how legitimate these decisions are and whether there has been a historical shift in the pattern of decision-making.

The ways in which animals are treated has, of course, become an issue area of considerable public concern in a number of Western countries. From an animal rights/liberation perspective, the vast majority of the ways in which institutions and individuals are permitted to treat animals – in research laboratories, farms, abattoirs, circuses, pet shops and so on – are regarded as morally illegitimate, and a considerable literature has evolved to condemn these practices.[2] My own views on the moral legitimacy of our present treatment of animals are also in the public domain.[3] This book accepts as given these philosophical challenges to what might be regarded as the moral orthodoxy. That is not to say that an animal rights perspective is absent from this book, but it will only be touched upon in the context of the political debate about animals; in the sense that they strike a chord with public opinion or inform the emergence and development of the movement which has arisen to seek greater protection for animals. At present, public opinion and governmental responses tend to be couched in the language of welfare rather than rights and, while recognizing that this situation may, and – to take off my objective hat for a moment – ought to change, a thorough assessment of the politics of animal protection must take the existing reality into account.

Although an issue of increasing importance, the sociology and politics of animal protection has been virtually ignored by social scientists in general, and political scientists in particular. In the inaugural edition of the journal *Society & Animals*, an innovative interdisciplinary social science publication, it was pointed out that 'socio-political movements, public policy and the law' is an area underrepresented in the animal studies literature.[4] It is incorrect to assert that little has been published on the socio-political character of the animal protection movement. Much of the available material, however, has been written by those active in the movement and often participants in the events they describe.[5] Although such work is often enlightening, valuable, and sometimes exceptional, it understandably tends to lack analytical rigour. Likewise, journalistic accounts tend to be descriptive, sensationalist, and sometimes inaccurate.[6] Academic accounts remain few and far between, one early exception being a chapter by Jeffrey Berry on the American group Friends of Animals.[7]

There is some evidence that this neglect is beginning to be rectified. Book-length accounts of the animal protection movement and the challenges it faces, almost exclusively focused on the United States, have appeared in recent years, written by those from the disciplines of sociology, anthropology, philosophy and the law.[8] There is also a growing interest in the psychological characteristics of the movement and social movement theory has been utilized to explain how animal protection organizations are created, organized and maintained.[9] What has been missing is the public policy input of political scientists. This book seeks to redress the balance by providing such a focus.

ANIMAL PROTECTION AND MAINSTREAM PUBLIC POLICY

The political science neglect of animal welfare can, at least partly, be explained by the assumption that governmental decision-making processes have had little to do with the protection of animals. Thus, it might be argued, the political-institutional focus proposed in this study is of little relevance. Certainly, it is the case that the animal protection movement has adopted a whole variety of strategies – from altering the behaviour of consumers to engaging in direct action against institutions involved in using animals – which are not dependent upon gaining greater legislative and administrative protection for animals.

The limited concern of decision-makers for the welfare of animals, then, coupled with the strategy of the animal protection movement, the argument goes, makes a public policy-orientated study of the issue inappropriately narrow and ephemeral.

I would disagree with the above assessment on a number of grounds. In the first place, even if it was accepted that relatively few significant and substantial animal protection measures have been adopted by national decision-makers, it is worth while to ask, particularly given the emergence of a strong animal protection movement and the generation of considerable public interest in the issue, why decision-makers have not done more. In political science terms, non-decision-making is as important as active decision-making.[10]

One might be forgiven for thinking that governments have entirely ignored animal welfare. This perception is undoubtedly partly the product of the emergence of a radicalized animal protection movement advocating far-reaching reforms which no government has come close to achieving. If the focus is on animal welfare, as opposed to rights, however, it becomes clear that, particularly in Britain and to a lesser extent in the United States, there is in reality a national legislative and administrative framework, often hidden but nevertheless extensive, designed to protect animals, or at least to give that impression. Of critical importance, too, is that this framework has changed considerably over the last two decades or so, at least partly as a direct response to rising public concern over the way animals are treated. As the animal protection movement further establishes its credentials, and the public's indifference is further eroded, additional developments can be expected.

In the context of the increasing importance of animal protection for decision-makers, it is not surprising that the animal protection movement has, to a certain degree, directed its attention towards more conventional lobbying activities. Indeed, it is possible to argue that this strategic shift marks the end of what might be regarded as the first stage of the animal protection movement's period of revitalization. Thus, in the 1970s in Britain and in much of the 1980s in the United States, the movement was able to gain advantages without concentrating upon, or being particularly successful within, decision-making arenas. The shock-value of its message and tactics was able to attract public support, generating shifts in consumption patterns and provoking revulsion at some of the well-publicized uses of animals. Change that did occur tended to happen as a result of the by-passing of the political arena or, at most, as a result of governmental action precipitated by the indirect use of popular protest. There is no doubt, however, that such popular protest tactics have become less effective. The message has become more familiar, and less likely to provoke outrage, and, equally importantly, as Chapter 2 in particular reveals, those non-state actors – such as the pharmaceutical companies, the biomedical research community and the meat industry – opposed to further controls on the way they treat animals, have mobilized against the animal protection movement, challenging its dominance within civil society. As Jasper and Poulson point out: 'Future success for the animal rights movement may come through Federal regulations and policies not by stopping individual experiments'.[11]

All of the above is not to suggest that conventional lobbying by animal protection advocates is a new phenomenon, nor is it to deny that mobilizing popular protest remains a key ingredient of animal protection politics, particularly in those policy arenas where animal advocates have less access and influence. It is, as with most social movements, something of a misnomer in any case to refer to a uniform animal protection *movement*. In both Britain and the United States, some – usually more moderate – elements have always tended to focus on so-called 'insider' tactics, seeking to forge links with politicians and bureaucrats, and some groups in Britain, such as the Royal Society for the Prevention of Cruelty to Animals (RSPCA) and the Royal Society for the Protection of Birds (RSPB), are extremely established and respectable organizations.[12] In the United States, likewise, lobbying members of Congress is an established and relatively simple affair which animal protectionists have long utilized. Indeed, some animal protection and wildlife conservation groups are now well known and respected participants on Capitol Hill.

Despite all of the above, it is the case that, in recent years, the access granted to animal protection advocates by decision-makers in most policy arenas has undoubtedly increased in both volume and depth. This, in turn, is a reflection, particularly in Britain, of the arrival of animal welfare into the political mainstream. The pressure on the actors within established policy arenas to further consider the welfare of animals, and to justify what they permit to be allowed to be done to them, has consequently increased. An examination of these processes provides a fascinating case study of how existing patterns of decision-making are affected by, and react to, the rise of a significant new social concern.

PLURALISM, POLICY NETWORKS AND ANIMAL PROTECTION

Much of the impetus for various types of, often illegal, forms of direct action in defence of animals has been based on the oft-stated suspicion within the animal protection movement that those with a vested interest in seeking to continue exploiting animals are powerful enough to be able to operate a veto power preventing significant reforms. Though much ink has been spilt in recent years in an attempt to demonstrate the moral case against exploiting animals, there has been no thorough assessment of the view that the *political* influence of the animal-use industry is similarly illegitimate.[13]

Political scientists, of course, have long been concerned with questions of interest representation and influence, and to aid explanation a number of models of governmental decision-making have been developed which attempt to postulate a particular relationship between organized groups and the state. For much of the post-war period, sustained debate has ensued about the relative merits of macro theories of the state which offer overarching theories of the power distribution in liberal democracies within which pressure group/governmental relations can be derived.[14] The initial stimulus for this debate was the development of the pluralist theory of the state. Although the antecedents of this approach can be seen before 1945, it was most fully developed in the first decade or so after the Second World War.[15]

Although the extensive pluralist literature is far from uniform, it is possible to identify a number of central components.[16] Firstly, pluralists argue that governmental outputs are best explained in terms of the interaction between organized groups and the state. Secondly, there is an assumption that the entry barriers to the system are low enough for any group of people to organize and get their voices heard. Finally, and crucially, pluralists argue that power in modern liberal democracies is dispersed amongst a wide variety of competing interests, and that the state's policy and administrative outputs reflect this fragmented power structure so that no one interest or small set of interests dominates, and all interested parties get at least some of their demands met in accordance with the saliency of their views within society as a whole. Pluralists argue that their theory represents not only an accurate description of political reality in Western liberal democracies, but also, in a world characterized by division and conflicts of interests, the only effective means of ensuring governments remain accountable in complex modern societies.

Pluralism has come in for a great deal of criticism on both normative and empirical grounds.[17] In particular, it has been argued by those, operating from alternative elitist or Marxist perspectives, that pluralist conclusions are a product of a flawed methodology which ignores the possibility that decision-makers are able to exclude particular interests from the political agenda or prevent interests which threaten existing power relationships from emerging in the first place.[18] More recently, the macro pluralist model has been increasingly discarded in favour of policy network analysis, which 'has almost become part of the orthodox conventional wisdom of contemporary political science'.[19] This shift has come about partly for methodological reasons and partly as a challenge to pluralist conclusions.

In terms of method, it is argued that macro theories are unable to take account of the variety of decision-making patterns within an increasingly sectoral policy process. Policy network analysis is based on the assumption that public policy is not the product of 'the government' as a whole but rather derives from a variety of different networks within government, each with its own set of governmental and non-governmental actors, norms of behaviour and power structure.[20] Thus, while some policy networks in an individual polity may exhibit openness, complexity and competition (key pluralist characteristics), others may be closed, specialized and consensual.[21] The adoption of a network approach can also be used to show that pluralist theory, by emphasizing the absence of a small number of interests dominating over a wide range of issue areas, has underestimated (or to be more precise undervalued) the extent to which particular interests can dominate within their own policy arenas. Policy network analysis, then, does not reject pluralism as such but simply argues that sectorized political systems may exhibit a wide range of power relationships. Some policy sectors, in other words, may be more pluralist than others.

Policy network analysis, then, is based upon the nature of the relationship between sectors of the state and those organizations with an interest in a particular sector's activities. What is important here is not so much the access which groups have to the state but the quality of that access. Access to politicians and bureaucrats can take many forms, from the occasional phone call or request for comment or information, at one end of the spectrum, to regular and formalized face-to-face participation in decision-making, at the other. It is the quality of access granted to organized interests which, above all, determines the character of a particular policy network.[22] A number of policy network typologies have been developed.[23] For our purposes, the most useful uses policy network as a generic term and identifies a continuum with the so-called 'policy community' at one end and the 'issue network' at the other. The position of any particular policy network on the continuum will depend upon such factors as the level of internal complexity in terms of the number and variety of participants, the frequency of interaction between the participants, the level of unity and the degree of functional autonomy, and the extent to which policies are formulated and implemented within the network.

A policy community, often described as a sub-government in the United States,[24] is one in which a limited number of participants exist in a close relationship with a shared set of beliefs, excluding those interests who do not share the prevailing ideology. Such a network might also be described as corporatist or elitist. An issue network, on the other hand, is a much more open policy network, although still with definable boundaries, with a variety of groups vying for influence. The government department or agency in this more pluralistic model is more likely to take on the role of a neutral arbiter seeking to balance the interests of the groups involved. Finally, there is an additional assumption that policy outcomes will be affected by the type of network. In the case of the policy community, policy continuity is the norm with the interests of the dominant groups protected and furthered. In the case of the issue network, there may well be policy stalemate as competing groups cancel each other out, accompanied perhaps by unpredictable and violent policy shifts.

A GUIDE TO THE CHAPTERS

Adopting policy network analysis in a study of animal protection decision-making would seem to be appropriate given the fact that it is a policy area which is particularly subject to sectorization. A variety of institutional structures have evolved to oversee the different uses to which animals are subject – as farm animals, laboratory animals, companion animals and wild animals – and an examination of these permits us to reach some conclusions about the power relationships involved in animal protection decision-making. Moreover, the policy network approach facilitates a cross-national analysis. A comparative study focusing, for instance, upon institutions is clearly problematic. Comparing animal protection policy-making in the American Congress and the British House of Commons, for example, is unlikely to produce many meaningful conclusions because they perform very different functions within their respective political systems. Policy network analysis, on the other hand, allows us to identify the key decision-makers in each country, which may cross-cut the traditional legislative–executive institutional divide, whilst at the same time employing a common framework of analysis.

A few words are necessary here about the decision to focus on Britain and the United States. To a certain degree, the choice was the product of convenience – ease of access of relevant material, a common language and so forth. It might be suggested that a more profitable comparison would be between Britain and one or more of those other European countries, particularly in the South of the continent, whose record on animal welfare is very poor. Britain's decision-making in animal protection is, of course – like many other issue areas – inextricably connected with membership of the European Union, and on numerous occasions throughout this book, reference will be made to this.

In actual fact, there are good reasons for focusing on the two countries chosen. The intriguing factor here is that animals are protected more stringently in Britain than they are in the United States. The majority of the federal legislation relating to animal protection relates to wild animals. Laboratory animals are covered by the Animal Welfare Act, originally introduced in 1966 and amended several times since, but, as we shall see, its scope is limited and the quality of enforcement questionable. Moreover, of all the OECD countries, only the United States and Japan have not taken action, with the exception of an extremely limited statute relating to transportation, on the welfare of farm animals prior to slaughter.

This discrepancy might be regarded as odd and worthy of examination for a number of reasons. Firstly, the two countries are at a comparable stage of economic development – unlike, say, Britain compared with Greece or Portugal. Concern for animals is often explained in terms of industrialization and urbanization, which has had the effect of separating people from the rural utilization of animals for human benefit.[25] This may or may not be a valid explanation, but it does not take us very far in seeking to distinguish between Britain and the United States. Most Americans (over 80 per cent) now live in urban areas and only 2 per cent earn their living through agricultural production, figures which are broadly equivalent to Britain.[26]

It is also instructive to note that there would seem to be a greater awareness of environmental issues in the United States, and this is reflected in the considerable amount of legislation (most notably the Endangered Species Act) which seeks to protect wild animals. Furthermore, both countries have visible animal protection movements which, as Chapters 3 and 4 illustrate, have evolved in strikingly similar ways. Moreover, the United States is a country which has stronger, and more deep-rooted, rights-based movements – for civil rights and women's rights in particular – than the more pragmatic and utilitarian British.

Finally, both countries have liberal democratic political systems. Indeed, it has been suggested that the American political system is, if anything, more open to the influence of groups, and particularly those with a cause to promote as opposed to an economic interest to defend.[27] Thus, in contrast to Britain, the federal nature of the American system, coupled with the separation of powers and the decentralization of, and the lack of party discipline in Congress, provides a much greater variety of access points for pressure group lobbying. The significant increase in promotional groups since the 1970s is regarded by some as an indication of the accuracy of a pluralist paradigm.[28]

The above factors lead us to make some interesting speculations worth testing. In particular, it might be the case that the different levels of protection afforded to animals by the legislative framework lies in the structure of the two country's respective political systems. If this is the case, two possibilities present themselves. Either the animal protection policy networks in the United States are less open than is suggested or there is not a clear relationship between policy networks and policy outcomes. That is, in the latter case, the existence of a more open network does not necessarily lead to a more equal distribution of benefits to its participants. As we will see, it is indeed possible to find both these processes at work in the politics of animal protection in the United States.

As well as utilizing policy network analysis to aid understanding of animal protection decision-making, a case study such as this enables us to comment upon the utility of the network approach itself. How far, that is, does a case study of animal protection decision-making confirm the assertion that decisions are taken in more or less autonomous sectors with relatively little outside interference? Further, is there a relationship between the outputs of a particular network and the pattern of relationships found within it? Finally, does a study of animal protection decision-making tell us anything about how and why policy networks change?

The vast majority of animal-related policy areas will be mentioned in the pages that follow. Particular attention, however, is devoted to the issues raised by the utilization of animals for food and for various laboratory procedures. There are a number of reasons for this. In the first place, these practices involve the use of a staggering number of animals. Secondly, the use of animals for food production and research procedures involve practices which inflict often severe suffering on animals, although the level of suffering and the benefits deriving to humans as a consequence are hugely contentious issues. Moreover, it is precisely these institutional uses of animals which the modern animal protection movement has tended to target. By so doing, a whole range of interests – from the economic benefits accruing to those myriad interests with a stake in animal use to the wider concerns of public health and diet – have been challenged. These factors – the number of animals used, the level of suffering inflicted, and the wide variety of interests at stake – has made the political battle in these two areas particularly fierce and important.

Chapter 1 of this volume sets the scene for subsequent chapters by describing the existing sectorized administrative framework (and the legislation which has given rise to it) within which decisions relating to the treatment of animals are made in Britain and the United States. In addition to the documentation of formal administrative structures and statutes, the growing political interest in animal protection is also traced through an examination of the way the issue has been treated generally in legislative bodies. The non-governmental actors are introduced in Chapters 2 to 4. In Chapter 2, an attempt is made to explain the political organization of those with an interest in utilizing animals, and the economic structure upon which this interest and organization is based. In Chapters 3 and 4, the development of the animal protection movement is discussed in terms of both its conventional lobbying capacity and broader questions of strategy and ideology.

The nature of animal protection decision-making is further explored in four chapters examining particular issue areas. Chapters 7 and 8 consider the politics of farm animal welfare in the United States and Britain and Chapters 9 and 10 the politics of animal research in Britain and the United States. Here, the aim is to build upon previous chapters by providing a detailed account of policy networks in action, describing and evaluating the nature, degree and quality of change over time.

The two remaining chapters, 5 and 6, have a slightly different focus. A clearly observable guide to the political saliency of an issue is the extent to which it has permeated into elected legislative bodies. These two chapters, therefore, seek to gauge the attitude of members of the British House of Commons and the American Congress towards animal protection issues. To this end, a database was created to record information on the number of resolutions (in the US), bills (in the US and Britain), parliamentary questions, and early day motions (in Britain) relating to animal protection introduced in a specific time period and the politicians responsible for them (see Appendix I). Information from this database is utilized at various points during this book. Of particular importance for Chapters 5 and 6 is the identification of those representatives who have displayed a notable interest in animal protection. From this information, an attempt is made to determine whether it is possible to isolate variables – in terms of, for instance, age, gender, geographical location, and party – which have some explanatory capacity.

PLURALISM, ANIMAL PROTECTION AND RESEARCH METHODOLOGY

It should be said at this juncture that documenting the extent of change is one thing, determining, and evaluating the legitimacy of, influence is quite another. On the question of legitimacy, establishing that animal protection decision-making is conducted in a pluralist environment would seem to enable us to accord some sort of legitimacy to it. In actual fact, as this book will reveal, it is by no means clear that such a pluralist label can be attached to at least some policy networks within which decisions relating to animal protection are made, and quite clear in one case – the network focusing on farm animals in the United States – that the pluralist label is inappropriate.

Nevertheless, to the extent that we can apply the pluralist label, it is important to recognize what follows from it. Advocates of animal rights would want to claim, at the very least, that the continuation of activities which cause animals pain and suffering – whether it be on the farm, in the slaughterhouse or in the laboratory – are morally illegitimate. In a pluralist political system where there is a consensus that non-human animals do not have rights in the sense that humans do, however, animal protection decision-making cannot be judged purely in those terms. Of course, our treatment of animals can and should be judged in terms of the infringement of rights and in that context, as many have shown, it is found seriously and tragically wanting. In a climate in which animal rights is not the dominant world view, however, we need another yardstick to judge what is done to animals, and pluralism, concerned with the degree to which decision-making takes account of the need to allow the representation and balancing of competing interests, provides such a yardstick.

A confirmation of the utility of pluralism in an examination of animal protection decision-making is an important corrective to the view, current amongst certain elements of the animal rights movement – particularly in America – that welfarist reforms are not worth having. This view, articulated most capably by the Rutgers law professor Gary Francione,[29] has challenged the utility of lobbying for welfarist reforms partly on the grounds that achieving limited improvements in the treatment of animals (larger cages, for instance, for battery hens) does not necessarily make the abolitionist goals of animal rightists (no battery cages at all) any closer; and may, by making – or appearing to make – the exploitation of animals more acceptable, obstruct the achievement of such goals. More importantly still for our purposes, Francione also argues that animal welfare – which seeks to balance animal suffering against the benefits likely to accrue to humans – does not in practice benefit animals because, due, in particular, to their status as property, their interests are almost always overridden in favour of the promotion of human interests.

The internal logic of this critique will be considered further in Chapter 3 since it has important implications for the future direction of the animal protection movement. The conclusions of this book as a whole, however, also stand as an assessment of the viability of animal welfare. This is because, in order to confirm the pluralist theory's utility in at least some areas of animal protection decision-making, it is necessary to show that the political system has acted to improve the welfare of animals, albeit short of recognizing their rights. This, of course, is a conclusion contrary to the analysis of animal rightists such as Francione.

Turning our attention to the empirical question, it is clear that determining the balance of power within policy networks is horrendously problematic. It goes without saying that such an exercise is not an exact science. In particular, the number of variables one has to consider raises problems of both manageability and interpretation. This is further compounded by the lack of documentary evidence. The policy network approach deemphasizes the role of legislatures, parties and the formal institutions of government, in favour of a study of informal political processes. By its very nature, lobbying involves personal contacts, and the contents of innumerable meetings – formal and informal – and telephone calls are rarely recorded, let alone preserved. The researcher is dependent, as is the case with this study, upon gaining direct contact with the political actors through questionnaires and more extensive interviews (see Appendix II).

Even if we have information – gained from such sources as questionnaires, interviews, and official publications – at our disposal, the methodological problems do not end there. Measuring influence remains extremely difficult. Obviously, one simple way of measuring influence is the extent to which organizations get what they want, or, as Gamson more eloquently describes it, the extent to which groups are able to achieve the 'distribution of new advantages to the group's beneficiaries'.[30] Two further questions arise from this.[31] In the first place, why did the benefit happen? Here, it should be pointed out that the motives behind a particular decision are never clear-cut and the views of the participants are unreliable guides to the exercise of influence. Governmental actors are unlikely to admit that their action in any particular case was determined by the pressure employed by non-governmental actors. Likewise, non-governmental actors will want to claim as much influence as possible (not least to impress their members and/or paymasters) and will, for the same reason, rarely admit to their ineffectiveness.[32] In reality, governmental decisions are the product of a wide range of variables some of which – such as international treaty obligations, public opinion, the electoral climate and the preferences of politicians and officials themselves – are not directly related to the specific pressure applied by organized groups.

The second key question is how beneficial have the 'benefits' been? Clearly, government action – and inaction – is an important guide to the power relationships in any particular policy area. In all but the most transparent cases, however, interpreting the effects of legislative and administrative outputs remains troublesome, and animal protection measures would seem to offer a paradigmatic example of this. It is difficult to say, for instance, whether the legislation designed to protect laboratory animals in Britain and the United States has resulted in a reduction of the suffering inflicted and/or a reduction in the number of animals used. Similarly, legislation is next to useless unless it is effectively enforced and assessing the level of enforcement, when a measure applies to the behaviour of thousands of individuals and is the responsibility of countless others, is much more difficult than judging the utility of the original statute.

The methodological problems inherent in detailed case studies make general theorising about public policy a particularly attractive alternative. We should bear in mind Moyer and Josling's sensible comment here that although no:

> single model or theory is likely to explain satisfactorily all the twists and turns of a complex policy...yet, if one does not have in mind some explanations of the motives and actions of decision-makers, then policy becomes a random process subject to description, but not to understanding.[33]

There is, however, no substitute for detailed empirical studies if the reality of decision-making is to be unearthed. A theoretical framework is important, but the dangers of becoming 'theory-bound', of trying to fit round pegs into square holes, are ever-present. The aim of this book, and the research upon which it is based, is to explore the political dynamics operating in a relatively new substantive issue area taking theoretical perspectives with us, as guides and not warders, along the way. It is hoped that, as a result, the politics of animal protection is better understood.

1 The Institutional Framework of Animal Protection

The initial task of this book is to document the structure – or, to be more accurate, structures – of animal welfare decision-making and the primary and secondary legislation that has created it, with particular reference to the frameworks concerned with farm and research animals. This is an essential first step if we are then to go on and adequately explain why things are as they are and attempt to predict future developments. What this chapter reveals is that, despite its supposed 'Cinderella' status, there is in reality a substantial body of legislation relating to animal welfare and a set of distinct administrative structures with responsibility for implementing and enforcing the law. A complete picture of the political system's absorption of concern for animal welfare also requires an examination of the extent to which the issue has been considered, with or without executive action being required, in both Congress and the House of Commons. Thus, the chapter begins by attempting to quantify this impact.

LEGISLATIVE SUPPORT FOR ANIMAL PROTECTION

In Britain and the United States, legislative activity on an issue is one indicator of its social and political importance. An examination of the British House of Commons reveals that increasing societal concern for the welfare of animals has been recognized by legislators. This can be seen if we look at the three primary ways in which concern for an issue can be expressed, the introduction of bills and early day motions (EDMs) and the tabling of questions which have to be answered by ministers. The total number of MPs responsible for raising animal protection through one or more of these routes during the 1987–92 parliament was 286 or 44 per cent of the 650 members of the House.

In terms of bills, as Table 1.1 shows, in the 30 years between 1950 and 1980, no less than 107, including some government bills but mostly ultimately unsuccessful private members' bills (PMBs), were introduced, followed by 63 in the 12 years between 1983 and 1995. To put this into perspective, the 42 PMBs on animal protection introduced between 1983 and 1995 constituted about 3 per cent of the total number of PMBs on all subjects introduced during this period.[1] Not surprisingly, given the public saliency of the issue, wildlife issues constitute the largest category and many of these bills were concerned with hunting in one shape or another. One interesting feature, and in contrast with the United States, is that more bills concerned with farm animal welfare have been introduced than bills concerned with animal experimentation, and from an earlier period too.

Other means by which MPs can make their voices heard and concerns felt are the asking of parliamentary questions and the

Table 1.1   Bills on animal protection introduced in the British Parliament, 1950–95

Year	Wildlife conservation	Animal experimentation	Domesticated animals	Farm animal welfare	Total[a]
1950–55	1	–	7	4	12
1956–60	3	–	2	2	7
1961–65	7	–	3	5	15
1966–70	12	5	8	6	31
1971–75	14	5	6	2	27
1976–80	8	5	–	2	15
1981–85	1	–	3	2	6
1985–87	1	1	5	1	8
1987–89	2	1	5	1	9
1989–91	10	–	4	4	18
1991–93	7	2	2	1	12
1993–95	3	–	5	3	11
Total	69	19	50	33	171

[a] This total does not include 19 petitions introduced between 1985–95. In addition, there were two general bills on animal protection which could not be classified in any of the specific areas.

introduction of EDMs. Between 1985 and 1994, MPs asked 2266 questions relating to animal protection which constitutes about 0.5 per cent of the total number of questions asked. This may represent a small fraction of parliamentary activity but given the huge array of subjects preoccupying MPs it still reveals a healthy concern for animal protection issues. Not surprisingly again, almost half the questions (1068) were concerned with wildlife issues but, as with bills, farm animal welfare questions were the next major area of concern with 575 (25 per cent) questions asked, followed by domestic animals (322 or 15 per cent) and animal experimentation (301 or 13 per cent).

MPs have often used the EDM procedure to raise animal protection issues. Indeed, between 1939 and 1984 only 21 EDMs secured 300 or more signatures and three of these (which also included issues as important as Sachsenshausen concentration camp, international assistance to Bangladesh and the Rhodesian situation) involved animal issues, one supporting a ban on whale product imports in 1979–80, one condemning the clubbing of baby seals in Canada in 1982–3 and one condemning whaling in 1983–4.[2] During the period 1985–94, a total of 105 EDMs concerned with animal protection were tabled. Nearly half of these (46) involved farm animal welfare issues, followed by 27 on domestic animals, 16 on wildlife, 11 on animal experimentation and five not in any particular category. This total represents about 0.8 per cent of the total number of EDMs tabled during this period (13 194) and, again, although this figure may seem small, given other priorities MPs have it is not an insignificant number.

Comparable information on the interest in animal protection demonstrated by members of the American Congress is shown in Tables 1.2 and 1.3. The proportion of Representatives involved in sponsoring or co-sponsoring the bills and resolutions on animal protection and wildlife issues listed in Table 1.3 was, on average between 1985 and 1994, about 50 per cent, although this disguises significant variations between Congresses (explored further in Chapter 6). This raw figure is broadly comparable with the proportion of British MPs demonstrating an interest in animal issues, although it is important to note that neither set of figures take into account the quality of this participation, an issue that is further explored in Chapters 5 and 6.

Table 1.2 Bills and resolutions on animal protection and wildlife conservation introduced in the US Congress in selected years between 1955 and 1968

	House				Senate			
	Wildlife conservation	Animal experimentation	Domesticated animals	Farm animal welfare	Wildlife conservation	Animal experimentation	Domesticated animals	Farm animal welfare
1955–6	29	–	–	3	9	–	–	1
1963–4	9	8	–	1	12	2	–	–
1967–8	39	15	1	–	7	1	1	–

Source: *Digest of Public Bills and Resolutions* (Washington, DC: US Government).

Table 1.3 Animal protection and wildlife conservation bills and resolutions introduced in the US House of Representatives, 1985–94

Congress	Wildlife conservation		Animal experimentation		Domesticated animals		Farm animal welfare		Total
	Bills	Resolutions	Bills	Resolutions	Bills	Resolutions	Bills	Resolutions	
99	7	1	3	0	14	6	0	1	32
100	9	1	2	3	21	4	4	0	44
101	7	1	3	4	38	6	1	0	60
102	4	1	4	2	29	2	3	0	47[a]
103	2	1	1	0	14	1	2	0	21
Total	29	5	13	9	116	19	10	1	204

[a] Total includes two general resolutions calling for the establishment of an 'animal rights awareness week'.

There are two significant differences, however, between the figures provided for animal concern in Britain and the United States. Firstly, bills and resolutions concerned with animal issues in the USA constitute a much smaller proportion of the total number introduced, never amounting to more than about 0.5 per cent of the total. Thus, in the 101st Congress, a total number of 14 353 bills and resolutions were introduced and only 60 (0.4 per cent) of these involved issues focusing on animal protection or wildlife conservation.[3] Secondly, as Tables 1.2 and 1.3 demonstrate, measures dealing with wildlife conservation predominate, constituting over half of the animal bills and resolutions introduced during the period 1985–94. A related point here is that very few measures dealing with the welfare of farm animals have been forthcoming compared to Britain, where they are almost as numerous as those concerned with wildlife.

SECTORIZATION AND THE STRUCTURE OF ANIMAL PROTECTION DECISION-MAKING

If we turn our attention to the institutional structure of animal welfare decision-making, we see part confirmation of the commonly-stated assertion that policy-making in complex industrial societies has become increasingly sectorized. Thus, it is possible to identify a distinct set of institutions and governmental actors responsible for different types of animal use. Indeed, animals are required for such a diverse range of activities that a surprisingly large number of separate governmental entities are involved. This becomes apparent if we look at the targets for parliamentary questions in the House of Commons. As Table 1.4 reveals, although three departments received over 80 per cent of the questions, no less than 17 separate governmental institutions were targeted in the period 1985–95.

The demarcation between different animal welfare structures, coupled with the anthropocentric world-view which, at present, dictates our treatment of animals, ensures that the level of protection afforded to an individual animal depends, not just – if at all – upon its needs and interests, but upon the institutional and legislative structure governing the particular use to which it is being put. To take one example, a rabbit raised for food would be subject to a totally different set of legislative criteria than

Political Animals

Table 1.4   Targets of Parliamentary questions
on animal protection and wildlife conservation,
1985–95

Department	No.	%
MAFF	966	43
Environment	416	18
Home Office	367	16
Scottish Office	125	6
Foreign Office	84	
Defence	82	
Welsh Office	64	
Trade and Industry	59	
Prime Minister	36	
Transport	21	
Treasury	21	
Education	12	
Health	5	
National Heritage	3	
Attorney General	3	
Social Security	1	
Employment	1	
Total	2266	

would one utilized in a laboratory or one existing in the wild or one owned as a pet. To see how this occurs, it is necessary to consider each structure in turn.

INSTITUTIONAL STRUCTURES AND ANIMAL PROTECTION IN BRITAIN

In Britain, there are now four main statutes each relating to a particular way we use animals or, in the case of wildlife conservation, the survival of particular species. This primary legislation has produced separate institutional structures, centring on different government departments and agencies.

Farm Animals

The treatment of farm animals is the responsibility of the Ministry of Agriculture, Fisheries and Food (MAFF). The modern structure, taking much greater account – at least superficially – of farm animal welfare, dates back about 30 years or so. Prior to 1968, specific regulations did exist for the transportation of animals and their treatment in slaughterhouses but the husbandry of farm animals was governed by a general anti-cruelty statute – the Protection of Animals Act – introduced in 1911, which itself built upon nineteenth-century antecedents.[4] Now, the treatment of farm animals from birth to slaughter is governed by two major statutes, the 1968 Agriculture (Miscellaneous Provisions) Act, and the Animal Health Act 1981 (designed to protect animals during transit and in markets) and one regulation, the Welfare of Animals (Slaughter or Killing) Regulations 1995, the purpose of which is self-evident.[5] The institutional structure which has arisen in parallel with this legislation includes a junior MAFF minister particularly responsible for farm animal welfare (at present Elliot Morley), the Animal Welfare Division (situated in MAFF) and the Farm Animal Welfare Council (FAWC). In addition, mention should be made of the European Union's increasing involvement in animal welfare issues which has widened the policy arena.

The centre-piece of the legislative framework is the 1968 Act. The first part of this statute provided specific protection for farm animals against the infliction of 'unnecessary suffering'. More importantly, in the second part, the Act also empowered the Secretary of State for Agriculture to introduce codes of practice on the welfare of farm animals and to introduce secondary legislation prohibiting or regulating particular practices. The codes are not legally binding but failure to comply can be used in evidence in any case brought against a farmer under the unnecessary suffering clause. There are now codes for the welfare of cattle, pigs, poultry and sheep which are regularly revised. Legally binding secondary legislation made under the 1968 statute includes regulations dealing with the removal of deer antlers, the tail docking of pigs and cattle, the inspection of intensive units, the prohibition on veal crates and sow stalls and tethers.

The 1968 Act also made provision for the creation of an advisory body, the Farm Animal Welfare Advisory Council (renamed FAWC in 1979), consisting of members, representing various interested parties, appointed by the secretary of state. The whole committee now meets four or five times a year and most of its detailed work is done through a number of subcommittees which usually meet bi-monthly. This body now resides within the Animal Welfare Division of MAFF, which provides its secretariat. Since 1989, the AWD has been part of the Animal Health and Veterinary Group which in turn is part of MAFF's Food Safety Directorate. It is situated in rather grey and functional Government buildings at Tolworth in Surrey, on the outskirts of London. Its head, at present Chris Ryder, is a Grade 5 civil servant (equivalent to an assistant secretary rank) whereas the head of the Food Safety Directorate has the higher deputy secretary rank. The function of the AWD is to advise ministers on animal welfare issues, to provide answers to parliamentary questions on animal welfare, and to liaise with other parts of MAFF on animal welfare issues. At present, the AWD employs 32 people and has a budget of £750 000.[6] Within the Animal Health and Veterinary Group, too, is the State Veterinary Service (SVS). Before 1968, the SVS was already responsible for inspecting animals being exported and after the 1968 Act came into force it also assumed responsibility for farm welfare inspections.

Although the junior minister responsible for animal welfare does consult extensively with the AWD, to this end using a video link between Whitehall and Tolworth, and the agency does 'take the lead' in drawing up animal welfare legislation and consulting with officials in other member states,[7] animal welfare is obviously also of concern to other sections of MAFF, and particularly the commodity divisions within the Livestock Group. Any decision, therefore, would be taken by the secretary of state in concert with the junior minister and these administrative divisions.

A final body to note is the Meat and Livestock Commission. Based in Milton Keynes, this quasi-governmental organization, established by the 1967 Agriculture Act, exists officially to promote greater efficiency in the livestock industry. A great deal of its time, however, is spent promoting the consumption of meat and, in this way, it is often criticized by the animal protection movement for obscuring the reality of modern meat production methods.

The European Union now takes a keen interest in farm animal welfare issues and, as Chapter 8 will show, membership severely constrains the ability of the British government to act independently.[8] The major institutions are the Directorate-General for Agriculture (DG VI) headed by a Commissioner and the Council of Agricultural Ministers, with the European Parliament playing a subordinate, although increasingly important, role. The first involvement of the EU occurred in 1975 when a directive required animals to be humanely stunned before slaughter. This was followed by directives in 1977, 1981 and 1991 which sought to protect animals during international transportation. Among other things, they stipulated that animals must not travel for longer than 24 hours without being given food and water and required each consignment of animals to be accompanied by a certificate.

There is little in theory to stop individual member states from adopting higher standards of farm animal welfare but, crucially, the advent of the single market has meant that it is very difficult, if not impossible, to prevent the import of (probably cheaper) animal products from member states with less stringent welfare standards. An additional, and – for animal advocates – a worrying constraint on national autonomy is the impact of the World Trade Organization (formerly GATT). This applies to a whole range of animal issues although up to now its impact has been most evident in wildlife protection. The encouragement of free trade the world over which the World Trade Organization embodies, will even limit the EU from being able to prevent the import of products derived from animals raised under welfare standards which it has deemed unacceptable.[9]

Laboratory Animals

The institutional structure directly concerned with protecting animals used for research in Britain has a longer history than is the case with the farm animal institutional framework. Indeed, there is a key difference between the two. Whereas concern for the welfare of farm animals has been grafted on to a department which was already centrally involved with the use of animals – and in a close relationship with those interests with a vested interest in continuing to exploit them – the institutional structure for regulating the use of animals for research was specifically created for the purpose. This structure, centring on the Home Office, was created by the 1876 Cruelty to Animals Act and has now been refined by its replacement, the 1986 Animals (Scientific Procedures) Act.

The 1876 legislation introduced a licensing system for those intending to use animals in experiments and the registration of facilities in which the work was to take place. Substantial restrictions were imposed upon licence holders but these could be removed by the granting of certificates granting exemptions from the restrictions.[10] The job of granting licenses and certificates as well as the inspection of research facilities, was given to the Home Office and the work is now done within the department's E Division.

As with the arena concerned with farm animals, research animal protection has been overhauled in the past few years. This has mainly been the product of the 1986 Act although some changes (such as the creation of an advisory committee) predated the legislation. In the absence of amending legislation prior to 1986, the Home Office inspectorate adapted its procedures to take into account the vastly changed nature of animal research in terms of the massively increased number of animals and variety of procedures used.

The 1986 Act retained the inspectorate but gave it more responsibility. Researchers were now to be subject to a dual-licensing system covering their personal competence to use animals and the specific project. Included in the legislation, too, was a clause explicitly detailing license applicants and the inspectorate to judge projects in terms of a cost–benefit analysis, with the implication being that an application where the cost to the animals used was greater than the benefits produced would be rejected. Finally, the legislation put the Animal Procedures Committee (APC) on a statutory footing which means it can choose to examine the topics it wishes and its annual reports to parliament are in the public domain.

An important point to note about the animal research institutional structure is that it also includes other government departments and agencies which conduct animal research themselves or represent clients who do. This includes MAFF – which oversees agencies conducting agricultural research involving the use of animals, the Ministry of Defence – which, particularly controversially, conducts military research (mainly at its Porton Down centre in Wiltshire) involving animals, the Department of Health – which is particularly concerned to protect the pharmaceutical industry – and, finally, the Department for Education which is responsible for funding university animal research. All government departments and agencies are subject to the provisions of the 1986 Act but, as subsequent chapters will show, they have tended to be peripheral members of the policy network, being subject to, as opposed to being involved in the development of, policy.

The direct impact of the EU on animal research is less than it is for farm animal welfare, but there is, of course, an international dimension to the issue which again limits the autonomy of the British government. There are two separate issues here. In the first place, the use of animals for product testing is subject to EU legislation and the single market would rule out a ban on the importation of products from countries with less stringent welfare standards. Secondly, biomedical researchers can, and have, claimed that the more stringent the controls are on the use of animals the greater the likelihood is that research, and personnel too, will go abroad. The economic consequences of this, particularly in relation to the pharmaceutical industry, is something that no government can ignore.

Domesticated and Wild Animals

Domesticated animals not kept on farms are used for a wide variety of purposes. In these cases – animals kept as pets, in zoos and exhibitions – national statutes developed by the Home Office apply but enforcement is left to the police, local authorities or voluntary agencies such as the RSPCA. The centre-piece of the legislative framework is the Protection of Animals Act originally passed in 1911. This statute includes a catch-all offence penalizing the infliction of unnecessary suffering on domesticated animals and captive wild animals. In practice, the courts have chosen to define 'captive' in such a stringent way that wild animals treated cruelly have been unprotected, although this loophole has now been closed (see below).

The policy arena surrounding wildlife conservation is complex. Laws relating to the protection of wild animals date back to the nineteenth century although a great deal of wildlife legislation was consolidated in the 1981 Wildlife and Countryside Act which incorporated Britain's obligations as members of international treaties such as CITES as well as the European Union. This legislation is enforced by the Department of the Environment, the centre of the institutional structure for wildlife issues. The emphasis in wildlife conservation has been on the protection of endangered species rather than individual animals so that the 1981 Act provides a very high degree of protection for those species listed as endangered and no protection at all for those common species which are not. However, some genuine anti-cruelty statutes do apply to wild animals, such as those which prohibit the use of certain particularly cruel devices – traps or poisons – to kill wild animals. In addition, the loophole mentioned above, whereby the 1911 Act did not really apply to wild animals – whether they were captive at the time or not – was closed with the passage of the Wild Mammals (Protection) Act in 1996.

The wildlife policy arena, however, includes much more than just the Department of the Environment and related interest groups. At the national level, as with more general environmental issues concerning, for instance, transport and industrial pollution, wildlife conservation is also affected by the activities of, and involves the participation of, other government departments. The Foreign Office, for instance, plays an important role in bringing wildlife issues to the attention of foreign governments. Likewise, the road-building activities of the Department of Transport can have a huge impact on wildlife. Most importantly of all, the impact of agriculture on wildlife conservation has been substantial and any attempt to promote it will involve impinging on the activities of farmers. For this reason, MAFF has a central role to play in wildlife policy-making.

At the sub-national level, the wildlife policy network also contains local authorities. Their main role involves the drawing up of local development plans in addition to assessing individual planning applications.[11] In reality, however, the executive power of local authorities in planning decisions is limited since ultimate authority lies with the Secretary of State for the Environment. One autonomous role local authorities have performed relates to what they allow on their land. Thus, some have prohibited hunting and/or circuses using animals on council-owned land.[12]

Finally, and most importantly of all, the British government in general and the Department of the Environment in particular is obliged to fulfil its international obligations in terms of both EU membership and as a signatory of numerous wildlife treaties. Again, as with farm and laboratory animal welfare, the impact of the World Trade Organization threatens to further remove the autonomy from one single national government.

It is not the purpose of this chapter to make authoritative judgements on the influence of the respective participants in the wildlife conservation decision-making arena, and this book as a whole is not primarily concerned with wildlife issues.[13] It is undoubtedly true, though, that post-war policy in areas such as transport and agriculture – emphasizing, in the former case, the need to build more roads to accommodate the ever increasing volume of traffic and, in the latter, habitat-destroying intensive farming methods – do seem to suggest that the conservation aims of the Department of the Environment have been submerged under other priorities. Having said that, as in the case of farm animal welfare (see Chapter 8), MAFF has shown greater regard for wildlife conservation in recent years and, in addition, the road-building programme has been severely cut back, albeit primarily for financial, rather than environmental, reasons.

INSTITUTIONAL STRUCTURES AND ANIMAL PROTECTION IN THE UNITED STATES

Policy arenas relating to animal protection in the United States differ from their British equivalents in important ways. These are partly products of historical accidents, partly a consequence of differing constitutional structures, and partly a reflection of the differing levels of priority given to animal protection. Like Britain, though, a whole range of governmental departments and agencies are involved in animal protection policy arenas and these policy arenas are centred around particular key pieces of legislation. As with Britain too, the sectorization of policy necessitates an examination of each policy arena in turn.

Farm Animals

The treatment of farm animals at the executive level is the responsibility of the United States Department of Agriculture (USDA). There are no federal statutes regulating animal husbandry, although from time to time USDA will introduce regulations affecting farm animals. There are three federal statutes which do impact on the welfare of farm animals in transit and at the slaughterhouse. First is the so-called '28-hour law', passed in 1873 and amended in 1906, which aims to protect livestock shipped by rail and over water by requiring that they be given rest, food and water if they are in transit for more than 28 hours. The 28 Hour Law is of little practical use now since over 90 per cent of animals are transported by road.[14]

The second piece of federal legislation is the 1958 Humane Slaughter Act, amended in 1978, which is administered by USDA's Food Safety and Inspection Service (an agency which, in 1991, employed approximately 6500 inspectors and 1200 veterinary medical officers[15]). The 1958 Act requires all meat-packers selling to the federal government to provide mechanical or electrical stunning prior to slaughter for all animals except, as in Britain, those animals being slaughtered for the kosher meat market. No penalty for non-compliance was introduced as such but it did have the effect of a compulsory law in the sense that those meat-packers who do not meet its requirements were not permitted to sell their products to the federal government. The 1978 amendment expanded the existing law to include all livestock in all federally-inspected plants. In addition, it required that all animals slaughtered for meat imported into the United States be humanely slaughtered. Also available to inspectors are the provisions of the Meat Inspection Act, which was amended in 1978 to empower the inspectors to stop the slaughtering line on the spot if any cruelty is observed, recommencement not being permitted until the deficiencies are corrected.

A further piece of legislation, the 1921 Packers and Stockyards Act, seems – at first sight – to add an additional layer of protection for farm animals. This legislation defines and empowers the Packers and Stockers Administration, the USDA agency which oversees stockyards. The 1921 Act requires 'reasonable care and promptness with respect to loading, transporting or otherwise handling livestock to...prevent avoidable loss'.

However, this 'avoidable loss' does not refer first and foremost to animal welfare but to the loss incurred by the producer. In reality, indeed, it has led to the big welfare problem of downed animals (those animals who reach stockyards or slaughterhouse in a poor physical shape). As a result of the Act, these downed animals are not euthanized on the spot but are taken to slaughter because to euthanize them, it is stipulated, would cause avoidable loss to the producer. In the last few years, a Downed Animal Protection Bill has been introduced in Congress which would make it illegal for stockyards to sell these animals to slaughterhouses and would require them to be euthanized.

USDA does not have the same power when it comes to policy-making relating to farm animals as the British MAFF. In the first place, the legislative role of Congress in the US political system is, because of the separation of powers, much greater than that of the House of Commons in the British unitary system. Indeed, as Chapter 7 will show, agriculture committees in the House and Senate play a fundamental role in determining the nature of agricultural policy in general. An additional crucial difference between the US and UK political systems is the federal nature of the former, which means that individual states have a great deal of autonomy in matters relating to the well-being of animals. All American states, for instance, had general anti-cruelty statutes by the 1920s (New York being the first in 1828, followed by Massachusetts in 1835) and, as you would expect from a fragmented polity, these laws vary widely in terms of quality and scope.[16]

In terms of farm animal welfare state anti-cruelty statutes have a limited impact. Twenty states, for instance, specifically exclude farm animals from coverage under their anti-cruelty laws. This is not surprising, not least since for one state to introduce much more stringent animal welfare measures when others do not is to introduce economic costs which are unlikely to be politically acceptable to the agricultural industry.[17] In addition, the vagueness of the term 'unnecessary suffering' (which anti-cruelty statutes seek to prohibit) has meant in practice that is very difficult, if not impossible, to bring successful prosecutions involving the treatment of farm animals.[18] Not only is it possible for farmers to justify almost any form of gratuitous cruelty as in some way necessary, it is also clearly the case, in particular, that intensive husbandry systems (such as veal crates or pig stalls) which do cause animals suffering cannot be touched by anti-cruelty statutes because a case can be made for their necessity. A final point is that, without a system of routine regulatory inspection, it is likely that most cases of wanton cruelty will, in any case, go unnoticed.

Some states have acted to introduce their own laws on farm animal welfare. Twenty-six states, for instance, have humane slaughter laws of their own and California in 1991 added poultry (not including laying hens) to their Humane Slaughter Act (poultry being totally excluded from the federal statute). Three years later, the same state passed a downed animal bill which outlaws the acceptance and sale of downed animals at stockyards and auction markets.[19] In addition, factory farming was sufficiently high up the political agenda in Massachusetts for an (unsuccessful) initiative to be introduced in 1988 which asked voters to ban certain practices such as the veal crate.

Laboratory Animals

Considerable emphasis in the United States has been focused on the issue of research animal protection and the institutional structure which has emerged is a reflection of this. The centrepiece of the policy arena is provided by USDA and the National Institutes of Health (NIH), an agency within the Public Health Service in the Department of Health and Human Services. Other elements involved include other federal departments and agencies involved in using, or requiring the use of, animals; congressional committees; state legislatures; the institutional animal care and use committees (IACUCs) which each institution using animals for research must set up; and, finally, the courts have been a significant player in this policy arena.

USDA's regulatory role was created in 1966 by what is now called the Animal Welfare Act and its role refined and expanded by amendments in 1970, 1976, 1985 and 1990. The purpose of the original Laboratory Animal Welfare Act passed in 1966 was primarily to regulate dog dealers through a licensing system. The legislation also provided for the registration of research laboratories and required research facilities to observe humane standards of care but this only applied when the animal was not being used for actual research or experimentation. Since research facilities were to decide for themselves when an animal was being so used, and presumably researchers would claim that they were being used throughout their stay in the laboratory, these standards did not generally apply. It was not until 1970, when the title of the legislation was shortened to the Animal Welfare Act, that the Act was extended to cover the care of all warm-bloodied animals (in terms, for instance, of the use of anaesthesia) in the laboratory environment (although, as we shall see in Chapter 10, USDA has taken a very narrow view of what 'warm-bloodied' means). The 1976 amendment extended the provisions of the legislation to include carriers, intermediate handlers and animal brokers, increased controls on the transportation of animals (excluding those being used for agricultural purposes), increased the penalties for violations of the legislation and required that all government agencies using laboratory animals show that they comply with the provisions of the Act.

The 1985 Improved Standards for Laboratory Animals Act represented the most far-reaching controls yet on the use of animals in American laboratories, although, as we will see in Chapter 10, its provisions are only peripherally concerned with the actual conduct of scientific procedures. Firstly, this legislation established an information service in the National Agricultural Library to provide data on alternatives to animal usage, to help prevent unintended duplication of procedures, and provide a record of humane techniques. Secondly, the legislation requires that each registered research facility must appoint an IACUC whose role is to oversee the procedures carried out on animals. Thirdly, researchers are required to consider alternatives to the use of animals and to consult with a veterinarian before beginning any experiment which could cause pain. Moreover, USDA was mandated to create regulations, which researchers are obliged to adhere to, on pre-surgical and post-surgical care, the use of pain relieving drugs and methods of euthanasia and the use of the same animal for more than one major procedure. Finally, in what became the most contentious part of the legislation, USDA was also instructed to set minimum standards for the humane handling, housing, care, treatment and transportation of laboratory animals including specific regulations to ensure 'an environment adequate to promote the psychological well-being of non-human primates' and to ensure the adequate exercise of dogs. Finally, the 1990 amendment in the form of the Pet Theft Act, requires pounds to hold animals for at least five days before releasing them to dealers, to inform owners

that pets taken to a pound may be used for research and to ensure that paperwork detailing the origin of each animal is kept
and made available.

USDA was given the job of implementing and enforcing the
Animal Welfare Act due to its independence from the animal
research community. The work is undertaken by a branch of an
USDA agency, the Animal and Plant Health Inspection Service
(APHIS), which resides in a new six-storey red-brick building in
suburban Maryland. Prior to 1989, enforcement of the Animal
Welfare Act was undertaken by the Veterinary Services section
of APHIS but a major reorganization resulted in the creation of a
new agency, Regulatory Enforcement and Animal Care (REAC).
At least partly due to complaints about REAC's poor record of
enforcement (see Chapter 10), the agency was reorganized in
October 1996. REAC was dissolved and a new Investigative and
Enforcement Services Unit (IES) was created separate from
Animal Care, which provides guidance for regulatory enforcement as well as liaison with the public and interest groups. Animal Care is but one of five major programme units within
APHIS and therefore has to share resources with, among others,
the Animal Damage Control and Plant Protection and Quar-
antine sections. IES has three regional offices throughout the
United States and it is their job to license facilities, to inspect
them and to investigate complaints.[20]

NIH, based at a large complex of buildings in Bethesda just
outside Washington DC, also plays a central role in the politics
of animal research. This agency, part of the Public Health Service in the Department of Health and Human Services, is the
primary allocator of federal funding for biomedical research.
NIH is divided into two major organizational units, an inter-
mural side, employing about 12 000 staff, which deals with research by NIH staff and an extramural side which allocates
research grants to scientists working in other public and private
sector institutions. Its research grants amount annually to about
$7 billion, about half of which involves some animal research.

NIH's importance for the welfare of laboratory animals derives firstly from its role in determining which research projects
to fund. When grant applications are received, a review group of
specialists in the relevant area will assess their scientific merit in
addition to being required to comment on the use of animals. If
the review committee has any concern about the way animals

are intended to be used, this must be reported to the Office for the Protection of Research Risks (OPRR) which then examines the issues before any grant is awarded. The OPRR, which employs about 40 staff, half of whom are directly concerned with animal welfare, is responsible for ensuring compliance with the Animal Welfare Act and NIH's own guidelines.[21] Since 1963 NIH has had a policy on animal welfare standards to which federally funded researchers must adhere and these, initially voluntary, guidelines were given statutory force by the Health Research Extension Act in 1985, a measure which accompanied the Improved Standards for Laboratory Animals Act.[22]

Many federal agencies have an interest in the animal research issue, either requiring scientific evidence from animal testing and/or themselves using animals to conduct their own research. USDA itself, for instance, uses data generated by animal tests and conducts its own animal research in the Agricultural Research Service. Likewise, since the passage of the 1938 Food, Drug and Cosmetic Act, the federal Food and Drug Administration (FDA) within the Department of Health and Human Services has controlled the admission of new drug and other products on to the market, and has required that all pharmaceutical products must be toxicity tested on animals. In addition, while the FDA does not explicitly mandate animal testing for non-pharmaceutical products, all companies are compelled to substantiate the safety of their products and the FDA does use data from animal tests. A number of other agencies – the independent Environmental Protection Agency, the Department of Labor, USDA, the Center for Disease Control, the Consumer Product Safety Commission, the Federal Trade Commission – also use data generated from animal tests.

Finally, mention should be made of the Defense Department which, controversially, uses animals for a variety of reasons relating to military effectiveness. According to evidence submitted to a Congressional hearing, the Department of Defense uses some 500 000 animals per year, the bulk (over 300 000) in 1992 being mice and rats but also, and more disturbingly, 2970 dogs, 813 cats and 1632 non-human primates.[23]

As in the case of farm animals, general anti-cruelty statutes do, except in the 19 states where research animals are specifically excluded, apply to research animals. Again, as in the case of farm animals, though, there are limitations because of the difficulty of demonstrating that an animal had suffered 'unnecessarily'. In the celebrated Silver Spring monkey affair, a researcher – Edward Taub – was initially found guilty under Maryland state law of cruelty to monkeys in his Silver Spring laboratory. This conviction, however, was overturned on appeal on the grounds that when the anti-cruelty law was initially drafted it was not intended to cover research animals.[24]

In a number of states, too, there have been legislative attempts to ban particular procedures. In California, for instance, a bill to ban the use of the Draize test for cosmetic and household cleaners passed the legislature twice but was twice vetoed by the Governor. Even at the city level, there can be variations in the application of federal regulations. In Cambridge, Massachusetts, for instance, the city council has taken a progressive view on the regulation of animal experimentation which has included a decision, in 1989, to appoint a commission to oversee and enforce the regulations in city laboratories.[25]

One important difference between Britain and the United States is the tradition in the latter whereby the courts play a much more prominent role in adjudicating disputes between state and non-state actors. In this regard, animal protection has been no exception. Thus, there have been numerous court cases – involving, in one case, the Supreme Court – dealing with the failure of USDA to draw up or enforce regulations concerned with animal research and the use of animals in biomedical education.[26] The effective use of the courts by the animal protection movement, however, is severely constrained by the regular denial of legal standing. This requirement, 'that a certain action has harmed the petitioner in a way that interferes with a legally recognisable right',[27] has prevented animal advocates from defending the interests of animals on numerous occasions.[28]

Domestic and Wild Animals

There is no federal statute designed to protect animals kept as pets, at least once they are bought from pet shops and breeders. Federal law, in the shape of the Animal Welfare Act, regulates breeders and the pet trade as well as prohibiting the promotion of, and participation in, fights involving mammals or birds, although state law allowing such activities takes precedence.

USDA is responsible for implementing and enforcing this legislation. Companion animals are covered by general anti-cruelty statutes and some states have prohibited specific cruel practices such as cock fighting and the use of decompression chambers to euthanize unwanted shelter animals. In addition, a number of states now require shelters to spray and neuter dogs and cats before adoption.

The wildlife conservation policy arena is the most complex of all the institutional frameworks designed to protect animals. A number of institutional arrangements have been created to administer legislation relating to wildlife. The Department of the Interior is regarded as the 'nation's principal conservation agency'.[29] The Fish and Wildlife Service within the department is responsible for administering and enforcing the Endangered Species Act originally passed in 1969, the Wild Birds Conservation Act 1992 and, jointly with the National Oceanic and Atmospheric Administration within the Commerce Department, the Marine Mammal Protection Act originally passed in 1972.

As in Britain, many other federal agencies (as well as Congressional committees) are involved in, and/or have an interest in wildlife policy. The National Parks service, founded in 1916, for instance, has an enormous impact on wildlife. In addition, The Bureau of Land Management is responsible for managing some public land and is specifically responsible for administering the 1971 Wild, Free-Roaming Horse and Burro Act, legislation which prohibits the removal or killing of wild horses and burros from the range without government permission. Moreover, USDA has, since 1915, operated the Animal Damage Control Programme and this has been responsible for killing millions of wild predators and 'nuisance' animals on public lands every year at the behest of cattle ranchers and other livestock producers.

At the state level, there is enormous scope for influencing wildlife policy. The fish and game commissions, for instance, have a great deal of autonomy from the federal government. Wildlife conservation is also the responsibility of state legislatures. A number of states, for instance, regulate trapping by, for instance, setting a maximum time period by which traps must be checked.[30] In addition, two states (Florida and Rhode Island) place severe restrictions on the use of the steel-jaw leghold trap and one state (New Jersey) has banned, since 1984, its use completely.[31]

The inclusion of wildlife protection initiatives on ballot papers has also become increasingly common and, with the limited opportunities available for the animal protection movement at the national level since the advent of a generally hostile Republican-controlled Congress, national groups have put a considerable amount of money and time into seeking the adoption of them. The first animal initiative occurred in 1920 and, as early as 1930, some success was achieved when Massachusetts voted to ban devices that 'cause continued suffering' to trapped animals.[32] More recently, in the 1994 elections, Oregon adopted a proposition banning bear baiting, and Arizona voters banned trapping on public lands.[33] In 1996, even more success was achieved when voters in Massachusetts and Colorado supported strong anti-trapping initiatives, voters in Washington state approved bans on baiting and hounding and voters in Alaska banned airborne hunting.

Our enquiry into the nature of animal protection politics has established so far that legislative interest in animal issues is now substantial, particularly in Britain but also, to a lesser degree, in the United States. Furthermore, the legislative and administrative strides that have been made have helped to build sectorized institutional structures designed, at least superficially, to mitigate the suffering of animals in the variety of ways in which humans have chosen to use them. This chapter, except in the brief analysis of the politics of British wildlife conservation, did not deal with two additional crucial questions. In the first place, it did not reveal the nature of the interest group system which surrounds each animal welfare policy arena. Secondly, it did not deal with the question of the balance of power within these policy arenas. The former question is dealt with in the following three chapters and the latter in Chapters 7 to 10.

2 The Economics and Politics of Animal Exploitation

In the last chapter, we identified a number of policy arenas responsible for decision-making impinging on the welfare of animals. The next three chapters build upon this analysis by examining the role of non-governmental organizations. The nature of the interest group system which surrounds each policy arena obviously has a key bearing upon both the extent of sectorization and the character of policy outputs. In this chapter the organizations with an interest in continuing to use animals are introduced, again with specific reference to farm and research interests. Essential to an understanding of the character of the animal use lobby is an examination of the industries and interests they represent, so this is our starting point.

As soon as we start examining the exploitation of animals, the staggering range of human interests served by it becomes quickly apparent. No one can question that animals are a source of significantly important economic interests. In addition, animals are used with the aim of improving human health, to ensure that humans are protected against potentially dangerous substances and products, and as a source of food, clothing and entertainment. While the economic benefits are indisputable, a ferocious debate also surrounds the utility of using animals in the other categories. Thus, the animal protection debate is not simply structured around the viability of according to animals a moral status sufficiently high to make certain, or all, human uses ethically illegitimate, whatever the consequences to humans. Rather, animal advocates challenge the very necessity of exploiting them, either on the grounds that their use does not produce the benefits claimed for it and/or that the use is unnecessary because trivial.[1]

Finally, and ironically, some animals are treated benignly by humans not, primarily at least, because we recognize their own interests in not suffering, but because – as in the keeping of animals as pets – we get companionship from them or because – as in the case of wildlife – we get some aesthetic pleasure from observing animals in their natural habitats.[2] In the latter case, conservationists are challenged by those (such as farmers, loggers, property developers and so forth) whose own economic interests are threatened by protecting wild animals.

THE POLITICAL ECONOMY OF WILDLIFE AND ANIMAL ENTERTAINMENT

The range of economic interests which gain through the exploitation of animals, and which stand to lose through more stringent animal protection standards, is formidable. We can start by mentioning those – such as breeders, organizers of rodeos (in America) and hunts, owners of pet shops, zoos, circuses, and marine entertainment complexes – who are in the business of using or providing animals for entertainment purposes.

All of these interests are organized to some degree and, when necessary, are prepared to make decision-makers aware of their views. The issue of wildlife conservation has produced an even more extensive range of interests. An example of this is provided by the list of witnesses who appeared in the Congressional hearings on the reauthorization of the Endangered Species Act in 1982 (see Table 2.1). Of the 40 organizations represented, only four can be regarded as animal protection groups, and the bulk of the rest are opposed to all or some animal protection objectives.

Table 2.1   Interested parties at selected Congressional Hearings on the Endangered Species Act, 1973–82

Wildlife Management Institute
Massachussetts Audubon Society
American Fur Resources Institute
Fur Takers of America
National Trappers Association
Wildlife Legislative Fund of America
Humane Society of the United States
Defenders of Wildlife

World Wildlife Fund
Pet Industry Joint Advisory Council
Reptile Skin Industry Trade Association
Safari Club International
Environmental Defense Fund
National Agricultural Chemicals Association
Nature Conservancy
National Forest Products Association
American Mining Congress
National Audubon Society
Western Geophysical Corporation
National Ocean Industries Association
Nuclear and Environment Division of Northeast Utilities
Western Regional Council
National Wildlife Federation
Edison Electric Institute
Water Resources Congress
Natural Resource Biologists Association
Trade Records Analysis of Flora and Fauna in Commerce
Natural Areas Association
Animal Welfare Institute
New York Botanical Gardens
National Parks and Conservation Association
Friends of the Earth
Sierra Club
International Primate Protection League
Fund for Animals
Southeast Alligator Association
French Taning Industry
Natural Resources Defense Council
Monsanto Agricultural Products Corporation
Pacific Power and Light Corporation

Source: *Hearings Before the Subcommittee on Fisheries and Wildlife Conservation and the Environment of the Committee on Merchant Marine and
Fisheries,* House of Representatives, 93rd Congress, First Session, 15,
26, 27 March 1973; 96th Congress, First Session, 6 April, 16, 20, 27
July 1979; 97th Congress, Second session, 22 February, 8 March 1982.

In the first place, the activities of trappers and hunters are
clearly anathema to animal rights advocates even when the
former, as they are increasingly doing, seek to profess their interest in wildlife conservation. The protection of species is very
different from the protection of individual animals and while

trappers and hunters – and the legendary pro-hunting National Rifle Association (NRA) in the United States to which many hunters belong – can claim, with varying degrees of credibility, to be on the side of conservation, there is a clear conflict with the individualistic animal rights position and often, because of the barbaric methods used, the animal welfare position too (see Chapter 5 for the case of the British hunting lobby).[3]

For the same reasons, it is also the case that the relationship between animal protectionists and general wildlife conservation organizations is often strained and rarely productive. This is not surprising because the origins of the wildlife conservation movement in the United States lay with hunting enthusiasts.[4] Thus, the Audubon Society was founded in 1905 by a hunter,[5] the National Wildlife Federation, formed in 1936, was for several decades dominated by hunting and fishing interests, and the Izaak Walton League of America, founded in 1922, still is.

Since the 1960s, however, some wildlife groups have tried to broaden their appeal to attract the support of those concerned with the protection of individual animals,[6] but their record on animal protection issues remains poor. For example, the Defenders of Wildlife refused to back the Refuge Wildlife Protection Act introduced in 1988 to ban hunting and trapping on national wildlife refuges.[7] A further example is the issue of the steel-jaw leghold trap. Proposals to abolish this vicious device which can inflict enormous suffering on animals unlucky enough to find themselves ensnared, have not been supported by any wildlife group, and in 1991 a bill to ban it was opposed vigorously by the Wildlife Legislative Fund of America and the Nature Conservancy, while the Wilderness Society and even Friends of the Earth had no position on it.

Similar conflicts have emerged in Britain. Greenpeace's refusal in the 1970s, for instance, to condemn the trapping of animals for fur led a number of activists, including Mark Glover, to leave and set up the anti-fur group LYNX (since superseded by Respect for Animals). The conflict between wildlife conservation and animal protection, however, has not been so acute in Britain. This is probably because hunting and shooting has always been less widespread in Britain. It is certainly the case that wildlife groups, and particularly the RSPB, tend to stand clear of hunting and shooting issues although this in itself weakens the force of the lobby against these practices.

Conflict between animal advocates and wildlife management agencies is inevitable too because of the ideological divisions described above. Such agencies, including state fish and game agencies, tend to be strongly in favour of hunting, not least because in many states they receive a considerable amount of their income from the sale of hunting and fishing licences. In the early 1990s, trapping was allowed as a wildlife management tool in 91 of the 452 National Wildlife Refuges managed by the Fish and Wildlife service.[8]

Another dimension to the issue of wildlife conservation is provided by the conflict over land usage. Here, animal protectionists and wildlife conservationists often find themselves on the same side as a range of economic interests, some of which are listed in Table 2.1, who stand to lose out if land, or water, is preserved for wildlife. For example, there has been considerable controversy in the United States over opening up public land to a range of activities – from mining to water-skiing – regarded as incompatible with wildlife conservation. An, unsuccessful, bill introduced by Bill Green in the 101st Congress, aiming to end commercial trapping and hunting in national wildlife refuges, was supported by the so-called Wildlife Refuge Reform Coalition, consisting of more than 30 animal protection and environmental organizations.[9]

THE ECONOMIC STRUCTURE OF INTENSIVE AGRICULTURE

The range of organizations who have an interest in the utilization of animals for the production of food is staggering. Farmers constitute only about 2–3 per cent of the population in both Britain and the United States, and the number of people employed on farms has decreased markedly over the past half century or so, but the collective economic value of the various components of the food production process is immense. In 1984 almost 20 per cent of GNP in the United States was derived from food production and all sectors of the process employed 18.5 per cent of the available civilian work force,[10] whereas in Britain domestic agriculture, food processing and food distribution account for 7.5 per cent of GDP.[11] Animal agriculture constitutes a large proportion of this activity. In 1980, for instance, livestock products accounted for some 56 per cent of the total value of agricultural production in the European Community.[12] Likewise, cattle production in the US has annual receipts in excess of $30 billion and represents the fourth largest manufacturing industry.[13] Meat consumption remains, despite the increase in vegetarianism over the past two decades, a central part of most people's diet in the developed world.[14]

Central to an understanding of interest representation in modern animal agriculture is the relatively recent development of intensive agriculture. Intensive agriculture aims at producing the largest quantity of food at the cheapest possible price. In order to achieve this goal, it was necessary to utilize as much land as possible for crop production and maximize the yield from that land. Both of these practices had severe environmental consequences in terms of the destruction of important habitats and in terms of the damaging effects of pesticides.[15] Central to intensification, of course, is the 'factory' farming of animals whereby rearing in an industrialized and mechanized fashion in order to maximize the productive capacities of animals has become the norm.[16] In practice, this means confinement and increased stocking densities both of which have serious implications for the welfare of animals and for the environment in general. In terms of its objectives, it should be said that agricultural intensification has been enormously successful. There has, for instance, been a 'spectacular' decline in the price of animal derived protein, thereby helping to provide for the urban working class a much larger disposable income.[17]

The food industry was always more than just farming but the growth of intensive agriculture has radically changed the volume and character of interests involved and, as a consequence, has reduced the importance of farming in the food production process. Intensification has not only drawn in a range of additional interests but has led to increasing horizontal and vertical integration as well as commodity specialization. The result has been the emergence of large and very wealthy agri-business corporations controlling 'both the supply of farming inputs and the disposal of farm outputs'.[18] Thus, in each stage of the food process – from farming to food processing, distribution and retailing – economies of scale have resulted in fewer, and larger companies. Furthermore, some companies now have a direct or indirect financial stake in most or all sectors of the process.

In the last half-century, then, agriculture has radically changed. It has changed from being a fragmented, labour-intensive industry to a capital intensive one which relies on a range of high-technology inputs requiring economies of scale to be commercially viable. Thus, there has been a significant rise in the size of farms and in the concentration of farm production. For example, the number of farms in the United States fell from 6.8 to 2.4 million between 1935 and 1980.[19] In the UK, similarly, some 254 300 agricultural holdings were recorded in 1987 and only about 11 per cent of these accounted for just over 55 per cent of output whereas the smallest 43 per cent produced only 2 per cent of the output.[20] Farmers now represent only a small part of the total financial value of the food production process and represent 'the tail of a very large dog'.[21] Thus, in 1979 the value of the farm sector's products in the United States was worth $70 billion but the total output of the food production process added $415 billion extra to this figure.[22] Those with a vested interest in the continuation of intensive agriculture now include the input industries (the feed industry, pharmaceutical and chemical companies, and the suppliers of farm machinery), those involved with the transportation of both live animals and finished products, slaughtering plants, the rendering industry, the food processing and manufacturing industries, retailers, advertisers, and, finally, those financial institutions with a stake in any one or more of these processes.

There are now, then, considerable financial incentives for the continuation of intensive agriculture, not least in the agrichemicals and pharmaceuticals sector. This sector produces a wide range of livestock feed supplements to accelerate growth, and increase the body weight of intensively reared animals. To give one example, four American companies – Monsanto, Eli Lilly, Upjohn and American Cyanamid – have invested nearly a billion dollars in research and development of bovine growth hormones, and in 1981, animal health products contributed 13 per cent to the total corporate sales of Pfizer and Eli Lilly.[23] In recent years, too, the potential of biotechnology has spawned a whole new range of interests whose activities impact sharply on the well-being, or even very existence, of farm animals.[24]

There is also an increasing tendency towards vertical and horizontal integration, and this is particularly apparent in the poultry industry. In Britain, for example, four companies control the vast majority of poultry production and over two-thirds of the national flock are on about 300 holdings with flocks greater than 20 000. By contrast, some 30 000 holdings with flocks of 50 hens or less account for just over one per cent of the national flock.[25] In the US, similarly, although there were over 30 000 broiler producers in the 1970s, about half of these accounted for 90 per cent of total output.[26] Likewise, since the 1950s, the number of pig farmers in the USA has fallen by over 80 per cent.[27] In the British dairy sector, to give another example, a small group of five companies buy two-thirds of the milk produced.[28]

A classic example of vertical and horizontal integration is provided by Unilever, the largest agribusiness corporation in Europe. Unilever produces a large range of food (and other) products, from margarines to meat and also owns plantations, trawler fleets, oil and timber mills, slaughterhouses, manufacturing and processing as well as wholesaling operations. In 1993, the company had a stock market value of £9.4 billion and a workforce of 283 000.[29] Its subsidiaries (it now owns 812 companies in 75 countries) include Birds' Eye frozen foods, Vesta packaged meals, Walls ice cream and meat products and Midland Poultry.[30] A further illustration is Hillsdown Holdings, Britain's biggest meat company. This company produces red meat, bacon, poultry and eggs. It has 150 subsidiaries, including Buxted Poultry and Daylay Eggs, and had a turnover in 1987 of over £3 billion. Its vertical penetration is assured by the ownership of feed mills, commercial hatcheries, abattoirs and food processing and distribution concerns.[31]

Vertical and horizontal integration is even more pronounced in the United States, where large corporations, such as Cargill (which processes meat and poultry as well as manufacturing animal feed), Castle and Cooke, and Ralston Purina, dominate the food production process. Another prime example is Con-Agra which has interests in animal feed, agrichemicals, food processing and retailing. In the last 30 years or so, it has also begun to acquire considerable interests in the beef sector so that by the end of the 1980s its annual red meat sales were over $7.5 billion. By this time too, three corporations – Iowa Beef Packers (now owned by Occidental Petroleum), Excel and ConAgra – owned about 17 per cent of all the cattle slaughtered in the USA and were responsible for slaughtering about 70 per cent of all the feedlot cattle in the USA.[32]

Even if corporate entities do not themselves own land or livestock, they can still exert enormous influence through 'contract farming' where farmers are contracted to one company. This can take the form of a 'full management transfer' where the buyer supplies the inputs, specifies how the production process is to take place and owns the commodity (particularly common in poultry production) or 'partial management transfer' where the buyer does not acquire ownership of the product until it leaves the farm (more common in the pig sector).[33] Over a third of all farmers in the USA are now tied to such contracts and for some commodities, most notably poultry, the figure is even higher.[34] The result, particularly of the full management transfer, is that farmers lose their independence. They are not only squeezed financially, but also have to engage in intensive production techniques since this benefits the companies they are contracted to as well as the consumer.

The final point to note about the character of intensive agriculture is that the developments described above have helped to facilitate agricultural specialization and, in particular, the dominance of commodity groups in agricultural production. In the United States, as a result, the influence of the general farm groups has declined whilst in Britain the dominance of the NFU is preserved through an elaborate system of committees where separate commodity producers can be represented.

THE ANIMAL RESEARCH COMMUNITY

There are a range of bodies with an interest in using animals for research purposes. Whether or not its reliance on animals is scientifically justified, the academic community – consisting of a range of disciplines through pharmacology and veterinary science to psychology – claim that their major concern is to defend their right to continue using animals in order to benefit humans in a variety of ways. While this may be so, it is also the case that the financial benefits to universities and research institutes from animal-based study can be considerable. Universities, in an increasingly harsh economic climate, rely to a great extent on the ability of their staff to attract research grants from the public and private sectors, and the future career prospects of staff depend to an equally large extent on the funds they can generate.

The demarcation between public health and profits is even more blurred in the case of pharmaceutical companies. The origins of the modern pharmaceutical industry date back to the eighteenth century in Britain and the nineteenth century in the United States, but in both countries there has been a massive growth in the pharmaceutical industry since the Second World War.[35] Central to the emergence of a buoyant pharmaceutical industry was the emergence of new chemical ingredients which began to replace the previous reliance on naturally occurring animal and vegetable ingredients. Such has been the development of the industry that over 95 per cent of the products available by the late 1970s were unknown 30 years previously.[36] By 1990, world production stood at $150 billion.[37] Both Britain and the United States have a 'sophisticated pharmaceutical industry and a significant research base'.[38] Indeed, the two leading pharmaceutical companies in 1988 were Merck & Co., a US company, and Glaxo, a British company, and 14 of the top 25 companies were American and three were British.[39] By 1976, UK output had reached £894 million and US world-wide sales were worth over $1 billion, with the latter having the biggest world market share (nearly 20 per cent) and the former the eighth largest (2.5 per cent).[40]

From this, it will be recognized that while the impact of drug companies on public health is undoubted, their contribution to the economy, in terms of employment, exports and so on, is also important. In 1980, the UK pharmaceutical industry, for instance, had 250 firms producing a gross output of £2028 million and employed 72 800 people.[41] Abrahams, for one, notes how important drugs were to Britain's exports in the 1950s and 1960s and he suggests that:

> the Ministry of Health had come to accept the basic philosophy that the export trade of the pharmaceutical industry was so precious that regulation of its affairs was to be avoided.[42]

There is no question that this had an impact on animal experimentation policy. In the first place, the pharmaceutical industry has a powerful ally in what was, in the 1970s, the Department of Health and Social Security (DHSS). Giving evidence to a select committee enquiry into animal research, for instance, the DHSS described itself as the 'sponsor' of the industry, 'responsible for monitoring the well-being of that industry and for representing its interests within the Government machine'.[43] During the passage of the 1986 Animals (Scientific Procedures) Act in Britain, it was undoubtedly the case too that the financial impact of greater regulation on drug companies' use of animals was an important factor in the government's deliberations on the legislation, not least because the importance of the economic dimension did not escape the pharmaceutical industry itself. Thus, in a memo to a House of Lords enquiry into animal research, the Association of the British Pharmaceutical Industry wrote that as well as therapeutic successes, the use of animals:

> have also conferred other substantial benefits on the community, such as the pharmaceutical industry's enviable record on exports, with a positive trade balance during the last year in excess of £450 million.[44]

It was no surprise, therefore, that very early on in the White Paper introducing the Government's plans to reform the 1876 Cruelty to Animals Act, it was emphasized that:

> The United Kingdom has a large pharmaceutical industry which makes a big contribution to our balance of payments and employs 67 500 people. In devising new controls it is very important not to put industry at risk unnecessarily.[45]

Separate from both the academic community and the pharmaceutical industry are the contract research laboratories who conduct toxicity tests on animals for a whole range of products such as drugs, pesticides, weedkillers, cosmetics and household and industrial products. The Huntingdon Research Centre in the East of England, for instance, had a net income of almost £2.5 million in 1984 and contracts with almost 500 clients. Likewise, the Hazleton Laboratories in Yorkshire, part of a worldwide group based in the United States, carries out toxicity tests for the pharmaceutical and agrichemical industries.[46]

Finally, the use of animals in research laboratories generates, in turn, a whole range of additional economic interests. In the first place, there are the suppliers of animals. In Britain, only purpose-bred animals are allowed to be used in research and this

requirement has spawned a number of commercial enterprises,
the most notable being Shamrock Farms based in Sussex. In the
United States, companies which provide purpose-bred animals
(the largest of which is Charles River, the organization which, as
we shall see below, was responsible for the creation of the
leading organization promoting animal research) co-exist with
so-called 'Class B' dealers who provide 'random source' animals
– gained from pounds, shelters and private individuals – for research. In addition, research laboratories are kitted-out by
companies who specialize in the relevant equipment, from cages
to restraining devices.

THE POLITICAL ORGANIZATION OF THE ANIMAL-USE LOBBY

Identifying the character of the interests served by the continuing utilization of animals provides us with the necessary framework within which to consider the political organization of these
interests. As with this book as a whole, the major focus is on the
issues of farm and laboratory animal welfare.

The first step here is a raw count of all those organizations who
might potentially have an interest in farm and laboratory animal
welfare decision-making.[47] In the USA this amounts to about
100 and in Britain about 80 organizations. The issue split is
broadly similar with agricultural groups dominating, although
less so in the USA, followed by those concerned with animal
research. In both countries, the common organizational structure is the trade association. Unlike Britain, however, a formal
lobbying arm is maintained in Washington DC by 26 individual
agribusiness and pharmaceutical companies. Similar companies
in Britain may well have discrete contacts with governmental
actors from time to time but there would seem to be a preference
for working on a day-to-day basis through the relevant trade
associations.

Of course, a raw count does not tell us very much. From the
information provided by a questionnaire (see Appendix II), interviews with the participants and other sources, we can attempt
to provide answers to a number of crucial questions. Obviously,
it is necessary to discover the extent of a particular organization's
concern with animal welfare issues. In addition, we need to ask

how far animal-use organizations are sectorized, each one focusing on a particular issue area and the governmental institutions concerned with it. Finally, in preparation for the accounts, in Chapters 7 to 10, of the participant's political influence, it is necessary to consider the organizational structure of the main defenders of animal use for food and research and a preliminary examination of the resources available to them.

The Major Participants

The evidence suggests that a surprisingly small number of the groups initially identified as being involved, directly or indirectly, with the fate of animals are actively involved in lobbying directly on animal protection issues. Questionnaire respondents were asked whether their lobbying involvement on animal protection issues was extensive, intermittent, or rare. In Britain, for the animal agriculture and research sectors, a total of 13 organizations (12 for the former and one for the latter) regarded their lobbying on animal protection issues as either extensive or intermittent, while in the USA the total was 10 (seven agricultural and three concerned with animal research). The response rate was about 75 per cent and so to avoid the possibility that relevant groups were being excluded through their failure to respond, evidence from other sources, such as appearances at committees and interviews with participants, was employed to provide a more accurate list. This exercise added a further 12 groups to the total list of organizations which appear, categorized according to their major interests, in Table 2.2.

Before we examine these groups in more detail, it is worth while examining the possibility that some organizations are not actively involved in lobbying because they do not regard animal protection as an important issue. It is certainly the case that pharmaceutical, biomedical and agricultural interests do have a huge range of concerns. Drug companies, for instance, have been preoccupied by the broader question of the safety of their products (which does, of course, involve the use of animals but goes much further than this), the price of their products and general questions relating to their profitability.[48] In these areas, individual pharmaceutical companies and their trade associations are extremely active. In Britain, a number of drug manufacturing and wholesale firms amalgamated in 1929 to form the

Table 2.2 Politically active animal use organisations in Britain and the United States

Britain

Agriculture

National Farmers Union
British Egg Industry Council
British Meat Manufacturers' Association
National Cattle Breeders' Association
British Pig Association
British Organic Farmers
National Sheep Association
National Federation of Meat Traders
Livestock Auctioneers' Association
UK Egg Producers' Association
British Poultry Meat Federation
Dairy Trade Federation

Research

Research Defence Society
Association of the British Pharmaceutical Industry
Medical Research Council
Cosmetic, Toiletry and Fragrance Association
Research for Health Charities Group

USA

Agriculture

American Feed Industry Association
American Farm Bureau Federation
American Meat Institute
National Grange
United Egg Producers
National Cattleman's Association
National Broiler Council
National Pork Producers' Council
American Veal Association
American Veterinary Medicine Association
Animal Health Institute
National Milk Producers' Federation

Research

National Association for Biomedical Research
American Medical Association
Pharmaceutical Manufacturers' Association
Putting People First
Americans for Medical Progress
Cosmetic, Toiletry and Fragrance Association

Wholesale Druggist Trade Association which was renamed the Association of the British Pharmaceutical Industry (ABPI) in 1949.[49] Its member companies (of which there are over 150) produce almost 100 per cent of the prescription medicines used in the National Health Service. Abrahams has noted how the ABPI has been extremely influential in the development of British drug safety policy, and has been well represented on the bodies designed to administer this policy. As a result, he argues, the interests of the producers have been prioritized ahead of those of the consumer.[50] Within the European Union, too, pharmaceutical and biotechnology companies have a powerful presence, with the Brussels-based European Federation of Pharmaceutical Industry Associations and the European Bio-technology Co-ordinating Group acting as the centrepiece of their lobbying effort.[51]

All of the above does raise the possibility that there is a 're-serve army' of organizations ready to join the fray if necessary. To a certain extent, these organizations do become more active at particular times. Thus, for instance, the witnesses appearing before the House of Lords select committee on animal research issues in 1979 included (as well as the Research Defence Society and the ABPI) the Royal Society, the Beecham Group, the Medical Research Council, the Association for the Study of Animal Behaviour, the British Psychological Society, the British Pharmacological Society and the Physiological Society.[52] In the USA, similarly, a variety of specialist scientific organizations – the American Heart Association, the Federation of American Societies for Experimental Biology, the American Physiological Society, the American Association of Medical Colleges, and the National Association of Life Sciences (a trade association representing contract testing laboratories) to name but a few – often appear at relevant Congressional hearings.

However, the questionnaire survey reveals that, of those who responded to the particular question, only one animal industry group (in the United States) explained their lack of lobbying involvement on the issue on the grounds that animal welfare legislation has little chance of becoming law, compared to 10 who said such legislation has little impact on them, 11 who said that other groups supporting their position are active on the issue and a further 11 who said that limited resources prevented them from lobbying on animal welfare.

Measuring the respective importance of those groups who do participate is a difficult task and is, to a certain degree, a subjective judgement. Nevertheless, based on their visibility in animal protection lobbying – including the number of times they are mentioned in secondary literature, in Congressional hearings or parliamentary debates and by other governmental and nongovernmental participants – it is possible to identify the major actors.

In both Britain and the United States, one group dominates the lobbying effort in each sector. In terms of animal research, specific groups – the National Association for Biomedical Research (NABR) and the Research Defence Society (RDS) – have been set up exclusively for the purpose of lobbying to promote the interests of animal researchers. In both countries too, the political organization of the animal research community dates back to the nineteenth century. In the United States, from the outset, the myriad organizations with an interest in animal research set up a separate entity to lobby on this issue. Thus, in 1899, the American Medical Association (AMA) appointed a Committee on National Legislation which had, as part of its remit, the monitoring of anti-vivisection legislation and in 1908, the AMA set up a Council for the Defense of Medical Research.[53] These were the antecedents of the National Society for Medical Research (NSMR) set up in Chicago in 1945 by the American Association of Medical Colleges and supported by the AMA.[54] At this time, the research community was on the attack. A primary aim was to lobby for so-called 'pound seizure' laws on a state-wide basis which would legally require animal shelters to turn their animals over to researchers (see Chapter 10 for more details on this issue).

The modern animal research lobby dates back to 1979 and the creation of the Association for Biomedical Research (ABR). Like its predecessors, ABR (now NABR) is a federal organization with a membership of universities, medical research groups and drug companies (see below). ABR was formed in the wake of the re-form of the Metcalf–Hatch Act in New York State which, as an important symbol of a revitalized animal protection movement, repealed the pound-seizure law originally passed in 1952. The NSMR by this time was perceived to be an inadequate vehicle for the promotion of animal use in biomedical research, partly at least because it was regarded as too extreme, seeking to justify the unrestrained use of animals for whatever purpose scientists deemed necessary.[55] A much more subtle organization, able to win the hearts and minds of an American public increasingly concerned about the use of animals, was deemed necessary, and ABR, founded by employees of Charles River, Inc. – the world's largest supplier of laboratory animals – was set up with this purpose and researchers were prepared to support it (see below).

The need for the research community to defend itself in the 1980s as a result of increasingly bad publicity and the possibility of further legislative restrictions (see Chapter 10), led to in-tensified activity. The ineffective NSMR was taken over by ABR in the mid-1980s and its name changed to the National Asso-ciation for Biomedical Research (NABR). In addition, both the Foundation for Biomedical Research (NABR's public relations arm founded in 1981), the AMA and other scientific organiza-tions actively sought to counter the animal protection movement with material for public consumption (often focused on school children) designed to promote the benefits of animal research to human health.[56]

NABR does the bulk of the lobbying on animal research, al-though its constituent organizations also participate at a sub-ordinate level. The Pharmaceutical Manufacturers Association (PMA), a trade association representing 100 drug companies, used to have its own animal welfare committee but now relies on NABR to which it is affiliated.[57] The same applies to the AMA. In addition, NABR and its constituent members have been joined by two other organizations, Putting People First and Americans for Medical Progress, founded in 1991 and 1992 re-spectively. The former was set up by Kathleen Marquardt and focuses on a range of animal issues including animal research. The latter, based in Alexandria, Virginia, was set up, and is largely financed, by the US Surgical Corporation, whose use of live dogs to demonstrate surgical staples has long been a target of the animal protection movement.[58] Both of these organizations, however, play a very small role in direct lobbying. Putting People First, which claims a membership of 30 000, specializes in grass-roots activism, mobilizing its members to write letters in support of animal research.

In Britain, the development of the research community's political organization has followed a similar course. As public concern about vivisection increased in the nineteenth century, researchers organized to counter it. In 1876, the British Physiological Society was founded and illustrious scientists such as Huxley and Darwin were enlisted to defend the use of animals. In 1882, in the face of continuing attacks on vivisection, the Association for the Advancement of Medicine by Research (AAMR) was founded at the behest of the presidents of the Royal Colleges of Physicians and Surgeons. Gradually, this organization became more concerned with setting itself up as the government's unofficial adviser than with promoting animal experimentation in public.[59] The AAMR's promotional, and eventually its lobbying role, was ultimately taken by the RDS founded by the surgeon Stephen Paget in 1908. The pharmaceutical industry is well represented within the RDS but it also has its own lobbying capacity on animal research issues. Thus, in 1975, due to growing public concern about animal experimentation and the possibility of legislative reform, the ABPI set up a working party on Laboratory Animal Regulations which aimed to represent the industry's interests to government.[60]

As in the United States, the research community in Britain did not, until the 1980s, campaign extensively in the public arena but the success of the animal protection movement in getting its message across precipitated a response. Initially, this role was performed by the RDS which, in the run-up to the passage of the 1986 Act, ran national advertising campaigns (their propaganda arm is now called the Biomedical Research Education Trust). The perceived failure of the RDS in mobilizing public opinion in favour of animal experimentation resulted in a much broader-based campaign. To this end, the ABPI set up the Animals in Medicines Research Information Centre (AMRIC) in the mid-1980s which produces glossy information packs, some designed for school children and their teachers, promoting the value of animal research. This was followed by campaigns in 1990 by the

British Association for the Advancement of Science, which issued a Declaration on Animals in Medical Research; and by the BMA in 1992, which launched a campaign 'informing the public of the importance of animal experiments in the fight against disease'.[61] Finally, in 1991 two new organizations with a campaigning edge were formed. One of these, Seriously Ill for Medical Research, was deliberately aimed at countering the sympathy generated by campaigns for animals. The other, the Research for Health Charities Group, is a coalition of the major medical research funding charities and one of this organization's objectives is to promote the benefits of animal research.

Like animal research, one organization in each country dominates the lobbying effort for agricultural interests. There is a significant difference here, though, in the sense that in Britain the leading group remains the National Farmers Union (NFU), a general farming organization, whereas in the United States the American Feed Industry Association (AFIA), a trade association representing the feed industry, holds pride of place.

The NFU's dominance in agricultural policy-making dates back to the period immediately after the Second World War (see Chapter 8) and it was natural for it to take responsibility for lobbying government when farm animal welfare became an important political issue. Other organizations, representing livestock auctioneers, meat manufacturers and virtually all commodity producers have a lobbying arm but they do not play an equal role. At the apex is the NFU followed by a number of commodity groups to which other organizations are affiliated. Thus, a number of organizations, such as the Bacon Meat Manufacturers' Association, are affiliated to the British Meat Manufacturers' Association. Likewise the British Poultry Federation (BPF) based in High Holborn in London is the chief lobbyist for a range of other poultry commodity groups including those representing chicken producers, goose producers, poultry breeders, turkey producers, hen packers, poultry merchants, and egg producers. Affiliated to the BPF is the British Poultry Meat Federation and the British Egg Industry Council. The latter is a trade association formed in 1986 which, in 1993, had ten member organizations including the British Egg Association, the British Egg Products Association and the British Poultry Breeders' and Hatcheries Association.[62] The Dairy Trade Federation also has a number of affiliates including the

National Dairyman's Association and the Creamery Proprietors' Association and affiliated to the latter are organizations such as the Association of British Preserved Milk Manufacturers and the Association of Cheese Processors.

The dominance of the AFIA in US animal welfare lobbying quickly became apparent in the course of my research. Initially, there was a certain reluctance among some agricultural groups to answer the questionnaire and it transpired that at least 12 of them had asked the chief AFIA lobbyist for his opinion. When I was able to assure him that the research was for genuine academic purposes he informed the others and they began to respond. Subsequent research confirmed the pre-eminence of the AFIA in this area.

The dominance of the NFU in Britain and the AFIA and commodity groups in the USA seems to have occurred for a number of reasons. In the first place, the general farming organizations in the United States have never been as influential as the NFU in Britain, the latter being particularly notable for its high density membership with over 80 per cent of farmers traditionally being members.[63] This is a reflection, in part, of the greater commodification and vertical integration of agriculture in the former. Thus, commodity groups in the USA developed as a consequence of the commodity price support programme introduced in the 1930s (see Chapter 7). It is not insignificant, therefore, that a trade association of firms that manufacture feed for other producers or for their own poultry or livestock operations plays such a central lobbying role and has close links with other agricultural groups representing commodity producers and veterinarians. We should not underestimate the degree of commodification in Britain. In this context, it is clearly the case that one reason for the NFU's predominance has been its ability to remain flexible enough to incorporate commodity producers as individual members within its organizational structure (see below), to develop close working relations with other commodity organizations and to take varying interests into account when determining its lobbying strategy.

One final point is that to some degree the AFIA's animal welfare role occurred by accident, or rather by the particular interests of those who have been employed as lobbyists. In the 1980s, the AFIA and the AFBF both recognised the potential political importance of farm animal welfare and sought to educate commodity groups. Ultimately, the AFIA took on the primary role as the defender of the agricultural community against the animal protection movement. This has been maintained by the AFIA's current chief lobbyist, Steve Kopperud, who has developed a particular interest in animal welfare issues and now regards himself as the 'eyes and ears' of the opposition. He not only represents the industry's view on the issue but is also prepared to debate with animal advocates on TV and radio shows.[64]

Policy Arenas and the Animal-Use Lobby

There is considerable evidence to support the view that the policy concerns of animal-use groups are sectorized, although, in the United States, there are important exceptions to this general rule. In order to assess the degree of sectorization, the questionnaire respondents in Britain and the USA were given a list of bills covering the whole range of animal welfare issues (see Table 2.3) and asked to indicate for each bill whether their lobbying was extensive, intermittent or rare and whether they opposed, supported or had no position on the bill.

In most cases, organizations indicated an interest in a small number of bills, lobbying and having a position on their particular sectoral interest. Indeed, there was a considerable degree of sub-sectorization here. In the agricultural sector, for example, the American Meat Institute, representing meat packers, lobbied and had a position on the Humane Slaughter of Poultry Bill and the Downed Animals Protection Bill but was not involved at all with the Protection of Veal Calves Bill. Likewise, the National Cattleman's Association had no position on the Humane Slaughter of Poultry Bill while the National Broiler Council, understandably, was only concerned with this bill. In Britain, similarly, the National Cattle Breeders Association and the UK Egg Producers' Association did not lobby or even have a position on the Pig Husbandry Bill. The NFU, likewise, while having an interest in all of the bills relating to farm animals – including the bill to introduce a dog registration scheme which does have a direct impact on farmers because of the damage that dogs can do to livestock – maintained 'its long-standing neutrality on the issue of hunting'.[65]

A similar pattern of subsectorization exists within animal research, where there is a tendency for biomedical and pharmaceutical organizations to distance themselves from the issue of non-pharmaceutical product testing. NABR does lobby on product testing issues but tends to leave the bulk of the work here to the Cosmetic, Toiletry and Fragrance Association (CTFA) – a trade association with a membership of more than 240 companies that manufacture or distribute about 90 per cent of the finished cosmetic products marketed in the USA – while the PMA was involved with the Animal Welfare Act but had no interest in the Consumer Products Safe Testing Bill. In Britain, similarly, the RDS avoids getting involved in the issue of toxicology testing for cosmetics, so, for instance, the organization was not active at

Table 2.3 Animal welfare bills in Britain and the United States used in questionnaire

Britain
Wildlife and Countryside Act 1981
Animals (Scientific Procedures) Act 1986
Dog Registration Amendment to the Environmental Protection Bill 1990
Dangerous Dogs Act 1991
Pig Husbandry Bill 1991
The Welfare of Animals at Slaughter Act 1991
Wild Mammals (Protection) Bill 1992
November 1992 EC Directive on Cosmetic Testing

USA
Protection of Veal Calves Bill 1990
Humane Slaughter of Poultry Bill 1993
Downed Animals Protection Bill 1993
Refuge Wildlife Protection Bill 1991
Improved Standards for Laboratory Animal Welfare Bill 1985
Pet Theft Bill 1990
Moratorium on Patents for Genetically Altered Animals Bill 1990
Consumer Products Safe Testing Bill 1991
Steel-Jaw Leghold Trap Prohibition Bill 1991
Dolphin Protection Consumer Information Act 1990
Endangered Species Act

all in lobbying on the Council of Ministers' decision on cosmetics testing in 1992. The RDS lobbyist does speak to his counterparts in the Cosmetic, Toiletry and Fragrance Association about once a year but no cosmetic organization has asked to join the RDS, and even if they did they would be refused.[66]

There are some important exceptions to the policy sectorization model. Significantly, these exceptions relate in particular to the animal research arena in the United States where the range of participants gives credence to the claim that the model of a closed and insulated policy community has little explanatory capacity (see Chapter 10 for a further discussion of this point). In the first place, as we have seen, organizations in the animal research sector have a range of other interests which involves them in consultation with other government agencies and, in the United States, congressional committees. Thus, when PMA were asked which executive agencies and departments the organization targets, the respondent wrote 'all'. Of course, the reason why NABR and the RDS were created in the first place was to distinguish lobbying on animal research from their constituent organizations' other concerns, itself a reflection of the disaggregated reality of policy-making.

A further exception is the lobbying of those organizations whose animal welfare interests cut across the sectoral boundaries we have identified. This includes the American organizations Putting People First and the American Veterinary Medical Association (AVMA). The former claimed to be active in wildlife, farm and research animal issues while the latter claimed to be active on bills concerned with farm and research animals. Two points need to be made about these cross-sectoral activities. In the first place, Putting People First is not a major player in any of the animal protection sectors, focusing, for the most part as previously indicated, on encouraging grass-roots legislative activism. As such, the organization does not need the expertise necessary to lobby effectively in areas requiring very different arguments and knowledge. Secondly, the AVMA is able to lobby effectively in the different issue areas precisely because it does have the resources to divide up its activities effectively.

The most striking difference between the political activity of the animal-use industry in the United States and in Britain is that in the former there are significant cross-sectoral links. In Britain, the NFU, as far as I am aware, has no – formal or informal –

links with the RDS. In America, cross-sectoral links centre upon the role of the AFIA and the chief lobbyist and senior vice president Steve Kopperud. He played a significant role in lobbying on the Animal Welfare Act, appearing at Congressional hearings and liaising with NABR on a joint approach. In addition, general farming organizations such as the American Farm Bureau Federation (AFBF), National Grange and the National Farmers' Union also participated in Congressional hearings on the subject, the National Grange revealing in a questionnaire response that they regarded themselves as extensively involved in lobbying on the Animal Welfare Act. By contrast, not one British agricultural organization I contacted had a view on the British animal research legislation.

To a certain extent, the Animal Welfare Act was of direct concern to agricultural interests because of the threat that agricultural animals would be covered by the legislation. The links, however, go further than this. Kopperud himself is concerned about animal welfare issues in general whether or not they threaten agricultural interests in particular. He was the main organizational force behind the creation of the Congressional Animal Welfare Caucus, consisting of members willing to defend industry against the animal protection movement. Moreover, Kopperud also chairs the Farm Animal Welfare Coalition, formed in 1983, an umbrella organization of some 45 organizations including NABR, and representatives from the fur industry, zoos and circuses. This body meets quarterly as a 'forum for collective strategizing', and crucially too, USDA officials are usually present at the meetings.[67] In turn, Kopperud is invited to meetings of the Washington Animal Research Network, a coalition of animal research groups which meets three or four times a year.[68]

It would be a mistake, of course, to attribute exclusive responsibility for these links to one organization, let alone one individual. Rather, a number of other factors are at play here. In the first place, co-operation was made more likely and desirable because the same Congressional committee has responsibility for both farm and laboratory animal welfare. Thus, it was necessary for NABR to seek out the assistance of agricultural lobbyists, and particularly the AFIA, to help gain access to members of the Agriculture Committee as well as USDA officials. In this regard, Steve Kopperud was happy to oblige

Frankie Trull, NABR's chief lobbyist, since he himself had been 'taught' to lobby against the animal protection movement by Trull.[69] There are two other more general ingredients worth mentioning. In the first place, the village-type atmosphere of Washington politics, largely absent in Britain, tends to push lobbyists with similar concerns together, as is also the case with animal protection lobbyists (see Chapter 4). Finally, for whatever reason, it is undoubtedly the case that there is a much greater sense of a common animal rights enemy in the USA – a reflection, perhaps, of the high visibility of PETA, an organization which attacks the exploitation of animals in all contexts. As an AFBF lobbyist said in his testimony to a Congressional hearing on animal research in 1983: 'We merely try to draw the parallel that some of the same people who are interested in the laboratory animal legislation are also interested in making changes in farm animal legislation'.[70]

Whatever the reasons for it, the unity displayed by animal-use lobbyists has produced a formidable opponent for the animal protection movement and undoubtedly increases the difficulty of their own lobbying efforts. The benefits of cross-sectoral alliances were seen in the lobbying effort to secure the passage of a statute in 1992 which aims to protect both research facilities and farms from attacks by animal liberationists. Significantly, this measure was lobbied for jointly by both agricultural and research groups which were part of a coalition of more than 70 organizations. It is inconceivable that a similar measure would be introduced in Britain, and even if it was, it is doubtful it would receive the kind of cross-sectoral support seen in the USA.

Organization and Resources

Organizations active in lobbying to defend the exploitation of animals have a number of different organizational structures. Trade associations, which have an institutional membership, dominate but there are also organizations which allow for a combination of individual and institutional membership, individual corporations, and, finally, those which are primarily or exclusively individual membership organizations.

It is clear that the interests discussed in this chapter have a number of advantages over the animal protection movement. In the first place, the existence of organizations with affiliated memberships provides for the multiple representation of some interests. Thus, a large agribusiness firm may belong to a number of trade associations as well as having its own separate lobbying capacity. Furthermore, a relatively small number of the organizations identified in this chapter were set up specifically to tackle the animal welfare issue and, as a result, most had a lobbying capacity long before animal welfare became a pressing issue. When this occurred, they were able to bring this existing lobbying capacity to bear on the issue.

An additional point is that all of the organizations concerned to defend the use of animals identified in this chapter either exist for reasons other than lobbying or are financed by those who so exist. As a consequence, they do not face the same kind of problems in mobilizing members and raising finance as do those animal protection groups that have been created specifically to promote the well-being of animals (see Chapter 3). This goes a long way towards explaining why the organizations identified in this chapter are able to achieve such a high density of membership. As we noted above, about 80 per cent of farmers, for instance, have traditionally been members of the NFU. Likewise, the British Poultry Federation speaks for almost 100 per cent of the breeding, hatchery and poultry meat sectors and claims 50–60 per cent of the national hen flock, the National Broiler Council in the USA represents 95 per cent of all broiler producers and the National Milk Producer's Federation accounts for about 60 per cent of all milk producers in the USA.[71]

The factors identified above can be illustrated if we look in more detail at the organizational structures and financial resources of the animal protection movement's major adversaries. An initial distinction worth making is that, unlike the AFIA and the NFU, NABR and the RDS were created to focus on the specific issue of animal research. NABR has an annual income of about $800 000 (FBMR's annual income is about $1 million) obtained almost exclusively from subscriptions paid by about 350 member institutions and companies. The RDS employs six full-time staff and has a membership of 10 000 individual and institutional members who provide the bulk of the organization's annual income which, in 1984, was over £400 000. In addition, the organization retains a firm of consultants (presently Market Access) to provide information and strategic advice at a cost of £2000 per year. Although animal experimentation has not been such a major issue in the EU as farm animal welfare, the RDS also provides the secretariat for the recently formed European Biomedical Research Association.[72]

The AFIA, in turn, differs from the NFU in that the former, as indicated above, is a trade association whose lobbyist is particularly interested in animal welfare issues. Founded in 1909, the organization now represents some 630 firms in 48 states and 13 foreign countries.[73] By contrast, the NFU is mainly dependent upon the annual subscriptions paid by individual farmers. In 1993, the NFU had 114 447 members, most (68 per cent) being farmers and the rest consisting of small-holders able to join under the 'Countryside' membership scheme introduced in the early 1990s.[74] The organization has a complex structure allowing for the representation of grass-roots opinion. The basic organizational units of the NFU are the local branches that elect delegates to the 49 county branches which, in turn, elect about 120 delegates to the National Council. The National Council meets about five times a year but most of its work is done within a number of committees (consisting of Council members and specialist members elected from the regions) with responsibility for a particular commodity or, as in the case of the parliamentary committee, general lobbying. Constitutionally, the committees serve as the 'political masters' of the permanent officials who are divided into departments reflecting the committee structure. At the apex of the organization are the president, deputy president and vice president, all of whom are subject to annual election by the council.[75]

Despite their different structures, both the AFIA and the NFU have considerable financial resources. Subscriptions from its affiliates allows the AFIA to maintain a headquarters in Arlington and a large office in Washington. In addition, the organization operates a PAC which, in the 1987–8 election cycle, contributed $30 400 to Congressional candidates.[76] In addition, the AFIA created the Animal Industry Foundation which, operating from its base in Arlington, distributes material promoting animal agriculture.[77] The NFU's income has been steadily increasing over the years, from about £500 000 in the mid-1960s to £2.5 million in 1975, £9.5 million in 1988, £15.5 million in 1990, £18.5 million in 1992, £18.9 million in 1993 and £19.9 million in 1994.[78] The vast majority of this income comes from membership subscriptions. In 1993, for instance – a typical year –

some £13.9 million of the total income of £18.9 million came
from subscriptions, with the next highest source being the £2.8
million gained from insurance commission.[79]

As a result of these financial resources, the NFU can afford to
maintain plush offices in a prime London location (previously in
Knightsbridge in a property it still owns, and now in Long Acre)
and to employ (in 1993) 808 staff – 178 at the headquarters, 173
in the regions and 457 group secretaries who run local offices.
According to the 1993 Annual Report, the NFU spends over
£1.4 million on 'members' representation' (consisting of meetings, elected officers' remuneration, overseas visits, COPA subscriptions, and membership retention and recruitment) and a
further £700 000 on 'public relations activities' (including national and regional shows, public affairs, and information services).[80]

Many British organizations spend a considerable proportion
of their time lobbying institutions of the European Union. We
have already seen that pharmaceutical companies are organized
on a European basis. The same applies to the NFU, which is
a member of COPA, a federation of over 20 national farmers'
unions which has a great deal of influence at the European level
(see Chapter 8). Since 1972, the NFU has also had its own permanent Brussels office, currently staffed by four people, and its
director is usually a member of the EU Economic and Social
Committee.[81] In 1993, the NFU spent almost £300 000 on its
permanent presence in Brussels and a further £184 000 went to
fund its participation in the work of COPA.[82]

While, as we have seen, the AFIA dominates lobbying on
animal welfare issues, other industry actors also have considerable resources which can be used to defeat the objectives of the
animal protection movement. In the late 1980s, the AFBF, for
instance – with a claimed membership of over three million –
employed an executive director in its Washington office in addition to 10 public affairs specialists and a total staff of 28. In the
same period, the National Cattleman's Association employed a
staff of 12, and the National Broiler Council nine.[83] In addition,
many individual agribusiness corporations employ professional
lobbyists and lawyers to represent their interests in Washington.
Finally, as will be explored further in Chapter 7, industry groups
also pour money into the coffers of Congressional candidates
and engage, far more than equivalent groups in Britain, in gen-

eral propaganda activities through the media and in schools. These activities involve a resource outlay by industry groups that is beyond the scope of animal protection organizations.

We have seen in this chapter that those who are generally hostile to the introduction of further restrictions on their ability to exploit animals have developed formidable lobbying and general public relations structures paid for by some of the wealthiest interests in their respective countries. Of course, it should be pointed out that the mere existence of financial resources does not guarantee success. Coupled, however, with a captive organizational structure, a shared purpose (particularly evident in the United States), the status of some of the participants (eminent scientists in particular) and the claim that animal exploitation produces many economic and health benefits for society as a whole, this lobby clearly has the potential to be extremely influential. The extent to which it has been and continues to be influential are issues to which we will return in Chapters 7 to 10. Before that, the next two chapters are concerned with the adversaries of those who seek to continue exploiting animals.

3 The Animal Protection Movement: Recruitment, Ideology and Strategy

The increasing political activity of the interests described in the last chapter is, of course, a reaction to society's growing interest in, and concern for, the welfare of animals. This increasing concern is a product of the interaction of various factors,[1] but one crucial ingredient has been the increasingly visible role played by the animal protection movement. Of course, organizational concern for the plight of animals dates back, in both Britain and the United States, to the nineteenth century. Over the past two decades or so, however, the animal protection movement has been revitalized and radicalized to the extent that it has become an important player in the social movement and pressure group universes.

As was indicated earlier, the arrival of this significant new social movement has produced a number of academic studies, and it is not the intention here simply to rehash the basic factual material contained within them. Instead, this chapter considers two related key issues which have arisen in the movement's development. The first relates to questions of recruitment and organizational maintenance. The second focuses on the debate between advocates of an animal rights-driven strategy and those who see the pursuit of welfarists means as compatible with the achievement of rights ends.

MANCUR OLSON AND MEMBERSHIP RECRUITMENT

The vast majority of the organizations concerned about animal protection can be categorized as cause, promotional or – as they are described in the United States – public interest groups.[2] This label is applied because such organizations aim to achieve collective benefits not restricted – as is the case for the vast majority of the organizations encountered in the previous chapter – to the narrow economic or professional interests of their members. This distinction, between interest groups defending their member's utilization of animals and cause groups promoting the issue of animal protection, is not entirely watertight. Those who defend the use of animals in biomedical research, for instance, would claim that by so doing they are promoting the public interest. Likewise, some organizations which promote the well-being of animals – such as retailers selling cruelty-free cosmetics or free-range eggs and veterinary organizations – are clearly also groups with a professional or economic interest in the issue. Nevertheless, since few animal advocates receive any direct economic benefit from their group activities, the distinction between cause and interests groups remains valid.

According to one theoretical approach, the distinction between cause and interest groups is important because of the recruitment and organizational maintenance problems faced particularly by the former type. The notion that such problems could exist for associations of individuals with common aims is a relatively recent phenomena. Up to the mid-1960s, the conventional wisdom was that it was completely natural for like-minded people to organize themselves into groups whenever common interests, grievances or deprivations arose and required public policy solutions.[3] This assumption changed, however, with the publication in 1965 of *The Logic of Collective Action* by the political economist Mancur Olson.[4]

Olson questioned the assumption that it is natural for individuals to join groups in order to achieve collective goals by arguing that it is actually against the self-interest of individuals to participate in the achievement of such goals (whether these goals will benefit the members of a particular group only or society at large). This is so, he suggests, because the rational individual will prefer to take a 'free ride' by calculating that it is not worth paying the costs of participation since she will enjoy the benefits gained by the group whether or not she is a member. This, of course, makes the process of organizing a group and recruiting members a problem since, if Olson is right, it is not clear how any group of people can be mobilized for collective action. Yet such groups do, of course, exist. Olson's answer to this apparent paradox is that membership recruitment is possible either because membership is compulsory (in a trade union, for instance) or because those seeking to recruit are able to offer 'selective incentives' which are not available to non-members.[5]

This theory has important implications for our understanding of the character and prospects of the animal protection movement in particular and cause groups in general. Interest groups are clearly much more likely, and much more able, to offer selective incentives. Indeed, for Olson, the lobbying capacity of large economic organizations is a product of their ability to offer selective incentives. As a result, they (including most of the adversaries of animal advocates) would seem to have crucial advantages deriving from their ability to recruit more easily. An obvious example of selective incentives is the various benefits – in terms of legal assistance, technical advice, pension schemes, insurance policies, and cut-price equipment – that agricultural organizations – such as the NFU in Britain and the AFBF in the USA – can offer exclusively to members. A classic example is the use of the 'lion mark' on eggs only available to those who subscribe to the British Egg Industry Council. Since the large retailers will only take eggs with the mark, membership becomes, in effect, compulsory.[6]

By contrast, cause groups are not generally organized for reasons other than campaigning or lobbying, and are unable to provide substantial selective incentives to their members. Some selective incentives – in the form, for instance, of magazines and other literature – are offered by animal protection organizations but these are hardly substantial given that they are usually worth less than the membership fee, and in addition, are often also available to non-members. Thus, as a result of the difficulties of organizing public interest or cause groups, it has been suggested, the few – in economic organizations – have significant advantages over the many.[7]

Another factor to note here is that, as we saw in the previous chapter, many organizations lobbying in defence of continued animal exploitation are either individual corporations or trade associations consisting of institutional, rather than individual, memberships. Such organizations have a distinct advantage over animal protection groups because they already have the necessary (and usually very extensive) financial and manpower resources at their disposal. Given the advantages held by economic interests, it is not a surprise to be told that no less than 70 per cent of all organizations having a Washington presence represent business interests, whereas public interest groups constitute only 4 per cent of all organizations active in Washington politics.[8]

In the context of the above, it is interesting to note that groups created specifically to lobby on animal research issues have faced some difficulties in recruiting members and income. Big universities in the USA, for instance, will only pay about $2000 as an annual subscription to NABR.[9] Likewise, the RDS in the early 1980s was regarded as 'peripheral' by the research community and had to gain 'credibility' before persuading some individuals and institutions to join. No doubt there are a whole variety of explanations for this, including researchers underestimating the threat of the animal protection movement, or not being prepared to risk the consequences of speaking out against animal research. It is worth speculating, in addition, that the reluctance of researchers to get involved was, and is, partly a product of a belief that they might as well leave it to others since they will gain in any case from any benefits and would not have to pay the costs – in terms, for instance, of being denigrated by animal advocates – likely to result from getting involved. In this context, it is no accident that both NABR and the RDS offer increasingly useful selective incentives, such as legal advice and representation as well as media training, which are only available to members.

RATIONAL CHOICE AND HUMAN INTERESTS

The collective action problem for the animal protection movement is arguably intensified by the specific character of the issue. If individuals are the self-interested utility-maximizers as painted by rational choice theorists such as Olson, then a cause which seeks to advance the interests of other species rather than any overt human interests – and indeed which is often painted, rightly or wrongly, as a cause which actually damages some human interests – faces peculiarly severe problems. Indeed, it is this emphasis which distinguishes the animal advocacy movement from virtually all other social movements. Thus, while it is true that not all members of the civil rights movement and the women's movement, for instance, have suffered directly as a result of racial or sexual discrimination, both movements are at least concerned with human interests. In the case of the animal protection movement, there can be no such similar species solidarity – although perhaps one of the reasons why campaigns in defence of the 'higher' non-human mammals tend to be more successful is precisely because we recognize their similarity to us.[10] Radical environmentalists face a similar problem to that of animal advocates when they seek to protect the natural world on the grounds that it has an intrinsic value which is not reducible to its value for us. It is precisely because of the difficulty inherent in such a position, however, that most (successful) environmental campaigning *does* focus on the human costs of environmental damage.

The greater propensity of humans to concern themselves with causes which benefit their own species might also help to explain why wildlife conservation is the most popular of all animal issues. We have seen that public policy outputs designed to conserve wildlife have been extensive and, in some cases, stringent. Likewise, in both the British House of Commons and particularly in the American Congress, interest in wildlife protection far outweighs all the other animal issues. This political concern, in turn, is a reflection of the greater public interest in the issue. Wildlife groups, on the whole, have larger memberships and greater wealth than those organizations concerned with the protection of food and laboratory animals (see Chapter 4).

A straightforward and convincing explanation for the popularity of wildlife conservation is that human interests are served by it. We might, of course, want to protect wild animals because we recognize their intrinsic value which requires that we treat them with respect. Accompanying this, though, are a variety of anthropocentric justifications for protecting wildlife. Thus, we might appreciate the aesthetic beauty of at least some species, or we might recognize their economic value – in terms of tourism or as a source of economic profit – which necessitates preserving a species.

The fact that much contemporary wildlife conservation is based on protecting species – rather than individuals – for unashamedly anthropocentric ends, has, as we indicated in Chapter 2, resulted in important conflicts between environmentalists and animal protectionists. It is for this reason too that there are few formal links between the two movements. Indeed, the roots of the animal protection movement lie in nineteenth-century social reformism (concerned with issues such as the abolition of child labour, improving the living conditions of the urban poor and the campaign to abolish slavery) which focused, like animal protection, on the exploitation of individuals.[11] Thus, the animal protection movement is, above all, a radical social justice movement, more akin to movements created to promote the interests of a long line of exploited groups – whether they be based on race, gender, sexuality or class – than the environmental movement.[12] The one crucial difference between animal protection and these other social movements is, of course, that its beneficiaries are not human, and this fact has tended, up to now, to minimize links between them.[13]

Human interests also dominate in the wildlife conservation policy arena. So, although it remains a competitive one – with environmentalists and animal protectionists on the one side and those who stand to lose economically, such as loggers, property developers and so forth, on the other – the dominant trend in the debate tends to be, not a conflict between animal and human interests, but a conflict between competing human interests. The fact that, in the United States, there is so much legislation concerned with wildlife conservation, but not one federal law or regulation concerned with how trapped animals may be killed, is a striking illustration of this point.

GROUP MAINTENANCE AND THE ROLE OF THE ENTREPRENEUR

Olson's work produced a major shift in the preoccupations of interest group scholars toward the analysis of organizational creation and maintenance. As far as the animal protection movement is concerned, there are two ways of reacting to the problem Olson identified. The fact that animal protection groups on both sides of the Atlantic have succeeded in surviving and, in some cases, prospering (as have many other public interest groups) would suggest either that Olson's rational choice model is wrong, and therefore we have to look in other directions for explanations of group recruitment and maintenance; or that groups are able to compensate in some way for their inability to offer selective incentives.

One approach to the creation and maintenance of groups from within the Olsonian tradition is to focus on the role of organizational elites. There are two strands to this argument. One is that group leaders:

> learned how to cope with the public goods dilemma not by inducing large numbers of new members to join the group through the manipulation of selective benefits, but by locating important new sources of funds outside the immediate membership.[14]

Thus, groups seek to attract large individual gifts and foundation grants as a means of overcoming the problem of attracting enough members paying subscriptions. Groups which are able to attract such patronage can then tolerate a greater number of free riders. The second strand focuses on the role of individual 'entrepreneurs' who are prepared to pay the costs of setting up organizations and providing a set of benefits with which they hope to attract members. In return, they expect to retain a senior staff position within the organization. The crucial point is that, according to exponents of both of these strands, most group activity 'has little to do with efforts to affect public policy decisions but is concerned rather with the internal exchange of benefits by which the group is organized and sustained.'[15]

Both of these strands do seem to have some explanatory capacity as far as the animal protection movement is concerned. Many groups have relied and some still do rely on a small number of large donations, particularly from bequests, and foundation grants. To give one example, only 50 per cent of HSUS's total budget of about $17 million in 1991 came from membership dues, the rest coming from gifts (40 per cent) and foundation grants (3 per cent).[16] The idea of entrepreneurs also has a good deal of resonance. The entrepreneurial politics of Ralph Nader in organizing American consumers gave this theory a boost,[17] as did the role of David Brower in creating Friends of the Earth, but it would seem to be equally applicable to the politics of animal protection. Indeed, it is remarkable how many animal protection organizations have been the responsibility of one or two individuals and how, even though many of these organizations now have a large staff-base and a considerable bureaucracy, they are still associated with their founders.

In the United States, for instance, the ASPCA was founded in 1866 by Henry Bergh, a wealthy New Yorker with family connections in the shipbuilding industry. In the modern movement, a classic case of an animal protection entrepreneur is Christine Stevens. Together with her father – Robert Gesell, at the time a professor of physiology at the University of Michigan – Stevens set up the Animal Welfare Institute (AWI), in 1951 and four years later its lobbying counterpart, the Society for Animal Protective Legislation, as a result of the humane lobby's refusal to get involved in the pound-seizure issue (see below and Chapter 10). The AWI today still operates from Stevens' large house in Georgetown, a salubrious suburb of Washington DC. Likewise, Alex Hershaft founded the Farm Animal Reform Movement (FARM) in 1981 and the organization is still based in his own property in Bethesda. Other examples include Cleveland Amory, responsible for creating the Fund for Animals in 1974; Alice Herrington's creation of the Friends of Animals in 1957; Helen Jones' role in the formation of what is now the International Society for Animal Rights; and, finally, the pivotal role played by Ingrid Newkirk and Alex Pacheco in the formation and subsequent development of PETA.

In Britain, the role of the policy entrepreneur is less pronounced but it is still an identifiable role. One can mention here Jean Pink's role in setting up Animal Aid, Mark Glover's work in setting up LYNX and, after he suffered personal financial hardship as a result of LYNX's demise, a new group, Respect for Animals. Bryan Davies' role in setting up IFAW is similarly notable as was that of Peter Roberts, who set up Compassion in World Farming in 1967.

One problem with the identification of such entrepreneurial figures is that they hardly fit the model of utility maximizers required by rational choice theory. Most of those creating animal protection groups did not need the staff job that advocates of this theory posit was their motivation, and one can only assume their main concern was the plight of the animals their groups were set up to ameliorate. On the other hand, it is apparent that organizational dynamics ensure that there is a keen rivalry between animal protection groups, which are determined to encourage loyalty to their 'brand' (see Chapter 4).

ANIMAL RIGHTS AND SOLIDARISTIC COLLECTIVISM
– A POST-OLSONIAN AGENDA

Despite the above arguments, it does remain the case that the
major characteristic of the revitalization of the animal protection
movement in the past few years has been not just the formation
of many new membership groups but also increasing memberships for the older ones too.[18] Nevertheless, it is the case that
compared to other public interest groups – concerned, for instance, with environmental and consumer issues – the 'pure'
animal protection groups, excluding those focusing primarily on
wildlife conservation, do have relatively small memberships.
Whether or not this is a product of the non-human focus of such
groups, as suggested above, there is undoubtedly a case for
building alliances with other groups when occasion arises. This
is a theme to which we will return. To the extent that animal
protection organizations have recruited many new members in
recent years, however, it would be churlish and, more to the
point, academically negligent, to ignore the motivations of those
who do join and actively participate as animal advocates.

One possible alternative explanation, which takes us beyond
the Olsonian emphasis on self-interested maximizers, is that
members are recruited into public interest groups because of the
solidary rewards that derive from associating in group activities.
That is, the very act of participating along with others is inherently satisfying, meeting deep-seated psychological needs,
irrespective of the external benefits accruing from it. Olson re-
jects this inherent satisfaction explanation as insufficiently precise to be included as a selective incentive. Nevertheless, if valid
as an explanation for group recruitment, it does, as indicated
below, have important implications for the political effectiveness
of the animal protection movement. The other viable explanation for involvement in group activities is the 'common sense'
view that individuals have purposive, ideological or issue-
orientated goals.[19] This explanation, of course, clearly takes us
beyond the Olsonian framework.

The, fairly limited, empirical research so far conducted on the
motivations of animal protection activists supports an issue-
orientated explanation. Shapiro's portrait of animal rights activists, for instance, is centred around such an assumption.[20]
Likewise, Berry's study of the Fund for Animals revealed that the

staff, who were either poorly paid at the New York headquarters or received no salary at all working in regional offices, did the work because of their love for animals.[21] In a similar vein, Jasper and Poulson, in a study comparing the animal rights with the anti-nuclear movement, have emphasized the role of ideas or moral sentiments as people are recruited into the former movement through the use of 'shock' symbols that raise 'such a sense of outrage in people that they become inclined towards political action even in the absence of a network of contacts'.[22] Thus, Jasper and Poulson suggest that these shocks tend to affect isolated individuals with little involvement in other progressive causes so that, unlike the anti-nuclear movement, a significant proportion of those recruited into the animal protection movement do not hear about the organizations and issues through a pre-existing social and organizational network but through public displays, direct mailing and media images.

These findings were confirmed by Herzog's research in which only a few of the animal rights activists he interviewed had a prior history of involvement in other social movements, and that whereas most were members of animal rights groups, 'group membership tended not to be a central focus of their involvement'.[23] Sperling, likewise, in a series of detailed interviews with animal rights activists, found that many of them had a prior concern for animals and: 'expressed a sense of excitement and surprise at finding that a movement existed which provided an arena for expressing their deeply held beliefs'.[24] Here, too, there is plenty of anecdotal evidence that the emerging animal rights movement in the 1970s was bolstered by the work of academic philosophers, such as Singer and Regan, who intellectualized the 'gut' feeling that something was seriously wrong with the way animals were being treated.[25]

The importance of the 'moral shock' explanation is that it suggests that, for some at least, concern about issues occurs prior to the desire to enjoy the benefits of participating in a group of like-minded individuals. Many activists, however, do belong to other social movements[26] and what is revealing here is that animal advocates do tend to share similar political values to those involved in other 'progressive' causes, such as civil rights, womens' rights and the environment, thereby suggesting an ideological rather than a social dimension to their activities. Greanville and Moss, for instance, found that 65 per cent of the animal advocates they surveyed were agnostics or atheists, and that 34 per cent and 32 per cent respectively described themselves as having liberal or radical political leanings.[27] Similarly, Sperling's study notes the explicit links her animal rights interviewees drew between animal abuse and, for example, feminism, imperialism, ecology, and anti-war and even anti-business attitudes, and many of them had been, or were still, involved with other protest movements.[28]

In so far as these issue-based explanations do account for membership recruitment, it is possible to bring into play the overarching explanations which seek to explain the increasing concern for the way animals are treated. Included here would be, for example, the greater knowledge of animal capabilities, the increasing scepticism about the ability of science and technology to solve problems and the emergence of post-material values or a 'sentimental anthropomorphism' that is a product of industrialism and the separation of most humans from the instrumental use of animals.[29]

It can be argued, however, that the issue-based reasons for involvement are not totally separate from those associated with the inherent satisfaction of group involvement. It is recognized that the development of a collective identity is crucial for the formation of solidary feelings and that this becomes a problem in groups with no common geographical, social, or occupational location.[30] Survey evidence does suggest that the demographic characteristics of animal advocates tend to be similar to those of other cause groups and social movements – largely white and middle-class and female. A survey conducted in the mid-1980s of the readership of the American animal rights magazine *The Animals' Agenda*, for instance, revealed that three out of four readers were between the ages of 21 and 49, over 60 per cent were female, 80 per cent lived in urban areas, 84 per cent were college graduates, and 80 per cent earned $25 000–$50 000 a year.[31] But even though there is a class and gender base to the animal protection movement, these social characteristics do not provide the rationale for membership in the same way, say, that female membership of the women's movement does.

Given the lack of a common social location for animal protection advocates, it is reasonable to assume that a collective identity is provided by an ideology (of animal rights) which internally unites movement members and sets the movement apart from others. As Jane Mansbridge writes in the context of the women's movement, 'Building an organisation on belief in a principle, when the world refuses to go along with that principle, produces a deep sense of us against them'.[32] In addition to its distinctiveness, there is the related point that animal rights ideology also has the effect of simplifying the debate. Accepting that animals have rights which cannot be infringed even if human benefits are likely to accrue by so doing, removes the need to get involved in complex technical debates concerned, for instance, with the degree to which animals suffer as a result of confinement or the degree to which animal exploiters will lose out financially as a result of reform. Reducing the technical complexity can lead to what Gormley refers to as 'hearing room' politics whereby regulators and business organizations can no longer hide behind a cloak of technical expertise.[33]

The problem with simplifying the debate in this way is that, for the present at least, the ideology of animal rights is not accepted – at least in its entirety – by mainstream opinion, and it merely serves to simplify the debate only for those who do accept the ideology. In so far as this is one of the functions performed by the ideology of animal rights then, coupled with the apparent need to recruit members through moral shocks, we might have stumbled upon a severe problem for the animal protection movement. This is because there may be a conflict between the needs of organizational recruitment and maintenance (requiring the use of a distinctive ideology promoting separateness and the identification of an implacable enemy – the 'sadistic' scientist and the 'money-grabbing' farmer) and the achievements of organizational goals (requiring, at least to some degree, the ability to reach consensus through negotiation with other governmental and non-governmental actors coupled with the need to attract the broadest measure of support for any particular campaign).

Seen in this way, an emphasis on welfare-based goals (the refinement of animal research reducing the amount of suffering inflicted, for instance, rather than the abolition of animal research) may be dysfunctional since it reduces the exclusiveness of the identity required for organizational maintenance (after all, virtually everyone can claim to be concerned about the *welfare* of animals). Conversely, the achievement of these self-same welfarist objectives, and the generation of widespread societal

support for these more limited objectives, may be hindered by
the need to recruit members through moral shocks and the need
to keep them through the articulation of an animal rights-based
group identity. As Jasper and Nelkin point out: 'the hubris of
self-righteousness has proven to be both a source of strength and
a potentially fatal flaw. The same moral confidence that attracts
so many recruits makes others wary of the new movement'.[34]

This tendency has also been noted by Michael Giannelli, a
well-known American activist, who has written about what he
calls 'the self-destructive politics of exclusion'. Some activists, he
writes:

> are vulnerable to the charge of being 'divisive', not because of
> their philosophy, but because of their intolerance, their mani-
> fest anger, and their impatience. They 'excommunicate' other
> rights activists for not sticking to 'abolition' campaigns. They
> alienate welfarists who might otherwise wish to work with
> rightists on common goals. They estrange the public for whom
> animal issues are not central to daily concerns. They turn off
> progressive politicians by their 'no compromise' agenda. This
> adds up to a terrible price to pay for ideological 'purism' and
> it is the animals who are stuck with the tab.[35]

Thoroughly assessing the empirical validity of the potential
conflict identified above is not easy. It is certainly the case that
many of the movement leaders to whom I have talked recognize
the dichotomy between recruiting and maintaining members on
the one hand and appealing to decision-makers and the general
public on the other. The editor of a movement newspaper in the
USA also commented that 'At least two lobbyists privately acknowledged putting a pure public image ahead of political success, believing compromise would not appeal to donors'.[36] It is
true, too, that those organizations – most notably the RSPCA –
with a ruling body made up of activists not on the organization's
payroll, have experienced conflicts generated by activist's perception that the paid staff are too willing to moderate their demands. One detailed study of the attitudes of a small number of
animal rights activists in the United States also provides partial
support for this thesis. Thus, the activists interviewed recognized
the importance of rights discourse in providing a sense of their
self-worth and definition. On the other hand, they also re-

cognized the limitations of rights by not demonstrating 'a false, unrealistic, or naïve hope' in them and by maintaining 'a strategic approach to advancing their ethics' through, for instance, the importance of the gradual achievement of animal rights objectives.[37] This latter finding was confirmed by another study incorporating a series of lengthy interviews with animal rights activists, the author being 'struck by the degree of pragmatism' among her interviewees.[38] Finally, the central argument of a major study of the animal rights movement in America by Gary Francione is that the leadership has sacrificed genuine animal rightism for an enlightened, but ultimately fatally flawed, form of welfarism.[39] In so far as he is right about this, it would seem to concur with the view that whereas leaders have recognized the need for a piecemeal approach necessitating compromise, this is seen as a sell-out by the grass-roots.

One crucial final point to make here is that the arguments above, postulating the existence of a conflict between the achievement of realizable goals and the non-public policy role performed by animal rights ideology, beg a central question. Obviously, this conflict only exists if it is accepted that welfarist goals are worth striving for, either on their own or as a stepping-stone to the achievement of rights goals. If they are not, then the needs of organizational recruitment and maintenance do not present a problem. It is to this debate, about the utility of animal welfare, that we now turn.

ANIMAL RIGHTS AND THE 'NEW WELFARISM'

Accounts of the animal protection movement have traditionally focused on the ideological distinction between rights and welfare. A more thorough typology, which enables a consideration of the key current debates within the animal protection movement, can be produced if we distinguish between ideology, strategy and method. This threefold typology enables us to make two crucial distinctions. In the first place, if we combine ideology and method it becomes apparent that while it is true that no animal welfarists (that I am aware of at least) advocate illegal direct action as a method, and there is a greater tendency for animal welfare organizations to focus on gaining direct access to decision-makers, the reverse is not true of animal rights advocates and organizations. Indeed, the animal rights movement contains some of the most fervent critics of such activity. Furthermore, while some animal rights groups – such as Animal Aid and the National Antivivisection Society (NAVS) in Britain and People for the Ethical Treatment of Animals (PETA) in the United States – do concentrate on general campaigning, there are some groups – such as the British Union for the Abolition of Vivisection (BUAV) in Britain – which have made strides in their attempt to gain insider status.[40]

Secondly, an important division is revealed if we examine the relationship between strategy and ideology. By combining these two factors, a threefold classification is apparent.[41]

1.　Absolutists in Strategy and Ideology

In this category can be placed those who see animal rights as providing a guide to both the means and ends of animal activism. This position is advocated most forcefully by Gary Francione[42] and consists of a number of separate, albeit related, arguments. Firstly, Francione suggests that there is no evidence in favour of the proposition that non-abolitionist animal welfare reforms will lead progressively to the eventual achievement of animal rights objectives. Furthermore, he also argues that such animal welfare steps are by themselves of very limited value since despite numerous welfarist steps over a long period of time, the pain and suffering endured by animals is greater now than it ever was.[43] Welfarism fails, for Francione, primarily because the balancing act between human and animal interests required by animal welfare is almost always decided in favour of the former since humans have rights whereas animals are assigned the status of property. As he points out:

> when we are faced with a human/animal conflict and use the prescribed 'balancing' method to determine whose interests should prevail, the answer is determined from the outset. In such a system, animals almost never prevail, irrespective of what might be the relatively trivial human interests at stake and the relatively weighty animal interest involved in the particular case.[44]

The pursuit of animal welfare reform may not just be worthless, Francione continues, but may also be counterproductive. This is because moderate reforms give the *impression* that something is being done to ease animal suffering and therefore make it more difficult to continue raising public concern. The Animal Welfare Act in the United States, for instance, may give the impression that the actual conduct of scientific procedures is being controlled when this is not the major purpose of the legislation.[45]

2. Philosophical Absolutists and Strategic Pragmatists

In this category come those, criticized by Francione, who seek the eventual achievement of animal rights objectives but who are also prepared to support non-abolitionist animal welfarist reforms as a means of achieving the ultimate abolitionist goal. As Francione would agree, it is fair to say that this represents the current strategy of many, if not all, national animal rights organizations. It has also been promoted by a number of authors and activists whom Francione labels as 'New Welfarists'.[46]

3. Animal Welfarists in Ideology and Strategy

Obviously, those individuals and organizations who accept the philosophic tenets of animal welfare – that we should take account of animal interests but those of humans must take precedence – do not face the strategic dilemma faced by advocates of animal rights, and can consistently support moderate reforming welfare measures without any qualms of conscience.

Before assessing the position promoted by Francione, it is important to note that conflict in the animal protection movement between what might be called the 'new fundamentalists' and the group Francione labels as 'new welfarists' has been evident from time to time. We should not exaggerate this because in many ways Francione's position is essentially a challenge to present practices in the animal rights movement, where, as Francione himself points out, the leadership in particular has tended to accept the new welfarist agenda.[47] Thus, even though animal rights leaders such as Newkirk, for instance, have criticized Henry Spira's strategy of courting cosmetic and meat industry leaders as fraternizing with the enemy, groups such as PETA, in Francione's view, have been no better in their readiness to support animal welfare measures and in their general campaigning, which has increasingly eschewed animal rights in favour of glossy (and even racist and sexist) campaigns emphasising a general requirement that implores people to care or be compassionate about animals.[48]

One instance of the conflict generated by the division between the view expressed by Francione and the new welfarism of those he seeks to criticize involved a heated exchange in 1996 between Francione himself and Michael Giannelli, the Executive Director of the Ark Trust, a Californian-based organization which seeks to promote the use of positive animal images in the media. Conducted initially on the Internet, the debate between the two, which became extremely personalized, centred on Francione's objection to the annual awards given by the Ark Trust to those in the media who have done most to promote animal causes. Francione's objection was based, partly at least, on his view that the use of animals in entertainment, however well they are treated, is to exploit them. The debate quickly widened to incorporate the general strategy debate between the new fundamentalists and the New Welfarists and the exchanges culminated in Giannelli writing and distributing a lengthy document designed to put his side of the case.[49]

The large amount of mail the dispute between Giannelli and Francione generated on animal rights e-mail networks demonstrates that it is of some interest to activists. More practical ramifications have also been a product of this ideological rift. For example, some activists, led by Francione and, initially, Tom Regan, called for a boycott of the 1996 'March for the Animals', a demonstration in Washington of animal advocates from throughout America, on the grounds that it promoted animal welfare rather than animal rights.[50]

Conflict along similar lines occurred over the pound seizure issue in the United States (see also Chapter 10). Here, a National Coalition to Protect Our Pets (ProPets), a coalition of 11 animal protection organizations, was formed in 1985 to campaign against pound seizure. Internal difficulties soon arose in this coalition between abolitionist animal rightists, on the one side, and new and old welfarists on the other. Both factions opposed pound seizure but disagreements occurred over the alternatives, with the former not prepared to advocate the substitution of purpose-bred for pound animals. As Finsen and Finsen point out: 'These differences reflect the fundamental ideological and strategic differences between humane organizations, which seek to reform and regulate animal experimentation, and animal rights organizations, which seek abolition'.[51]

Gary Francione has produced a considerable and impressive literature seeking to justify his position and because some of his arguments have been written in response to my own previous work and because the implications for the animal protection movement of accepting his position are profound, it is worth while assessing the arguments in some detail.[52] The first point to make here is that it would be unfair and simplistic to describe Francione's position as utopian or unrealistic since he does suggest that animal rights advocates can adopt incremental strategies, through either engaging in general campaigns to shift public consciousness towards an animal rights position, or supporting incremental legislative reforms that meet a number of criteria, not least that they are reforms which seek to prohibit particular practices – for example, the abolition, rather than the refinement, of cosmetic testing. Such reforms are acceptable if they avoid the need to engage in the trading of human and animal interests (which always, Francione thinks, works to the advantage of the former) and the replacement of one exploitative regime by another – for example, larger battery cages rather than no cages at all.[53]

Difficulties with this position, however, still remain. An initial point is that the adoption of his position can, as we saw above, be a source of division within the animal protection movement. Here, I do take Francione's point that unity is the responsibility of all sides and one should not, as often happens, blame animal rights advocates for failing, for instance, to support a lobbying stance put forward by moderates.[54] Having said this, unity does remain, whether one likes it or not, a crucial pressure group resource and it is still worth speculating what might have happened in particular circumstances had the movement been more united. For instance, it is still possible to maintain that the British Government might have been prepared to offer more in the law reforming animal experimentation had the RSPCA and the Committee for the Reform of Animal Experimentation (CRAE) been able to forge a consensus. CRAE, it should be noted, can be criticized for this just as much as the RSPCA Council, which passively opposed the legislation on the grounds that it would continue to allow pain to be inflicted on animals (see Chapter 9).

Similarly, the benefits of adopting a broad strategy, where no one is excluded merely because they have failed to articulate an abolitionist rights-based strategy, are clearly apparent. Interestingly, Francione writes of the campaigns against live animal exports from Britain in favourable terms as representing the abolitionism of which he approves.[55] In actual fact, there are difficulties with regarding this as abolitionist because the calves not exported still exist and have to be dealt with in some way.[56] More importantly, the language of rights was conspicuous by its absence in the campaign and profitably so. As Benton and Redfearn point out:

> the limiting of the protests to identifiable 'welfare' targets has been crucial in maintaining the breadth of public support which the campaign continues to enjoy. A large poster draped from a Colchester pub read 'You Don't Have to Stop Eating Meat to Care – Ban Live Exports'.[57]

Furthermore, it is significant that Benton and Redfearn's study of the campaign against live exports revealed that some of the participants did not see animal protection as the main issue at stake and very few saw it as the only one. As a result, the animal protection movement was able to draw in those concerned about local democracy, civil liberties and police powers, thereby creating a powerful constituency.[58] To have made this an issue of animal rights, with the exclusivity that often involves, might well have threatened this alliance of views.

A further problem with Francione's position is that the distinction between abolitionist measures and reformist measures falling short of abolition, is not always clear-cut. The abolition of cosmetic testing does not, for instance, rule out the possibility that animals previously utilized in this way will not then be exploited in other procedures. Likewise, the abolition of battery cages does not imply that hens will no longer be utilized to produce eggs. Furthermore, if such abolitionist measures were to be introduced, they might also be subject to the criticism, levelled at welfarists by rightists, that improving the conditions in which animals are kept without challenging the underlying institutional exploitation, might make it more difficult to move on to the next stage and abolish such exploitation entirely. In such situations, then, it seems the only really consistent course of action for an animal rights advocate following Francione's position is to reject these incremental measures in favour of a complete prohibition on animal research and animal agriculture. But then we are back to the charge that this represents utopian aspirations.

In reality, Francione does doubt the ability of animal rights advocates to achieve any meaningful abolitionist objectives through existing legislative and judicial channels, particularly given that lobbyist's success in influencing decision-makers is dependent upon their willingness to compromise. In effect, too, his stipulation that support for incremental reforms cannot involve the advocacy of alternatives to present practices (the replacement of one trap, for instance, with a more humane alternative)[59] rules out of court one of the key pressure group resources. That is, decision-makers are more likely to listen to a pressure group if it can offer solutions to problems and offering alternatives is often a useful negotiating position. In the case of animals, of course, Francione is right to say this is likely to mean that the exploitation continues, but it is hard to deny that animals can benefit. In the case of traps, for instance, surely it is better to outlaw traps which can cause enormous pain and suffering even if animals will still be trapped?

As a result of Francione's doubts about the viability of an incremental reformism which is consistent with animal rights, animal advocates, he thinks, can best use their time by engaging exclusively in campaigns to change public opinion.[60] Francione is right to suggest that fundamental changes are unlikely to come about, particularly in the United States, without extensive public campaigns designed to alter the public's consciousness. As Berry accurately remarks: 'Policies are inextricably tied to prevailing values; when those values are changed, mountains can be moved'.[61] To say, however, that traditional lobbying is pointless involves adding the assumption that all welfarist-based reforms short of abolition are not worth having. This too, I think, can be challenged.

Francione is obviously correct to say that, while animals are regarded as the mere property of humans, the animal rights agenda cannot be fulfilled. He is not justified, however, in making two further assumptions. Firstly, while the abolition of property rights in animals is a necessary condition for the achievement of animal rights, it is by no means clear it is a sufficient condition. The abominable treatment of many supposedly free humans throughout the world is an important reminder that granting formal rights does not necessarily result in better treatment in reality. Indeed, the imposition from above of edicts abolishing the property status of animals is unlikely, without a change in social values relating to their moral status, to have the effect desired.

Secondly, to go on to say that no welfarist-based reforms can have any major effects on the way animals are treated is also extremely debatable. In the first place, abolitionist measures prohibiting particular practices can, and, more to the point, have been justified on animal welfare grounds too. Francione attacks in particular general anti-cruelty measures which seek to protect animals against unnecessary suffering. As we have seen, basic anti-cruelty statutes in Britain and the United States fall into this category and I, like Francione, think, for some of the reasons he espouses, that these measures are problematic. This is not, however, the only animal welfare model. Thus, abolitionist measures could be justified on the grounds that the benefits to humans of continuing with a particular practice is outweighed by the suffering inflicted on animals. I have argued elsewhere that improvements to the treatment of animals, particularly in Britain, have been a product of this type of calculation rather than a widespread acceptance that animals have rights which should be protected at all costs.[62]

Thus, the value of the major animal welfare statutes in Britain – the 1968 Agriculture (Miscellaneous Provisions) Act and the 1986 Animals (Scientific Procedures) Act – is not so much in the basic unnecessary cruelty provisions they both contain, but in the potential they afford for abolitionist regulations to be added (see Chapters 8 and 9 for further details). In the case of the latter, the abolition of veal crates and sow stalls and tethers in Britain would come into this category as measures, introduced under the 1968 Act, which the agricultural lobby did – particularly in the latter case – challenge as economically damaging to their industry but which were accepted by government because of the strength of public opinion. Future possible reforms now very much on the agenda as a result of Labour's victory in the 1997 general election – such as the abolition of fox hunting and fur farms – would be justified on similar grounds. In the context of the USA, Francione criticizes Henry Spira for not pursuing, except in his early campaigns, an abolitionist strategy.[63] But some of Spira's most recent campaigns have involved demands which involve the abolition of particular practices such as the campaign to persuade USDA to abolish the face branding of cattle (see Chapter 7).

Most animal welfare measures, it must be admitted, have fallen short of the strict criteria he adopts for incremental measures animal rightists can support. By itself, however, this does not mean they are not worth having. It *is* surely possible to distinguish between adequate and inadequate welfare reforms. For example, a regulation which insists upon environmental enrichment for all laboratory animals is, all things being equal, of greater worth than one which requires it only for particular species, which in turn is better than having no regulation at all, effective enforcement notwithstanding. Here, it might be argued that the rights versus welfare debate is nowhere near as prevalent in Britain as it is in the USA, precisely because in the former country it is recognized that welfarism is a viable strategy producing genuine improvements in the way animals are treated. Francione may be right to say that the pain and suffering endured by animals is greater than it was say 50 years ago and that more animals are now exploited than in the past. This does not, however, prove that animal welfare measures do not work, since it might be suggested that things would be worse still without these measures. This might equally lead to the conclusion that if we want to improve the condition of animals what is required is more animal welfare measures, whether they be abolitionist or otherwise.

Francione also seeks to undermine the viability of animal welfare by pointing, quite correctly, to the fact that the exploiters of animals are increasingly using animal welfare language.[64] Of course, this can and has been used as a public relations device and as a stick with which to beat advocates of animal rights. On the other hand, we should perhaps see the use of animal welfare language by animal exploiters as a mark of the animal protection movement's progress in legitimizing the use of the term. Francione presents the dichotomy between animal welfare and animal rights as the only two positions one can adopt, but this is not the case. Orlans, for instance, wants to distinguish between animal exploitation, animal use and animal welfare.[65] The first is a Cartesian position recognizing no moral responsibility towards animals while the second recognizes moral responsibilities but favours self-regulation. By contrast, animal welfare demands regulatory control by the state. It is possible to argue, then, that the acceptance of an animal welfare position does represent a distinctive position and, in so far as regulatory control has been accepted by animal exploiters, it does represent a shift from their previous denial of any moral responsibility or the belief that they can be relied upon to ensure the well-being of animals without state intervention. The final point here is that, even if the animal protection movement's opponents have attempted to hijack the animal welfare label for their own spoiling purposes, this does not devalue the concept itself. This would be like saying we should not use the label socialism because the Nazis described themselves as National Socialists!

Francione's major objection to non-abolitionist welfare measures is that they are usually undermined because human interests take precedence. Thus, for example, researchers will fight against a regulation requiring the provision of environmental enrichment for laboratory animals on the grounds that the animal suffering produced by not having such a regulation is necessary because extra research costs are inimical to human interests. Moreover, even if such a regulation was introduced, the property status of animals means that animal advocates find it difficult to acquire legal standing in the courts to challenge non-enforcement or inadequate enforcement. As we shall see in Chapter 10, this mirrors accurately the fate of regulations demanded by the 1985 amendment to the Animal Welfare Act in the United States.

It is important to understand, however, the circumstances in which animal welfare does fail to improve the well-being of animals. Here, contrary to Francione, I would argue, and this view is illustrated in the course of this book, that the answer lies not just, or even primarily, in the concepts of property and legal standing but rather in the political weight exercised by those with a vested interest in exploiting animals coupled with the absence of sustained social pressure for change. In this view, it is necessary to distinguish the legal constraints that protect the exploiters of animals from the social and political climate that largely determines the effectiveness of these constraints. In other words, the weight given to the property status of animals will depend upon the prevailing social and political climate existing in a particular culture at a particular moment in time. In Britain, for example, it is undoubtedly the case that deference to property ownership in general, and the ownership of animals in particular, has been less powerful than it has been in the United States. It seems more compelling, however, to argue that this deference to property ownership is a product of prevailing social norms than to argue the converse, that these social norms are a product of existing forms of property rights.

To illustrate this point, it is instructive to compare what animal abuse is tolerated in Britain and the USA. Francione places great weight upon the fact that, despite decades of campaigning by the animal protection movement in the USA, animals are still sacrificed for trivial purposes, the infamous annual pigeon shoot at Hegins in Pennsylvania being a prime example.[66] He is quite right here, of course, but I would suggest that the scale of animal abuse for so obviously trivial ends as occurs in the USA would not be tolerated to anything like the same degree in Britain. There is a very good chance, for instance, that the hunting of foxes and stags by hounds and hare coursing will be abolished over the next five years and such practices have been massively opposed by public opinion for some years now.[67] Interestingly, in the light of Francione's argument, the anti-hunting lobby makes enormous capital by labelling hunting as a sport, thereby suggesting that it is trivial, and the hunting fraternity have responded by emphasising that hunting has a more 'noble' purpose in terms of conservation and habitat protection (see Chapter 5). Yet the legal status of animals is exactly the same in the two countries and cannot therefore be used to explain the differential treatment of, and concern for, animals.

Likewise, Francione, correctly, points to the unity of animal exploiters in the United States (a point confirmed in Chapter 2) and he explains this in terms of the 'narrow common interest' they have in not having their property rights interfered with.[68] This same degree of unity does not exist in Britain, however, despite the fact that the property status of animals is the same. Again, we must look for alternative reasons – such as the nature of the political system and prevailing social values – which would seem to have greater explanatory value than the legal status of animals.

The animal rights movement in the USA, then, faces a much more difficult task because it seeks to challenge deep-seated American values – in particular, the sanctity of individual property, and a frontier mentality which corresponds to a belief in unlimited opportunity and progress – which can, and have been, used to justify the exploitation of animals on farms and in laboratories.[69] It can be admitted that one response to this is to try and ensure that animals are accorded the same rights as humans. But then it might also, with a great deal of justification, be argued that, in reality, there are human casualties of these values (from a Western European perspective, at least, the 'American Dream' was always a sham), and these humans are supposed to have the very rights which Francione claims will protect animals.

We have considered in this chapter some central issues relating to the formation, mobilization and strategy of the animal protection movement. It has been suggested that, whilst there may be mobilization difficulties, it is worth while for the animal protection movement to pursue reformist strategies whether or not they can be seen as means to the end of abolitionist animal rights objectives. As animal welfare gravitates further towards the political mainstream, these reformist objectives are likely to involve a greater concentration on conventional lobbying activities. The next chapter examines the character of the movement's lobbying to date.

4 Lobbying for Animals

Whether or not it is deemed to be worthwhile, the fact remains that the animal protection movement has increasingly sought to engage in conventional lobbying activities. The aim of this chapter is to document the nature of this activity. In order to enable a comparison with the animal protection movement's adversaries, a set of categories similar to those adopted in Chapter 2 is utilized. That is, following a raw count of the groups involved, an attempt is made to identify the most important and influential groups, examine their organizational resources and establish the degree of sectorization evident in their working practices.

THE DEVELOPMENT OF THE MODERN ANIMAL PROTECTION MOVEMENT

The animal protection movement's pattern of development has followed very similar lines in Britain and the United States. In both countries humane organizations and anti-vivisectionist societies emerged in the nineteenth century and in both countries the movement went into decline in the early part of the twentieth century before expanding again from the 1950s onwards. Finally, in more recent times – the 1970s in Britain and the 1980s in the USA – the movement was revitalized and radicalized by the appearance of national groups and grass-roots activism informed by the language of animal rights or liberation.

In the USA, the catalyst for the emergence of new groups in the 1950s and 1960s was the controversy surrounding the pound seizure issue. As we saw in Chapter 3, the biomedical community was successful in persuading state legislatures to pass laws granting them access to shelter animals. The animal protection movement was at such a low ebb that it either stood back and watched this happen or, as with the American Society for the Prevention of Cruelty to Animals (ASPCA), actively co-operated in the sale of pound animals to laboratories. It was this passive response that led to the formation of a number of more radical groups – such as the Humane Society of the United States (HSUS), the Society for Animal Rights and the Animal Welfare Institute (AWI).[1] In Britain, likewise, a number of new groups – such as Compassion in World Farming (CIWF), and the Fund for the Replacement of Animals in Medical Experiments (FRAME) – were formed in the 1950s and 1960s as the welfare of farm and laboratory animals began to take a higher priority.

The final stage in the development of the modern animal protection movement occurred in the 1970s with the emergence of grass-roots-orientated animal rights groups. In the United States, there were two streams to this development, one centring on New York and Henry Spira's well-documented campaigns against laboratory animal exploitation,[2] and the other centring on the origins of People for the Ethical Treatment of Animals (PETA). In the latter case, an important role was played by Alex Hershaft who, in the 1970s, organized a series of vegetarian conferences at which he and a number of others agitated for the inclusion of an animal rights agenda. From these conferences, and in particular one held at Allentown, Pennsylvania, in July 1981, a number of animal rights groups – most notably PETA, Hershaft's own Farm Animal Reform Movement (FARM) and Trans-Species Unlimited – emerged.[3]

In Britain, some new animal rights-based groups – such as Animal Aid, LYNX and Zoo Check – were formed and there was a greater emphasis on grass-roots campaigning. Perhaps more significant in Britain was the reinvigoration of older groups as dormant organizations, such as the British Union for the Abolition of Vivisection (BUAV), were revitalized by new activists with an animal rights agenda and a harder campaigning edge.[4] In both countries, the emergence of more radical activist groups has undoubtedly had the effect of radicalizing the older established groups in terms of their objectives and strategies. In Britain, for instance, the Royal Society for the Prevention of Cruelty to Animals (RSPCA) was dogged in the 1970s by internal disputes as animal rights activists sought, with some success, to change the society's direction.[5] More recently still, the increasing visibility of campaigning groups such as Animal Aid and CIWF has been an important factor in the RSPCA's continued campaigning focus on farm and laboratory animal welfare.

In the United States, similarly, PETA's ability to recruit members and its continual scrutiny of the policy positions of the older established groups, in particular, has kept the latter on their toes. As a result, the HSUS, for one, has hardened its approach over the years. In 1993, for instance, HSUS ran a campaign against factory farming which produced a furious response from industry groups, which complained that the campaign 'places HSUS squarely in the lead among animal rights groups seeking a vegetarian society by using emotionalism to adjure the public to both "reduce" and "replace" the animal products...with other foods'.[6]

KEY POLITICAL ACTORS

Not all animal protection groups, of course, place a great deal of emphasis on lobbying activities. In the United States, there are about 40 animal protection and wildlife conservation organizations with a significant Washington DC presence, whereas in Britain there are about 30 substantial national groups with an interest in animal issues of one sort or another. This initial analysis can, in addition, be further refined through the utilization of four separate indices of a group's importance in the political process, the first two relating to British and American groups and the latter two relating to British groups alone. These are the views of the animal protection movement's adversaries; the perception that animal advocacy groups have of each other; surveys of British MPs' attitudes of group influence and, finally, each individual group's evaluation of its own role.

By combining the first two indices it becomes clear that some groups are regarded as much more important political players than others. Questionnaire respondents were asked to name four groups that they thought were the most influential. In the USA, a total of 18 groups and in Britain a total of 13 groups were cited, and these are listed in Table 4.1 in rank order of the number of mentions they received. What the table does not reveal is that a small number of groups received a disproportionate number of mentions. In the USA, five groups – HSUS, PETA, the National Wildlife Federation (NWF), the Sierra Club and the American Humane Association (AHA) – stood out, receiving over 60 per cent of the total number of mentions. In Britain, even more starkly, three groups – the RSPCA, CIWF and the Royal Society

Table 4.1 Reputional survey of British and American animal protection and wildlife conservation groups

Britain
Royal Society for the Prevention of Cruelty to Animals
Compassion in World Farming
Royal Society for the Protection of Birds
World Wide Fund for Nature
Royal Society for Nature Conservation
Humane Slaughter Association
World Society for the Protection of Animals
British Union for the Abolition of Vivisection
Animal Aid
Greenpeace
Friends of the Earth
League Against Cruel Sports
International Fund for Animal Welfare

USA
Humane Society of the United States
People for the Ethical Treatment of Animals
National Wildlife Federation
American Humane Association
Sierra Club
Animal Welfare Institute
Defenders of Wildlife
Audubon Society
Fund for Animals
Massachusetts Society for the Prevention of Cruelty to Animals
American Society for the Prevention of Cruelty to Animals
Environmental Defense Fund
World Wildlife Fund
Farm Animal Reform Movement
Farm Sanctuary
Nature Conservancy
Greenpeace
Animal Liberation Front

for the Protection of Birds (RSPB) – received almost 60 per cent of the total number of mentions.

These lists should be treated with some caution since not every group asked responded. In addition, it may be that the importance of the broader environmental and wildlife conservation groups is underestimated because not all of the myriad organizations with an interest in wildlife issues – property developers, house builders, loggers and so forth – were consulted. There is no doubt, too, that there was a tendency in the responses to equate influence with a high profile. Thus, PETA, for obvious reasons, scored highly in the American survey but as will be suggested below, the organization does not place a great deal of emphasis on formal lobbying. By contrast, no one in the British survey mentioned FRAME, an organization which had an important role in the formulation and passage of the 1986 Animals (Scientific Procedures) Act.

Having raised these doubts as to the representative nature of the surveys, however, it is significant that the conclusions of the reputational surveys accord fairly accurately with other qualitative evidence and, in the case of Britain, with questionnaire information on the scope of a group's lobbying range and, finally, with surveys of MPs' evaluation of animal protection organizations. Thus, on the extent of lobbying, each British group was asked what the targets of its lobbying were (MPs, government departments, European Union institutions) and whether it regarded the lobbying of each as extensive, regular or rare. Only four groups – the RSPCA, the RSPB, CIWF and Advocates for Animals – said that they lobbied all three targets extensively. Only the latter does not coincide with the list provided by the reputational study. This discrepancy is no-doubt partly a product of differing interpretations of what 'extensive' means. In addition, Advocates for Animals (formerly the Scottish Society for the Prevention of Vivisection) did play a key role, through the participation of its then director Clive Hollands, in the process leading to the reform of the British law on animal experimentation, but it was a role, as with FRAME, which did not result in the organization receiving a particularly high profile.

Surveys of MPs tend to concur with the conclusions arrived at above. For example, an Access opinion poll conducted for the League Against Cruel Sports (LACS) in 1994 asked a cross-section of MPs to comment on how favourably their impressions were of LACS, the RSPB and the RSPCA and 'how effective or otherwise' the three organizations were in communicating with MPs.[7] No less than 97 per cent of MPs had either very favourable or favourable impressions of the RSPB, while the figures for

LACS and the RSPCA were 53 per cent and 77 per cent respectively. In terms of effectiveness, 84 per cent of MPs thought that the RSPCA was either very effective or effective, whereas the figures for the RSPB were 80 per cent and 72 per cent respectively.

These conclusions are confirmed by a MORI poll of 124 MPs conducted for the RSPCA in 1993.[8] No less than 78 per cent of MPs said they knew the RSPCA very well or fairly well compared to 73 per cent for the LACS, 71 per cent for the RSPB, 39 per cent for BUAV, 30 per cent for IFAW and 28 per cent for CIWF.[9] When asked how favourable they regarded these groups, however, the RSPB and RSPCA were much further ahead, with 94 per cent saying they regarded the RSPB very favourably or mainly favourably and 80 per cent for the RSPCA. Far below this were approval ratings for the LACS and CIWF (38 per cent), the International Fund for Animal Welfare (IFAW) (37 per cent) and BUAV (30 per cent). Likewise, when asked whether they had been in contact with a particular group in the past year, 63 per cent indicated they had been in touch with the RSPCA, 55 per cent LACS, 52 per cent the RSPB, 31 per cent the BUAV, 27 per cent CIWF and only 25 per cent IFAW.

The RSPCA's role as the major animal protection organization in Britain is clear-cut and the importance of this will be referred to below. In the United States, while there is greater equity between organizations in terms of reputation and financial resources, it is widely recognized that HSUS has become the most visible animal protection organization in Washington politics, one guide to public interest groups describing it as 'the General Motors' of the animal protection movement.[10] The organization, formed in 1954, now employs over 100 full-time staff and claims a membership, of subscribers and supporters, of over two million and an annual budget of, in 1996, over $30 million (see Table 4.2 for details of group incomes). HSUS's development as the key player in animal protection politics is symbolised by its regular recruitment of the 'rising stars' in the movement, the latest example being Wayne Pacelle's move from the Fund for Animals to a senior role within HSUS.[11]

In terms of public recognition, HSUS is rivalled by PETA. However, although PETA is now a large organization, with about 250 000 members, an annual budget, in 1996, of over $13 million and a staff of about 90, its lobbying presence is not as high as other animal protection groups. It has, it is true, adopted an increasingly centralized approach, choosing in the mid-1980s to close its local chapters and concentrate on the maintenance of one organizational base close to Washington DC.[12] Moreover, it does also take advantage of the lobbying opportunities presented by the fragmented American system. Despite all this, it does remain the classic example of an outsider group, more concerned with mobilizing public opinion than directly seeking to lobby decision-makers itself. In this context, it is worth quoting from a letter I received from Ingrid Newkirk in reply to a request for an interview. Newkirk wrote, without apparent irony, that 'As I am not a political animal, I believe you would not benefit from visiting me'.[13]

Table 4.2   The budgets of the major animal protection and wildlife conservation organizations in the United States, 1996

Name	1996 budget $m.
American Humane Association	6.5
American SPCA	18.1
Defenders of Wildlife	6.8
Doris Day Animal League	1.8
Environmental Defense Fund	24.6
Friends of Animals	4.4
Fund for Animals	3.3
Greenpeace	24.1
Humane Society of the United States	31.6
International Fund for Animal Welfare	7.3
Massachusetts Society for the Prevention of Cruelty to Animals	22.7
National Audubon Society	42.4
National Wildlife Federation	100.6
The Nature Conservancy	312.4
People for the Ethical Treatment of Animals	13.4
Sierra Club	43.9
Wildlife Conservation Society	66.2
World Society for the Protection of Animals	5.3
World Wildlife Fund	63.5

Source: *Animal People* (December 1996).

It is the case, then, that the animal protection movement's lobbying capacity has increased markedly over the past two decades or so, and there is no doubt too that they are taken much more seriously now by governmental actors. Andrew Rowan, for instance, who lobbied for the HSUS, comments how in the early 1980s he usually ended up talking to the junior aides or summer interns of members of Congress whereas ten years later 'there are senior aides who have animal issues as part of their beat'.[14] It is also interesting to note that as the animal protection movement has increasingly focused on conventional lobbying activities, it has tended to recruit lobbyists with relevant professional qualifications and/or political experience. In Britain, for instance, the RSPCA recruits those with expertise in science and agriculture for its farm and research animal sections, as well as experienced parliamentary lobbyists with backgrounds in political parties or other pressure groups. Thus, in the process of conducting interviews in Britain I came across a (since elected) Labour Party prospective parliamentary candidate (LACS), a former Labour party agent (RSPCA), an Oxford Politics, Philosophy and Economics graduate with trade union experience (BUAV), and a lawyer (CIWF). In the USA, likewise, there is a trend towards greater professionalism, particularly as the original founders are replaced by career employees. Animal protection lobbyists now tend to be highly educated professionals with backgrounds such as working in Congress and the executive branch, the law and lobbying for other organizations. To name but three examples, Adele Douglass the chief lobbyist for the AHA, was formerly a Congressional aide, Holly Hazard (the director of the Doris Day Animal League) is a lawyer, and Wayne Pacelle (HSUS) a Yale graduate.

FINANCIAL RESOURCES AND POLITICAL INFLUENCE

The financial resources of the animal-use industry are, as we have seen, considerable and resources can be provided not just for lobbying capability but also for propaganda purposes. The animal protection movement cannot really compete with this. The resources of animal advocacy organizations (as Table 4.2 illustrates) do seem considerable, but the image often painted by their adversaries – of a limitless supply of funds – is clearly a fiction. Three points in particular should be borne in mind here. Firstly, unlike corporations and trade associations, animal protection groups do not have a clearly-defined and easily manageable source of finance (in the form of either individual members working for a corporation or constituent organizations of a trade association) from which to draw, and nor do they have a pre-existing corporate structure from which a lobbying capacity can be created. As a consequence, money has to be raised, often through direct mailing techniques, to create both a general organizational structure and a lobbying adjunct. In some cases, as with the ASPCA and the AHA, the organization's head office is not in Washington DC and a separate office has to be created for lobbying purposes, whereas others – such as PETA, AWI and HSUS – are situated in the nation's capital, so extra expenses are avoided. In Britain, it is not quite so essential to have a London base although some – such as the LACS, the BUAV and Friends of the Earth – do. Even in a country as small as Britain, however, extra expense and time is incurred by having to travel in from Sussex (RSPCA), Bedfordshire (RSPB), Hampshire (CIWF) or Devon (where Richard Ryder, the political consultant for the Political Animal Lobby – the lobbying arm of IFAW – lives).

The second factor which ought to be borne in mind when considering the financial resources available to animal protection organizations is that the wealthiest of them tend to be those who also maintain a costly and time-consuming service to directly aid suffering animals. The ASPCA and the RSPCA, for instance, both perform extensive secondary functions in managing animal shelters, maintaining clinics and providing an inspectorate to root out cases of animal cruelty. Likewise, the AHA, which campaigns on children's issues as well, represents animal care and control agencies throughout the country, many of whom are affiliated members of the organization, as well as maintaining a Los Angeles office which monitors the use of animals in the entertainment industry. Many other animal protection organizations perform additional functions other than campaigning.[15]

Finally, the wealthiest of all animal advocacy groups tend to be those concerned with wildlife conservation, and these groups do not primarily concern themselves with farm or laboratory animal issues, and, as we saw in Chapter 2, there can be

significant ideological-based conflicts between them and mainstream animal protection organizations.

Because of the organizational needs of animal advocacy
groups and the additional secondary functions many of them
perform, the resources available for direct lobbying are severely
restricted. It has been reported, for instance, that direct-mail
costs account for about 90 per cent of every dollar raised by the
Doris Day Animal League. Likewise in 1990, the lobbying
budget of the HSUS represented only about 6 per cent of its total
spending.[16] The financial inequalities identified above are real
enough but we should be careful about assuming, of course, that
money is the only, or even the most important, factor determining political influence. It is difficult to show conclusively,
for instance, that the availability of PAC money in the United
States buys a group political influence (see Chapter 7), and the
general evidence provided by the case studies in Chapters 7–10
of this book tend to suggest that public policy outcomes are the
product of a number of factors, some of which are not, directly at
least, related to financial clout. The success that the animal
protection movement has achieved in state initiatives (see
Chapter 1) has come about, for instance, despite the financial
advantages of its opponents.

The recent partial decline of the NRA would seem to represent a classic example of the truism that extensive financial
resources and a large membership does not always win the day.
In 1992, the NRA had a staff of 550, a lobbying arm – the Institute for Legislative Action – a budget of $86.9 million, 2.65
million members, 50 state affiliates, 16 000 affiliated clubs and a
PAC.[17] Despite this, it is widely recognized that with growing
public concern over the proliferation of gun-related deaths, the
legislative influence of the NRA has begun to wane. As the
Foundation for Public Affairs, a Washington think tank, pointed
out:

> with its antagonists better organized than ever before, with
> many law enforcement groups willing to actively lobby on
> gun control measures that the association opposes, and with
> the nation shaken by an epidemic of violence, lawmakers and
> others are questioning whether the group's influence has di-
> minished on Capitol Hill.[18]

It is difficult to make comparisons between the financial strength of animal advocacy organizations in Britain and the United States. For one thing, there is a much larger potential pool of supporters (and therefore money) in the latter, but, at the same time, the costs of running a national organization are that much greater. The RSPCA's regular annual income of around £20 million seems formidable in the light of these factors. It should be remembered, however, that – if we exclude the wealthy wildlife group such as the RSPB and the World Wide Fund for Nature (WWF) – the RSPCA has a dominant place within the animal protection community in Britain. Most of the other groups have much more moderate incomes and consequently far fewer administrative, scientific and lobbying staff.

ORGANIZATIONAL ALLIANCES AND POLICY SECTORIZATION

An examination of animal protection lobbying in Britain and the United States shows that though there is a considerable degree of formal and informal interaction between organizations, the evidence still largely confirms the sectorized model of policymaking. In Britain, organizational alliances in the modern period date back to the 1970s. The period between August 1976 and August 1977 was designated by the movement as Animal Welfare Year and the unity fashioned by this event was instrumental in the creation of a number of joint consultative bodies.[19] One of these was the Farm Animal Welfare Co-ordinating Executive – consisting of representatives from animal protection groups such as CIWF, the Farm and Food Society, the RSPCA and the World Society for the Protection of Animals (WSPA) and chaired by the Labour MP Robin Corbett – which, among other things, gave joint evidence to the Commons Agriculture Committee's enquiry into animal husbandry in 1981.[20] The classic example was the Committee for the Reform of Animal Experimentation (CRAE) formed in 1977 under the leadership of Lord Houghton. CRAE was joined in 1993 by FRAME and the British Veterinary Association (BVA), which jointly lobbied government on a common set of objectives (see Chapter 9 for more details). This unity was continued up to the 1979 election campaign when the five joint bodies created during Animal

Welfare Year (together with LACS) formed the General Election Co-ordinating Committee for Animal Protection (GECCAP) with the aim of lobbying the parties on animal welfare issues and generally 'putting animals into politics'.

Much of the campaigning in the 1970s remained sectorized with different joint bodies focusing on different animal protection issues. In addition, serious divisions remained within the animal protection movement despite the attempts at unification. For instance, only 42 out of 79 organizations contacted initially participated in Animal Welfare Year, the others declining to attend mainly on ideological grounds.[21] Furthermore, it proved impossible to keep abolitionist groups such as the National Antivivisection Society (NAVS) and the BUAV within the alliance promoted by CRAE and, during the passage of the 1986 Animals (Scientific Procedures) Act, they, together with Animal Aid, formed an oppositionist organization against the legislation.

Before and since, most organizational alliances have tended to be much more informal than the CRAE alliance, more concerned with information sharing than the creation of a common policy position and joint lobbying. It needs to be stressed here that, as indicated earlier, the British animal protection community is dominated by the RSPCA and the nature of organizational alliances has tended to be shaped by its priorities. Thus, it is evident that the RSPCA is very aware of the need to preserve its 'brand' name (and maintain itself as the 'Heinz Baked Beans' of animal protection, as one senior RSPCA employee told me[22]) and this has made it reluctant to dilute its identity in formal coalitions. Before the 1979 election, for instance, the RSPCA published a booklet called a 'Charter for Animals' without consulting GECCAP, a move which, Clive Hollands – a leading exponent of movement unity – argues, confused the voters since it adopted a different line from GECCAP objectives.[23]

Likewise, the RSPCA, although formally a member of CRAE, tended to go it alone during the run-up to the passage of the 1986 Animals (Scientific Procedures) Act rather than throw in its lot with the CRAE Alliance, and met Mellor separately[24] (see Chapter 9). This was partly a matter of policy differences – the RSPCA (dominated by its radical council) refusing to budge from its publicly stated opposition to all experiments on animals which cause pain – partly a desire for its identity not to be absorbed within a coalition and partly because at the time it was involved in internal battles and did not place much emphasis on lobbying or campaigning. The desire for independence did cause problems. For example, during the House of Lords select committee enquiry into animal experimentation in 1979, Lord Houghton, speaking on behalf of CRAE, was annoyed that the RSPCA's evidence was being taken before CRAE's thereby undermining CRAE's claim to be providing the 'main evidence on behalf of the animal welfare organizations'.[25]

Nevertheless, the RSPCA has joined forces with, most notably, CIWF on specific farm animal welfare issues and with a number of other organizations (the LACS, the National Federation of Badger Groups, WWF, and the Royal Society for Nature Conservation) in the Coalition for Badgers designed to support PMBs introduced in the early 1990s. In addition, in its capacity as the major player in Eurogroup for Animal Welfare, the RSPCA holds regular meetings in London, to which representatives from other organizations are invited, at which the latest developments in the European Union are outlined and debated.

In the United States, there is, paradoxically, both greater and lesser scope for organizational co-operation. The geographical enormity of the USA tends to militate against sustained coalition building. The logistical difficulties of organizing animal protection marches on Washington, held in 1990 and 1996, for instance, is an illustration of this factor at work and was at least partly responsible for the relatively small turnout of a few thousand in the latter case. In addition, as we had cause to note in Chapter 3, ideological divisions – between advocates of rights and advocates of welfare – have been more prominent in the USA and have also obstructed organizational unity.

Attempts to secure unity is, however, a regular preoccupation for animal advocates. At the leadership level, unity is sought through the annual (since 1985) Summit for the Animals where groups founders, chief executives and lobbyists meet to discuss common concerns and to develop co-ordinated responses. At the 1997 summit, for instance, a concerted effort was made to develop a common platform on a number of issues. This meeting, which I attended, was cordial enough and certainly valuable in terms of the networking possibilities made available. It was of much more limited use in policy terms, however, partly because of organizations' desire to maintain their own identity and

Political Animals

autonomy but also because of disputes over policy objectives. At the grass-roots level, the National Alliance for Animals, headed by Peter Gerard, exists to co-ordinate local activism and it was responsible, for instance, for organizing the two marches on Washington, in 1990 and 1996.

At the level of Washington politics, there is greater scope than in Britain for co-operation between the lobbyists of animal protection organizations simply by virtue of the fact that their offices are located in close proximity in Washington DC. At an informal level, animal protection lobbyists know each other very well and there is a regular ad-hoc sharing of information through fax machines, telephone conversations and meetings. At a more formal level, the so-called 'Tuesday Group' – consisting of lobbyists from various organizations including AHA, ASPCA, the Fund for Animals, AWI, the HSUS and the Doris Day Animal League – was created in the late 1980s and meets monthly when Congress is in session to discuss pending legislation. In addition, groups will come together on species issues (marine mammal protection and the Endangered Species Act, to give two examples). Although groups will co-operate for the achievement of shared objectives, the coalitions remain informal, based more on the sharing of information and lobbying work-load (best defined as networking) than some form of organizational unity and a detailed attempt to work out common policy positions (prerequisites for genuine coalition-building).

The degree of policy sectorization in the animal protection lobby is considerable. As with the animal use lobby, animal advocacy groups were asked how far they lobbied on key pieces of legislation (see Table 2.2 for list of bills). A number of single issue or single sector groups revealed, not surprisingly, that they only lobbied on bills which were of particular interest to them. Thus, FARM in the United States only lobbied on farm animal issues, and LACS in Britain only on blood sports issues and so on. More surprisingly, both the Sierra Club and the Wildlife Legislative Fund of America claimed to have lobbied on animal research issues as well as wildlife issues. This does not fit in with the sectoral pattern of policy-making and, it should also be said, there is no other evidence – their participation in Congressional hearings, for instance, or being mentioned by other actors who were involved – that they were, centrally at least, concerned with animal research legislation.

More significantly, we should also mention those more general animal welfare organizations, such as the RSPCA, the BVA, Advocates for Animals, and the Universities Federation for Animal Welfare (UFAW) in Britain, and HSUS, the Doris Day Animal League and the AHA in the United States, which would, superficially at least, appear to lobby in a cross-sectoral fashion. Indeed, the AHA and HSUS lobbied on all 11 bills. In addition, animal rights groups – such as PETA and Animal Aid – tend to lean towards a more general coverage of animal issues, since their operational principle is that all animals, whatever they are used for, are deserving of protection by very virtue of the fact that their possession of rights makes human utilization illegitimate.

Three points need to be made about these apparent exceptions to the sectorized model of lobbying. In the first place, general animal rights groups tend to concentrate on campaigning and they therefore do not require the specialization necessary for effective personal lobbying of officials. Secondly, those general groups who do more extensive lobbying are more sectorized than is at first apparent. The RSPCA organization, for instance, has a number of separate sections, each headed by a director, based upon issues, lobbying targets and secondary functions. In terms of issues, the Chief Veterinary Officer heads a division responsible for companion animals whilst the Director of Scientific Affairs (at present Dr Tony Suckling) heads a division with sub-sectors responsible for wildlife, farm animals and research animals. Staff in these sectors are primarily responsible for liaising with relevant ministers and civil servants whilst a separate division exists for lobbying parliament. At the apex of the organization is the director general, Peter Davies, through who any correspondence with ministers must go.[26] Another example of a sectorized organizational structure is the BVA, which is governed by a council elected by 28 territorial divisions and, more significantly for our purposes here, by 20 non-territorial divisions representing particular areas of veterinary medicine, such as the British Laboratory Animals Veterinary Association and the Pig Veterinary Society.[27] The permanent staff are, likewise, organized into specialist divisions that brief the elected officers fronting the lobbying effort as well as attending meetings with government officials themselves.

The final point is that, although some of the smaller general animal protection groups may lobby on cross-sectoral issues, they tend to participate to a greater degree on issues of particular interest to them. Thus, the AHA chief lobbyist Adele Douglass, for instance, was particularly interested in, and played a central lobbying role on, legislation designed to deal with pet theft, this reflecting her organization's preoccupation with companion animals.

The last three chapters have considered the nature of those non-governmental organizations that participate in the policy networks surrounding issues relating to the protection of animals. It can be concluded that those interests concerned to defend their right to continue exploiting animals are wealthy and, particularly in the USA, united. The animal protection movement, by contrast, has apparently severe organizational, financial and ideological problems. Before we go on, in Chapters 7–10, to examine the effects these weaknesses have in particular policy networks, the next two chapters take a slight detour to examine how animal protection is regarded in the British and American legislatures.

5 Parliament and Animal Protection

It is a commonplace to argue that parliament's role in the British political system has declined. This is largely confirmed by an examination of its role in animal welfare decision-making where the animal welfare legislative and administrative framework has developed largely independently of the parliamentary sphere. But while parliament's direct legislative impact may be minimal, it will also be argued in this chapter that the legislative branch has played a role in the development of animal welfare as a political issue. Moreover, this chapter also examines the characteristics of those MPs most interested in animal welfare. The conclusions, most notably that party and gender are important explanatory variables, have potentially important consequences for the future direction of the issue.

PARLIAMENT'S LIMITED ROLE

Much has been written about the decline of the British parliament.[1] With the emergence of a disciplined party system in the latter part of the nineteenth century, governments became able to rely on a whipped Commons majority which guaranteed that the bulk of their legislation would receive the royal assent. Conversely, it is now rare for backbenchers to make a legislative impact, particularly when they do not have government support or at least acquiescence. The trend towards executive dominance is confirmed by a study of animal welfare policy-making. As we saw in Chapter 1, major government departments have the responsibility for administering policy relating to the welfare of farm and laboratory animals, and the primary legislation giving rise to the administrative structure was government sponsored. Because of this, as we shall see in later chapters, the system of animal welfare interest group politics has increasingly been focused on the executive. Thus, in drawing the boundaries of animal welfare policy networks in Britain, parliament plays, with the exception of the hunting issue, a peripheral role.

Parliament has been further marginalized by Britain's membership of the European Union and its participation in international wildlife treaties. In the case of farm animals in particular, decisions relating to the welfare of animals are increasingly being taken at the European level. Not only has this had the effect of limiting the British government's ability to act independently of other member states (see Chapter 8), it has also meant that private members' bills (PMBs) can be rejected on the grounds that they conflict with directives. Furthermore, MPs cannot amend, or even influence to any great extent, legislation determined by the Council of Ministers. In this way, control over decision-making is even further removed from Westminster.

Parliament's direct legislative impact – whereby the executive is forced to accept measures which it would prefer not to – has, then, been negligible. Thus, of the 59 PMBs introduced by backbenchers between 1983 and 1995, only 39 got as far as the first reading stage in the Commons and only nine eventually received the royal assent and became law. Even more significantly, none of these nine were opposed by the government of the day. Indeed, not once in the whole post-war period has an animal protection bill opposed by the executive succeeded. In recent times, the closest a government came to a defeat on animal welfare was over the issue of a dog registration scheme. This proposal – which would have made it compulsory for all dogs to be registered, thereby enabling the owners of strays to be located – was supported not just by animal welfare organizations but also by a whole range of influential groups, from the NFU to the Police Federation. In its first vote on the issue in April 1990, 49 Conservative MPs voted against a three-line whip and the government's majority was significantly reduced from over a 100 to just 12 (the proposal was defeated by 275–263). As a result of pressure, particularly from the NFU, the Lords reinstated the dog registration amendment (to the Environmental Protection Bill) and when it was sent back to the Commons the amendment was defeated by only three votes (274–271), the Thatcher government's narrowest majority when applying a three-line whip.[2]

The one possible exception to parliament's legislative impotence was the fate of the Pig Husbandry Bill introduced in

1991 by the Conservative backbencher, and noted critic of intensive agriculture, Richard Body.[3] Written by the animal protection group Compassion in World Farming (CIWF), the bill – which sought to ban sow stalls and tethers, devices which are used to restrain sows throughout most of their lives – gained considerable support in the Commons. Just before the second reading debate, the government announced it would accept the bill and, should it fail, would introduce regulations under the 1968 Agriculture (Miscellaneous Provisions) Act to achieve the same objectives.[4] In the event, this proved necessary when the bill failed at the report stage as a result of time-wasting tactics by its opponents.[5] Body's PMB failed then, but it is possible to argue, although difficult to prove, that the government acted only when it saw how popular the bill was.[6] Indeed, in providing a longer phase-out period for stalls and tethers (eight years) than Body's bill proposed (five years), the government might be seen here to be representing agricultural interests by engaging in a damage limitation exercise, providing more time for pig farmers to move to alternative systems. A more charitable, and extremely significant, view is that Commons support for the reform enabled MAFF to act despite the opposition of the Pig Breeders' Association and the NFU (for further discussion of the relationship between MAFF and organized interests see Chapter 8).

PARLIAMENT AND HUNTING

The one animal protection issue which has not been subject to executive dominance is hunting. Traditionally, MPs have been allowed a free vote on abolition bills and parliament has been at the centre of the debate.[7] Indeed, given the variety of non-governmental actors involved, seeking to compete on a relatively equal footing for the ears of MPs, hunting would seem to represent a classic case of an open and pluralistic issue network. It has proved exceedingly difficult, however, for anti-hunting bills to make significant progress.

The hunting lobby (consisting mainly of the British Field Sports Society) has been able to garner enough opposition from MPs and peers who are either landowners themselves or represent rural constituencies where support for hunting remains strong. As a result, PMBs have either been defeated by a vote or have fallen victim to a variety of procedural devices. An additional factor benefiting the pro-hunting lobby has been the shift in their campaigning focus. Originally, hunting was justified primarily on the grounds that it was an effective means of pest control, an argument that was popular with many farmers. Nowadays, hunting tends to be justified on the grounds that it promotes conservation. Thus, without the hunting community, it is argued, there would be no incentive for landowners to preserve the habitats which the hunted animals rely upon. This switch in focus causes problems for the anti-hunting lobby because it divides animal protectionists from many environmentalists whose ideological emphasis is on preserving species and not protecting individual animals against cruelty (see Chapter 2 for a further discussion of this point). The significant role of the hunting lobby in the creation of the Countryside Movement, a body promoting a whole range of countryside issues including hunting and farming, in 1996 is another illustration of this clever reorientation.[8]

There are some signs, however, that the previously strong position of the hunting lobby is waning. More Conservative MPs are now prepared to support abolition bills and this in turn is a product of the fact that fewer MPs now represent rural constituencies and those that still do have increasingly to take into account the growing number of new middle-class rural dwellers who are more likely to oppose hunting. Above all, public opinion has hardened considerably against fox hunting and hare coursing. Thus, a MORI poll in 1978 found that 54 per cent were opposed whereas 16 years later this had increased to 69 per cent. Significantly, in support of the view that there is not a rural/urban divide on this issue, the poll also found there was only a marginal difference in opinion between those living in rural and urban constituencies.[9]

Given the relative ease with which PMBs can be sabotaged by a small number of MPs, however, coupled with the considerable support for bloodsports which still exists in the House of Lords, the best hope for the anti-hunting lobby rests with the Labour government taking action. In this context, it is crucial to note that as well as being centred on the legislature, the hunting issue is also unusual, from an animal welfare perspective, in the sense that a clear party divide exists. Support for hunting comes almost exclusively from the Conservative Party whereas Labour MPs have been generally hostile. Thus, at the second reading stage of the Labour MP Kevin McNamara's abolitionist Wild Mammals (Protection) Bill introduced in the early 1990s, no Labour MPs voted against and of the 190 who did, all but six were Conservatives.[10]

More significantly still, abolition of hare coursing and deer hunting became official Labour Party policy in 1979 and in the 1983 election fox hunting was added. By the 1997 election, Labour's commitment had been diluted to a promise of support for a PMB.[11] As a recognition of Labour's support, the anti-hunting lobby has tended to make no secret of its party preference. The League Against Cruel Sports (LACS), for instance, contributed £80 000 towards Labour's election campaign in 1979. More recently, the International Fund for Animal Welfare (IFAW) gave Labour a staggering £1 million in the run-up to the 1997 election primarily because of the party's anti-hunting stance.[12] This was the largest single donation from a body not affiliated to the party in its history.

In 1997, a Labour backbencher did introduce a bill to abolish hunting but at the time of writing the Labour government had shown itself unwilling to ensure the bill's passage through the Commons by granting it extra parliamentary time. Despite this, with a huge Labour majority the bill will probably clear all of its hurdles in the Commons. The Lords, however, is another matter and a bill which lacks the legitimacy of executive sponsorship is likely to be mauled by the upper House. Indeed, there is even some opposition to an anti-hunting bill from Labour Peers. Baroness Mallalieu (a hunter herself), for instance, heads the Labour pro-hunting group Leave Country Sports Alone, formed in 1994, which also includes Lords Donoughue and Shackleton and celebrities such as John Mortimer and David Puttnam among its supporters. Whether there would be sufficient time, or inclination, on the part of the government to invoke the provisions of the 1949 Parliament Act and override the Lords' veto, is, at the time of writing, an open question. The initial signs, in May 1997, did not look too promising, with Jack Cunningham, the new Minister of Agriculture, suggesting that the Labour government, while accepting the Commons' verdict on hunting for pleasure, would still allow 'licensed' hunts to exist in order to control the fox population.[13]

LEGISLATION, SCRUTINY AND AGENDA SETTING

Despite parliament's limited legislative role, it does still perform a number of useful functions in the British political system. It can be argued, for instance, that parliamentary debates initiated by backbenchers function as part of an on-going legislative process.[14] The various anti-hunting bills, for instance, might be seen as an essential part of the process which will eventually lead to its abolition. The same might be said of the dog registration proposal mentioned earlier. These assertions, of course, are only speculative since they have not yet resulted in legislative change. If we examine the development of policy in farm and laboratory animal welfare, however, it can be seen that parliamentary debate has preceded governmental action.

In the case of animal research, two PMBs introduced virtually simultaneously in the 1979–80 session (one in the Commons and one in the Lords) had the effect of keeping the issue in the public domain, and were arguably a contributory factor in provoking and shaping eventual executive action. The Laboratory Animals Protection Bill introduced by Lord Halsbury was particularly important in this regard since it resulted in the creation of a select committee of peers who deliberated extensively on the bill before producing a lengthy report.[15] The Conservative government, who had promised to reform the existing law dating back to 1876 in their 1979 manifesto, rejected both bills. What was significant here, though, was that Home Office ministers were regularly forced to justify their decision by reference to the fact that a government-sponsored version would be preferable. In addition, certain elements of the select committee's report – such as the creation of a statutory advisory committee – were eventually adopted in the 1986 legislation; for further details on the origins of the 1986 Animals (Scientific Procedures) Act see Chapter 9.

In the case of farm animal welfare, a similar pattern can be observed. The Body bill mentioned above provides one example of a PMB precipitating an, in this case, rapid governmental response. Prior to this bill, in addition, there had been a number of parliamentary initiatives in farm animal welfare. In addition to other PMBs, the Agricultural Select Committee has regularly concerned itself with farm animal welfare. Significantly, a number of its recommendations in a major report published in 1981 – most notably relating to sow stalls and tethers and the veal crate – have since been acted upon by government (for further details see Chapter 8).[16]

As well as being part of the on-going legislative process, parliament also exists as a forum for highlighting issues of public concern and for publicizing and scrutinizing the activities of the executive. This has clearly been its major contribution to animal welfare. MPs cannot fail to appreciate the level of public concern for the welfare of animals given the size of their post bags on the issue. A MORI poll conducted for the RSPCA in 1993, for instance, revealed that 60 of the 124 MPs interviewed received more mail on animal welfare than any other issue. On only one other issue – housing – did more MPs (73) receive the most letters.[17] We saw in Chapter 1 – in terms of the number and proportion of PMBs, petitions, parliamentary questions and Early Day Motions concerned with the issue and the number of MPs involved in tabling them – that parliament has responded as an accurate barometer of public interest.

THE EXTENT OF ANIMAL ADVOCACY IN PARLIAMENT

In Chapter 1, the extent of parliamentary activity on animal protection and wildlife conservation was outlined in terms of the number and type of bills, parliamentary questions and EDMs introduced. The rest of this chapter considers the number and character of the MPs responsible for them during the parliamentary sessions between 1985 and 1994. In terms of raw numbers, a total of 352 MPs showed some concern (measured by the asking of parliamentary questions, the introduction of bills and the tabling of EDMs), however intermittent, for animal protection and wildlife conservation between 1985 and 1994. By the end of the 1987 General Election, 14 of these had either retired, died or were defeated. A further 53 were elected for the first time in 1992. This leaves a total of 286 MPs sitting in the Commons between 1987 and 1992, representing 44 per cent of the 650 members of the House.

These raw figures can be refined in two important ways. In the first place, it is worth asking to what extent wildlife issues were more popular among MPs and the degree to which those who

were involved with wildlife issues were different from those expressing an interest in mainstream animal protection issues.
Here, we find that out of the total number of 352 MPs, 75 were
only involved with wildlife issues and a further 135 did not express any interest in wildlife issues. As a consequence, and
somewhat surprisingly given the greater public saliency of
wildlife issues, 277 MPs showed an interest in animal protection
issues whereas only 217 showed an interest in wildlife issues.

The second, and even more crucial, piece of refining is to
measure the intensity of support for animal issues. The raw figures we have been discussing so far are misleading in that many
MPs are included by virtue of a minimum commitment to animal issues. Over 200 (out of the 352) MPs, for instance, asked a
relatively small number of parliamentary questions, only 44 introduced a bill and/or petition and only 41 an EDM. By utilizing a scoring system (explained in Appendix I) it is possible to
be far more selective and identify those MPs with a greater
commitment to animal issues.

Refining the list of MPs in terms of their commitment to animal issues produces a list of 36 MPs in the 1987–92 parliament
who demonstrated an extensive or moderate commitment to
animal protection and wildlife conservation (see Table 5.1). This
figure represents 13 per cent of the MPs showing any kind of
interest in animal issues during the 1987–92 parliament and 6
per cent of the whole House.[18] This list can be further reduced to
include 12 MPs who were exceptionally committed to animal
issues (the first 12 names in Table 5.1). In turn, four of these –
Tony Banks, Ron Davies, Elliot Morley and Harry Greenway –
were well ahead of the others. The minimum requirement for
inclusion in the list of 36 is equivalent to asking 14 parliamentary
questions or sponsoring one bill and asking four questions. Below this, many of the others asked only one or two questions in
the House.

PROFILE OF ANIMAL ADVOCATES IN THE HOUSE

Having identified the MPs who raised animal protection and
wildlife issues in the House, it is possible to examine the characteristics of these MPs. Not only does the identification of
particular characteristics help us to explain the past development

Table 5.1   The top 36 animal advocates in the House of
Commons, 1987–92

Name	Party	Score
Tony Banks	Labour	148
Ron Davies	Labour	134.5
Elliot Morley	Labour	96.5
Harry Greenway	Conservative	92
Harry Cohen	Labour	58
Simon Hughes	Liberal Democrat	40.5
David Amess	Conservative	32.5
Alan Meale	Labour	32
Andrew Bowden	Conservative	30.5
David Clark	Labour	28
Janet Fookes	Conservative	27.5
Richard Body	Conservative	22.5
Robin Corbett	Labour	19.5
David Hincliffe	Labour	19
Roger Gale	Conservative	17
Tam Dalyell	Labour	16
James Dunnachie	Labour	15
Greg Knight	Conservative	14
Martin Redmond	Labour	12.5
Jeremy Corbyn	Labour	12.5
Chris Mullin	Labour	11.5
Alan Williams	Labour	11.5
Teddy Taylor	Conservative	11.5
Peter Hardy	Labour	11.5
Terry Lewis	Labour	11
Kevin McNamara	Labour	10.5
Ronald Boyes	Labour	10.5
Donald Coleman	Labour	10
Roy Hughes	Labour	8
Norman Godman	Labour	7.5
Geoffrey Steinberg	Labour	7.5
Paul Flynn	Labour	7.5
Emma Nicholson	Conservative*	7.5
Alex Carlile	Liberal Democrat	7
James Wallace	Liberal Democrat	7
Rhodri Morgan	Labour	7

* She defected to the Liberal Democrats before the 1997
election.

of animal welfare in the Commons, it also provides us with some guide to the future of the issue in both the legislature and the executive. Indeed, the adage that today's backbencher is potentially tomorrow's minister has been confirmed in this case since a number of the key backbench supporters of animal protection in the 1987–92 parliament are now members of the Labour government (see below). Another key question is the extent to which those MPs supportive of animal protection represent a new divide in British politics not based on party. Finally, by comparing the results of this survey with a similar analysis of members of Congress (the results of which can be found in Chapter 6) it is possible to isolate key variables which might help us to explain the differential animal welfare achievements of the two countries.

At this point, it should be noted that there may be something of a bias in the survey by dint of the fact that during this period the Conservatives were the governing party. About 100 Conservative MPs, therefore, were not in a position to engage in backbench activities – such as tabling parliamentary questions – which constitutes the major focus of this survey. This may distort the results particularly in relation to the importance of party and, since the average age of government ministers tends to be higher than that of backbenchers, age too. Having said this, many ministers were in a position to introduce government bills and there is little evidence that any members of the Thatcher administrations – with the possible exception of Alan Clark[19] – would have been vociferous defenders of animals but for the constraints of ministerial office. Conversely, Elliot Morley's pre-eminent position at the top of the list is largely a product of his role as Labour's front-bench spokesman on animal welfare but his appointment to that position, and his willingness to take it, is equally a product of his well-known interest in and concern for the welfare of animals.

Geography and Party Profile

As Table 5.2 reveals, the geographical locations of MPs most interested in animal issues were disproportionately skewed towards constituencies in London, the North of England and Wales. This is almost entirely, however, a product of the party variable, since Labour's strength was in these areas. More difficult to explain is why almost half of the 12 most committed animal advocates in the Commons represented seats in London. Labour certainly had more representation in London than the South as a whole (the party won 23 out of the 84 London seats in 1987) but this does not, by itself, explain the disproportionate representation on our list. It may, of course, be mere coincidence, but it is also worth speculating that it reflects in some way the link between animal welfare and an urbanization (more greatly personified by Inner London than anywhere else) which cuts people off from the utilitarian uses and abuses of animals. Further evidence for the importance of urbanization is that few of the MPs on our list (five out of 36 to be precise) represent constituencies that can be described as rural, and only one of these MPs – Richard Body, the Conservative MP from Holland with Boston in East Anglia – is in the top 12.

A much more significant variable is the party label of MPs. In terms of the total number of MPs showing any kind of interest in animal issues, there is a slight bias towards Labour. Thus, while the Conservatives won 58 per cent of the seats in the 1987 election, only 48 per cent of those MPs elected in 1987 showing some concern for animal welfare were Conservatives compared to 41 per cent Labour (35 per cent of the seats overall) and 7 per cent Liberal or Social Democrat (3 per cent of the seats overall). The bias towards Labour is much more pronounced in the list of moderately and extensively committed MPs (see Table 5.3). Thus, no less than 67 per cent of the top 36 MPs were Labour as opposed to only 22 per cent who were Conservatives. In the top 12, this bias is less pronounced, although still considerable, with

Table 5.2   Geographical profile of MPs interested in animal issues, 1987–92

Region	% in House	Top 12		Top 36	
		no.	%	no.	%
London	13	5	(42)	6	(17)
S. England	28	3	(25)	6	(17)
Midlands	16	1	(8)	3	(8)
N. England	20	2	(17)	10	(28)
Wales	5	1	(8)	7	(19)
Scotland	11	–	–	4	(11)

Table 5.3   Party labels of MPs interested in animal issues, 1987–92

Party	Whole House		Top 12		Top 36	
	no.	%	no.	%	no.	%
Labour	229	(35)	24	(67)	6	(50)
Conservative	375	(58)	8	(22)	5	(42)
Liberal Democrats*	22	(3)	4	(11)	1	(8)

* At the time of the 1987 election, the Liberal Party and the Social Democratic Party.

50 per cent Labour and 42 per cent Conservative. This Labour bias is also noticeable beyond 1992. Of the 63 new Labour MPs elected in 1992, 32 (or over 50 per cent) had promoted an animal protection or wildlife conservation issue by the end of the 1994 session of parliament.

Age and Gender

Age was not a significant variable in terms of the top 36 MPs. Most of them (around 70 per cent) were clustered around the 40 to 60 age range as are MPs in general. In the top 12, however, no less than five (42 per cent) were aged between 30 and 40 in 1987. Since the average age of Labour and Conservative MPs was about 50 and 60 respectively in the 1987–92 parliament, there is some evidence that animal welfare is of particular interest to younger MPs. However, no MPs among the 36 were under 30 compared to about 12 (or 2 per cent) in the House as a whole.

For the 1987–92 parliament, gender was also not a significant variable in terms of animal protection. That is, there is little evidence that female MPs are more likely to be interested in animal issues than their male counterparts. Of the total number of 286 MPs who showed some interest in animal protection in the 1987–92 parliament, for instance, 9 per cent were women as opposed to just over 6 per cent in the whole House. Likewise, as Table 5.4 shows, there is little difference between the proportion of women in the top 36 and top 12 animal advocates and the Commons as a whole. This disguises, however, potentially significant developments after 1992. In the 1992–4 period no fewer than 11 new female MPs, first elected in 1992, were recorded as

Table 5.4   Support for animal issues in the House of Commons by gender, 1987–92

	Whole House		Top 12		Top 36	
	no.	*%*	*no.*	*%*	*no.*	*%*
male	609	(94)	11	(92)	34	(94)
female	41	(6)	1	(8)	2	(6)

having contributed to the promotion of animal protection, and this represents more than 50 per cent of the new female intake in the election (11 out of 21).

The major conclusion of the research results presented in the latter part of this chapter is that party label is the most significant indicator of support for animal protection. While it is true to say that some of the most committed animal advocates in the Commons are Conservatives, the evidence points to a previously unappreciated predominance of Labour MPs. It is certainly not entirely accurate, therefore, to describe animal protection as a cross-party issue. Labour's resounding victory in the 1997 general election, therefore, is encouraging for animal advocates. Some of those who did most to promote the well-being of animals from the backbenchers in the 1980s – Tony Banks, Ron Davies, Elliot Morley and David Clark – now find themselves in a Labour administration. Moreover, the evidence also suggests that, from 1992, female MPs, and particularly female Labour MPs, began to play a greater role in the advocacy of animal issues in the Commons. With the election of an unprecedented number of, mostly Labour, female MPs in 1997 (101 in all representing nearly 25 per cent of the entire parliamentary Labour Party), there is every chance that animal protection will become a more important parliamentary issue in the years leading up to the millennium.[20]

6 American Legislators and Animal Protection

For reasons already explored, Congress plays a much more important legislative function than the British House of Commons and because of this, the general role of Congress in animal protection decision-making is considered further in Chapters 7 and 10. This chapter is limited to an examination of the characteristics of those members of Congress who have displayed an interest in animal protection issues in the period 1985–1994.

By assessing the relative importance of a number of variables – geographical location, age, party and gender – it is possible to provide evidence for the existence of particular traits likely to be found in Congressional supporters of animal welfare. From this we can go on to ask how far support for animal welfare is consistent with support for other 'progressive' issues, most notably environmentalism, and therefore how far support for animal welfare represents a new and independent force in Congress. Finally, by comparing the Congressional results with the British survey, it might then be possible to go at least some of the way towards explaining why American Congressional members have been less willing to raise animal welfare issues and what kind of Congressional member needs to be elected to improve the legislature's record in the future.

THE SCOPE OF CONGRESSIONAL SUPPORT

Before we examine particular characteristics of those most willing to support animal protection and wildlife conservation initiatives in Congress, it is necessary to provide an account of the scope of this support. The figures, shown in Table 6.1, are, superficially at least, quite impressive. On average, between 1985 and 1994, more than half of Representatives sponsored or co-sponsored bills or resolutions concerned with wildlife conservation and animal protection, the number reaching a high-point of over 70 per cent in the 101st Congress and never falling

Table 6.1   Congressional supporters of animal protection and wildlife conservation initiatives, 1985–94

Congress	House				Senate	
	Wildlife conservation		*Animal protection*		*Wildlife conservation*	*Animal protection*
	No.	%	No.	%		
99	256	(59)	256	(59)	41	58
100	232	(53)	253	(58)	39	38
101	323	(74)	315	(72)	60	57
102	303	(70)	210	(48)	63	6
103	171	(39)	108	(25)	24	4

below one quarter. In the 102nd and 103rd Congresses, there was a decline in the number of interested members in both Houses. This occurred partly because there were fewer Democrats in the House after the 1992 elections, but mainly because fewer animal-related bills were introduced (see Table 1.3).

There are two important factors to note about the raw figures reviewed above. In the first place, as with British MPs, accounting for intensity of support for animal protection and wildlife measures reveals that many members only had a peripheral interest. A maximum number of points (based upon a scoring system explained in Appendix I) was available for each Congress depending upon the number of relevant bills and resolutions introduced. As Table 6.2 demonstrates, most members of the House whose interest was recorded scored under 10 points (equivalent to supporting less than three bills and one resolution and representing no more than 8 per cent of the

Table 6.2   Intensity of support for animal protection and wildlife conservation measures in the House of Representatives, 1985–94

Congress	Max. points	50–69	30–49	20–29	10–19	0–9
99	160	–	6	27	82	195
100	232	3	33	47	73	146
101	316	11	48	58	87	173
102	254	2	41	57	69	159
103	118	–	1	9	34	153

points available in each Congress between 1985 and 1994 and, in the 101st Congress, as low as 3 per cent) and many scored much lower than ten by only co-sponsoring one or two bills.

More significant, and manageable, lists of interested members of Congress are arrived at by including only those with an extensive record of sponsoring and co-sponsoring wildlife conservation and animal protection bills and resolutions. By so doing, a much smaller group of members results. For example, only six Representatives scored over 19 per cent of the available points in the 99th Congress, followed by 3 over 22 per cent in the 100th, 11 over 16 per cent in the 101st, 2 over 20 per cent in the 102nd and one over 25 per cent in the 103rd. The highest scores for each Congress were dominated by two Representatives, Edolphus Towns, the black Democrat from New York (a 19 per cent score – 60 out of 316 – in the 101st Congress and 27 per cent – 69 out of 254 – in the 102nd Congress) and Gerry Studds, the long-serving and influential Democrat from Massachusetts. In the one remaining Congress, the 99th, the leading Representative was Sala Burton, a female Democrat from California. For each Congress, a list of the most supportive members (see Table 6.3), followed by a list of those demonstrating both extensive and moderate commitment was drawn up and these have been used as the data for the assessment of a number of variables discussed below.[1]

The second point to note about the raw figures indicated above is that they incorporate support for animal protection *and* wildlife conservation bills and resolutions. As previous chapters have noted, advocates of these two issue areas in the United States are often distinct and sometimes in conflict with each other. In view of this, it is worth examining the extent to which Congressional supporters of wildlife conservation and animal protection also represent similarly distinct groups. The evidence is presented in Tables 6.4 and 6.5.

It is clear from these figures that wildlife conservation and animal protection were regarded by some members of the House as distinct issues. In particular, a relatively high proportion of the Representatives recorded as sponsoring or co-sponsoring bills and resolutions relating to animal issues in the 102 and 103 Congresses (39 per cent and 52 per cent respectively) were only involved with wildlife issues. The converse, exclusive support for animal protection issues, was less evident, with the

Table 6.3 Representatives displaying the greatest interest in wildlife conservation and animal protection bills and resolutions in the House, 1985–94

99th	100th	101st	102nd	103rd
S. Burton (D-Ca)	G. Studds (D-MA)	E. Towns (D-NY)	E. Towns (D-NY)	G. Studds (D-MA)
R. Mrazek (D-NY)	A. Jacobs (D-Ind)	W. Lipinski (D-IL)	A. Jacobs (D-IND)	G. Ackerman (D-NY)
R. Roe (D-NJ)	E. Towns (D-NY)	F. Pallone (D-NJ)	R. Dellums (D-CA)	J. Fields (R-TX)
E. Towns (D-NY)	T. Weiss (D-NY)	R. Dellums (D-CA)	G. Studds (D-MA)	T. Manton (D-NY)
R. Torricelli (D-NJ)	R. Mrazek (D-NY)	A. Ravenel (R-SC)	A. Ravenel (R-SC)	A. Jacobs (D-IND)
D. Burton (R-Ind)	R.C. Smith (R-NH)	C. Schneider (R-RI)	P. Stark (D-CA)	G. Brown (D-CA)
T. Lantos (D-CA)	M. Martinez (R-CA)	C. Collins (D-IL)	G. Brown (D-CA)	A. Beilenson (D-CA)
F. Horton (R-NY)	G. Ackerman (D-NY)	J. Bates (D-CA)	N. Pelosi (D-CA)	E. Towns (D-NY)
S. Levin (D-Mich)	M. Owens (D-NY)	R. Roe (D-NJ)	F. Guarini (D-NJ)	A. Ravenel (R-SC)
G. Anderson (D-CA)	R. Dellums (D-CA)	J. Lewis (D-GA)	R. Machtley (R-RI)	P. Deutsch (D-FL)
R.C. Smith (R-NH)	R. Dornan (R-CA)	P. DeFazio (D-OR)	C. Bennett (D-FL)	
T. Weiss (D-NY)	T. Lantos (D-CA)	T. Weiss (D-NY)	A. Beilenson (D-CA)	
M. Martinez (R-CA)	W. Fauntroy (D-DC)	A. Jacobs (D-IND)	T. Lantos (D-CA)	
M. Levine (D-CA)	T. Manton (D-NY)	C. Atkins (D-MA)	R. Mrazek (D-NY)	
	N. Pelosi (D-CA)	N. Pelosi (D-CA)	J. Jontz (D-IND)	
	H. Fish (R-NY)	C. Wilson (D-TX)	W. Lipinski (D-IL)	
	J. Feighan (D-OH)		J. Scheuer (D-NY)	
	W. Hughes (D-NJ)		E. Norton (D-DC)	
	J. Howard (D-NJ)			

Political Animals

Table 6.4   Support for wildlife measures in the US House of
Representatives, 1985–94

Congress	Members supporting wildlife measures only	% of total no. of members supporting wildlife measures
99	54	21
100	49	21
101	62	19
102	118	39
103	89	52

Table 6.5   Support for animal protection measures in the US
House of Representatives, 1985–94

Congress	Members supporting animal protection measures only	% of total no. of members supporting animal protection measures
99	54	21
100	70	28
101	54	17
102	25	12
103	26	24

proportion exceeding a quarter in only one Congress (28 per cent in the 100th). It is not surprising that wildlife bills should attract Representatives who would not ordinarily support measures concerned with animals. As we have pointed out, bills designed to conserve wildlife and, to a lesser degree, protect wildlife from suffering have greater public saliency and Representatives would be less inhibited in supporting them. There were, after all, many more wildlife initiatives introduced into the House between 1985 and 1994 (135) than all the other animal issues put together (67). Moreover, a number of wildlife bills were concerned with the creation of refuges in particular areas which were likely to gain the support of the local Representatives who would not necessarily have a general interest in animal issues.

It is unquestionably significant that so many members of the House who were prepared to support wildlife measures did not support other animal issues. Persuading them to do so would seem an easier task than those Representatives who have shown absolutely no interest in any animal issues. Having said this, the key point to note for our purposes here is that an average of 70 per cent of members who supported wildlife initiatives over the ten-year period under consideration also supported other animal issues. Moreover, those members of the House who displayed a moderate or high commitment to animal issues tended also to support both wildlife conservation and animal protection initiatives. As a result, with the exception of the 103rd Congress where much fewer animal protection measures were introduced, excluding the points gained through supporting wildlife initiatives did not produce significantly different lists for each Congress.

Geographical Profile

Examining the geographical profile of those Representatives most supportive of animal issues reveals a number of clearly distinct characteristics (see Table 6.6). The first point to note is that there is no great discrepancy between the geographical locations of those in the most committed lists and those containing the most and moderately committed, except for a slightly greater incidence of New York and Californian Representatives in the former. Secondly, Representatives from Southern and Mid-Western states have greater representation amongst members supporting animal issues in the 103rd Congress than in the preceding four, 40 per cent in the most committed list and 34 per cent in the most and moderately committed list. This can be explained by the paucity of animal protection measures as compared with those concerned with wildlife conservation which allows those Representatives solely interested in the latter to score as highly as those concerned with more broadly-based animal issues.

On all the lists, the most striking characteristic is the disproportionate appearance of those representing voting districts in North Eastern states and, to a lesser extent, Western states. Thus, in the House as a whole, North Eastern and Western states are allocated about 20 per cent of the seats each. However, as

Political Animals

Table 6.6   Geographical profile of Representatives interested in
animal issues, 1985–94

Congress	Region								Total
	NE	(%)	MW	(%)	South	(%)	West	(%)	
(a) Extensively and moderately committed members									
99	38	(57)	6	(9)	7	(10)	16	(24)	67
100	28	(50)	9	(16)	6	(11)	13	(23)	56
101	28	(46)	6	(10)	8	(13)	19	(31)	61
102	31	(53)	4	(7)	8	(14)	14	(24)	58*
103	16	(36)	5	(11)	10	(23)	13	(30)	44
Total	141	(49)	30	(10)	39	(14)	75	(26)	286
(b) Extensively committed members									
99	8	(57)	1		–		5	(36)	14
100	11	(58)	2		1		5	(26)	19
101	6	(38)	3		3		4	(25)	16
102	7	(39)	2		3		6	(33)	18
103	4	(40)	1		3		2	(20)	10
Total	36	(47)	9		10		22	(29)	77

* Total includes a delegate from American Samoa.

table 6.6 reveals, on average almost half of the Representatives
in the lists of extensively and moderately committed members
represented voting districts in the North East and between a
quarter and a third represented voting districts in the West.

In turn, Representatives from New York and California were
disproportionately represented both nationally and within their
regions. In the larger lists of extensively and moderately committed members, this trend is less marked with, on average, 19
per cent of the names on the list representing New York (compared to about 7 per cent in the whole House) a figure constituting 39 per cent of all the Representatives on the list from
states in the North East (compared to 31 per cent in the whole
House). Similarly, 20 per cent of concerned members represented California (compared to only about 10 per cent in the
whole House) and these members represented 76 per cent of all

the members on the lists from Western states (compared to over 50 per cent in the whole House). There is much greater disproportionality, however, in the lists of the most committed members (see table 6.6). On average, 25 per cent (19 out of 77) of these represented New York and no less than 27 per cent (21 out of 77) represented California. New York and Californian Representatives dominated the contingent from their regions with the former constituting 52 per cent (19 out of 36) and the latter 95 per cent (21 out of 22).

The geographical evidence presented above is much as one would have expected. Support for animal issues is strongest amongst members representing the most urban, and traditionally more liberal, parts of the USA and weakest among members representing the most rural, agricultural, and traditionally more conservative, regions (see below). Thus, no Representatives from the five states with the highest agricultural populations (South Dakota, North Dakota, Nebraska, Montana, Iowa and Idaho) appear on the lists of the members most or moderately committed to animal issues, despite the fact that these states elected 15 members to the House between 1986 and 1990 and 13 after 1990. Similarly, as Table 6.7 illustrates, only 7 per cent of the Representatives scoring extremely or moderately highly were from rural states and only two of the most committed members (Robert Smith, R–NH and Arthur Ravenel, R–SC) represented rural states.

Table 6.7   Rural and urban profile of Representatives interested in animal issues, 1985–94

Congress	Rural	Urban	Total
99	4	63	67
100	4	52	56
101	3	58	61
102	5	53	58
103	4	40	44
Total	20	266	286

Party Profile

If we turn our attention to the party profile of animal protection-supporting Representatives, an equally distinctive pattern becomes clear. As Table 6.8 shows, during the five Congresses under study here the Democrats, of course, had a majority, so one would expect a preponderance of Democrats in the lists of Representatives supporting animal protection and wildlife measures. What we find, however, as Table 6.9 illustrates, is a massive preponderance of Democrats over Republicans in all five Congresses, averaging out at over 80 per cent. Animal protection, therefore, is quite clearly a Democrat issue, and the Republicans capture of that House in the 1994 elections, and their subsequent holding of a majority in the 1996 elections, goes a long way towards explaining why animal protection issues do not have such a high profile as they did during the ten-year period with which this study has been concerned.

Party divisions in the USA are much weaker, of course, than in Britain where it is still broadly possible to infer an ideological position from an individual's party label. In the USA, party labels tend to be less important for a Congressional candidate than representing the particular interests of major groupings within states and voting districts. In many ways, as indicated above, the geographical location of Representatives is a better guide to their political leanings with a preponderance of (Democrat and Republican) liberals in the urban areas of the North East and the West and a preponderance of (Democrat and Republican) conservatives in the rural areas of the South and Mid West. In as far

Table 6.8   Party strength in the House of
Representatives, 1985–94

Congress	Democrats		Republicans	
	No.	%	No.	%
99	253	(58)	182	(42)
100	258	(59)	177	(41)
101	260	(60)	175	(40)
102	267	(61)	167	(39)
103	258	(59)	176	(41)

Table 6.9   Party labels of Representatives interested in
animal issues, 1985–94

Congress	Democrats		Republicans		Total
	No.	*%*	*No.*	*%*	
(a) Extensively and moderately committed members					
99	56	(84)	11	(16)	67
100	47	(84)	9	(16)	56
101	51	(84)	10	(16)	61
102	51	(88)	7	(12)	58
103	34	(77)	10	(22)	44
Total	239	(84)	47	(16)	286
(b) Extensively committed members					
99	10	(71)	4	(29)	14
100	15	(79)	4	(21)	19
101	14	(88)	2	(12)	16
102	16	(89)	2	(11)	18
103	8	(80)	2	(20)	10
Total	63	(82)	14	(18)	77

as this is the case, this study confirms animal protection as an issue much more likely to be supported by those with liberal leanings. For example, in the 103rd Congress, of the 34 Democrats who scored highest on animal issues, no less than 41 per cent of them were returned from voting districts in the North East and 32 per cent from Western states, whereas Democratic Representatives from these two regions in the House as a whole constituted only 19 per cent and 21 per cent respectively.

Gender Profile

Concern for animals is often regarded as an issue of particular concern to the female gender and, as we saw in the previous chapter, there is some, albeit not particularly significant, evidence that this is the case in the British House of Commons. In the US House of Representatives there is even less evidence of a gender bias. The evidence, illustrated in Table 6.10, shows that the proportion of women that has been identified as supporting animal protection and wildlife conservation measures accurately reflects the proportion of women in the House as a whole, so that as the number of women members rose so did the proportion supporting animal issues. Between 1985 and 1994, 49 female Representatives out of a total of 651 sponsored or co-sponsored at least one animal protection or wildlife conservation bill or resolution, and at 8 per cent this is also broadly accurate with the proportion of women to men in the House during this period. In the list of the members most committed to animal issues, there is a slightly higher representation of women compared to the House as a whole particularly in the 101st Congress where three of the top 16 were females, but this can be contrasted with the 103rd Congress where none of the top 10 Representatives were women.

The female Representatives concerned, listed in Table 6.11, confirm the general characteristics of those legislators most likely to support animal issues. Of the 14, 11 were Democrats and most represented urban areas in the North East and West. The female Representative demonstrating the most commitment to animal issues during this period was Nancy Pelosi, the Democrat legislator from San Francisco, who scored the 14th highest number of points in the 100th Congress, the 15th highest in the 101st and the seventh highest in the 102nd Congress. Following hard on her heels was Patty Schroeder, the Democratic Representative

Table 6.10   Women in the House of Representatives and animal issues, 1985–94

Congress	In whole House		Extensive and moderate commitment to animal issues		Extensive commitment to animal issues	
	No.	%	No.	%	No.	%
99	22	(5)	4	(6)	1	(7)
100	23	(5)	3	(5)	1	(5)
101	25	(6)	4	(7)	3	(19)
102	29	(7)	4	(7)	2	(11)
103	47	(11)	6	(14)	0	(0)

Table 6.11 Female Representatives most
interested in animal issues, 1985–94

N. Pelosi	D–CA.
P. Schroeder	D–CO.
S. Burton	D–CA.
C. Schneider	D–RI.
C. Collins	D–ILL.
E. Norton	D–DC
M. Kaptur	D–OH.
B. Mikulski	D–MD.
H. Bentley	R – MD.
C. Morella	R–MD.
C. Weldon	R–PA.
E. Furse	D–OR.
C. Maloney	D–NY.
L. Roybal-Allard	D–CA.

from Denver, who has been particularly keen on promoting alternatives to the use of animals for product testing.

Age Profile

One might have assumed that animal issues would be particularly attractive to younger members of the House of Representatives. After all, the issues involved are a relatively recent addition to the Congressional agenda and there is considerable support for the objectives of the animal protection movement among the young in the wider population. Given this, it is surprising to note that relative youthfulness is not a particularly important determinant of support for animal protection measures in the House. Indeed, even more surprisingly, as Tables 6.12 and 6.13 illustrate, there is a tendency for animal protection supporters in the House to be slightly older than Representatives in general and this age discrepancy is even more pronounced amongst the most committed supporters. Thus, in the 99th and 102nd Congresses, as many as 29 per cent and 39 per cent respectively of those who scored the highest animal protection and wildlife conservation ratings (four out of 14 and seven out of 18) were 60 years of age or above (compared to 18 per cent and 25 per cent in the House as a whole). Conversely, only two Rep-

Political Animals

Table 6.12   The age profile of Representatives, 1985–92

Congress	Under 40		40–49		50–59		over 60	
	No.	*(%)*	*No.*	*(%)*	*No.*	*(%)*	*No.*	*(%)*
99	71	(16)	154	(35)	131	(30)	78	(18)
100	63	(15)	153	(35)	137	(31)	82	(19)
101	41	(9)	163	(37)	133	(31)	96	(22)
102	39	(9)	153	(35)	133	(31)	110	(25)

resentatives (Robert Torricelli and Frank Pallone, both Democrats from New Jersey) appearing in the lists of members most
committed to animal issues between 1985 and 1992 were under
40.

Why this age discrepancy should exist is not altogether clear,
but the future survival of animal protection as a Congressional
issue of any weight could be seriously affected by the age profile

Table 6.13   Age profile of Representatives interested in animal issues,
1985–92

Congress	Under 40		40–49		50–59		over 60	
	No.	*(%)*	*No.*	*(%)*	*No.*	*(%)*	*No.*	*(%)*
(a) Extensively and moderately commited members								
99	11	(16)	19	(28)	23	(34)	14	(21)
100	5	(9)	17	(30)	19	(34)	15	(27)
101	2	(4)	19	(31)	21	(34)	19	(31)
102	2	(3)	22	(38)	19	(33)	15	(26)
Total	20	(8)	77	(32)	82	(34)	63	(26)
(b) Extensively committed members								
99	1	(7)	5	(35)	4	(29)	4	(29)
100	–	–	6	(32)	10	(53)	3	(16)
101	1	(6)	6	(38)	6	(38)	3	(19)
102	–	–	8	(44)	3	(17)	7	(39)
Total	2	(3)	25	(37)	23	(34)	17	(25)

of its supporters. Some of the most indefatigable advocates of animal welfare in the House (Tom Lantos, Edolphus Towns, Ronald Dellums, Robert Dornan, Andrew Jacobs, Tom Manton, Arthur Ravenel, Bill Lipinski, George Brown and Tony Beilenson) were born in the 1930s or before and are reaching, or are rapidly approaching, the twilight of their careers. Few members of the House seem to be ready to step into their shoes.

Animal Protection and Progressive Politics

We have already seen that those members supporting animal protection and wildlife conservation measures in Congress tended to represent voting districts in the North East and West, and that this leads us to suspect that there is a correlation between such support and general liberal leanings. This is further confirmed if we examine the approval ratings given to members of the House by organizations generally regarded as liberal. To take one example, of the 325 members in the 103rd Congress (excluding freshman), 93 (29 per cent) were given approval ratings of 75 per cent or over by the organization Americans for Democratic Action (the higher the score, the greater the approval).[2] By contrast, of the 37 members (excluding freshman) who scored highest on animal issues, no less than 19 (51 per cent) received approval ratings of 75 per cent or over from Americans for Democratic Action. In addition, it is most likely that the score of 51 per cent underestimates the proportion of liberals amongst supporters of animal protection in the entire period from 1985–94 since the proportion of Northern Democrats supporting animal issues was smaller in the 103rd Congress than it had been in the four previous Congresses (see Tables 6.6 and 6.9).

It is also possible to compare the record of members of Congress on animal issues with their rankings on broader environmental topics. Of particular relevance here is Jeremy and Carol Rifkin's study of the environmental voting records of members in the 101st Congress and part of the 102nd.[3] This study divided environmental bills and resolutions into eight distinct areas, of which 'animal rights' was one, for each of which members of Congress were allocated points.[4] The total number of points was then computed to provide the basis for a list of the 'Greenest' members, the so-called 'A' list followed by lists B–F.

What the Rifkins' study reveals is that legislators with good environmental records have many similar characteristics to the main supporters of animal protection issues. In the first place, those with the best environmental records were overwhelmingly Democrats, tended to represent districts in the East and West of the USA and were predominantly liberal, with a close affinity, in particular, between support for 'Green' issues and those of most interest to the organized labour movement.[5] Given the similar characteristics noted above, it is not surprising to find that those who scored highest on animal issues also tended to score highly on broader environmental issues. Thus, in the 101st Congress, no less than 13 of the top 16 Congressional animal advocates in my survey were in the Rifkins' A list consisting of the 39 highest scoring environmental advocates, and the other three (W. Lipinski, R. Roe and C. Wilson) were in the B list consisting of the 40th to the 118th highest environmental scorers (see Table 6.3).

CONCLUSION

This chapter has identified a clear profile of the type of Representative most likely to support animal protection and wildlife measures in the House. This person is most likely to be a middle-aged male Democrat representing a voting district in the North East or the West of the USA. This person is also likely to have liberal political leanings and be someone who is also generally supportive of environmentalism. A contrast with the British House of Commons is illuminating. In the first place, although there was, as we saw in Chapter 5, a greater, and previously unappreciated, preponderance of Labour MPs amongst animal advocates in the Commons, there is greater cross-party support than exists in the USA. Moreover, while age is not really a factor in determining support, as it is in the USA, there is some evidence that after 1992 gender did become a more important factor.

This chapter began, for animal advocates at least, in an optimistic fashion. A large proportion of Representatives were involved in sponsoring or co-sponsoring bills and resolutions concerned with animal protection and wildlife conservation between 1985 and 1994. As the chapter progressed, however, the picture became less and less rosy. Relatively few members of the House have consistently supported animal issues moderately and even fewer have been more extensive supporters. Most of this latter group, with one or two exceptions, do not hold important positions in the House which could be used to promote animal welfare. Furthermore, many Representatives have supported wildlife conservation bills only and the animal protection movement has been unable to secure their support for farm or laboratory animal measures.

As a result, even though support for animal issues was strongest amongst liberal-inclined Democrats from the West and North West, many Democrats representing voting districts in these areas, and many with liberal political leanings, have not been regular and consistent supporters of animal issues. To a certain degree, this has also been the case with broader environmental issues. Thus, the Rifkins' study discussed above identifies over 300 Representatives in the 101st Congress who had sponsored at least one environmental bill or resolution, but their overall analysis: 'shows a small but committed group of Green legislators scoring well above their colleagues and a large contingent of representatives and senators who are ideologically opposed to bills that reflect the new Green orientation.'[6]

Committed support for animal issues alone, and particularly those excluding wild animals, however, is even more of a minority occupation. For example, over 100 Representatives in the Rifkins' survey scored no points in their animal rights category but did score, sometimes quite highly, on non animal-based environmental measures. Similarly, nine Representatives scored relatively poorly in the animal rights section (10 points or below) but finished up with a B ranking when their support for other environmental issues was included.[7]

The conclusion to this chapter, then, is something of a depressing one for animal advocates. To make matters worse, the situation has got worse as the 1990s have progressed. There are now fewer Democrats in Congress than there were during the time-frame of this study. Furthermore, the animal protection movement has not (unlike, as the Rifkins' found, the environmental movement) benefited greatly from the gradual increase in the number of women elected to the House. Finally, the age profile of committed animal protection supporters in the House is worryingly high and there is little evidence that younger members have any great enthusiasm for the issue. By contrast, with Labour's landslide victory in the 1997 general election in Britain and the unprecedented number of female MPs returned, the situation in that country is much more promising. Future success for animal protection in the House of Representatives depends upon reaching out to those members who have liberal and progressive political leanings but who, so far, have not included the protection of animals as an issue worthy of their support. Achieving that goal, however, is not so easy.

7 The Politics of Farm Animal Welfare in the United States

A glance at the politics of farm animal welfare in Britain and the United States, the topic to be considered in the next two chapters, reveals a striking anomaly. On the one hand, as was illustrated in Chapter 1, decision-makers in Britain have introduced seemingly comprehensive primary and secondary legislation concerned with the welfare of animals from the farm to the abattoir. Conversely, the legislative protection of farm animals in the United States is, in some areas, patchy and, in others, non-existent. Yet, on the other hand, it appears that the farm animal policy arenas in both countries are similar, with farming and agribusiness interests given a privileged position and animal welfare and environmental interests kept at arms length. The function of this and the following chapter is to assess the two possible answers to this anomaly. In the first place, it might be suggested that the British legislative framework is less impressive than it might first appear. A second scenario is the claim that legislative reform in Britain can be explained by a change in the policy arena whereby a closed and insulated policy community, dominated by agricultural interests, has weakened to the point where a more open and pluralistic policy arena has begun to emerge.

Whatever the position in Britain, there is little doubt that farm animal welfare in the United States is a victim of the policy-making process. There could not be a clearer example of a policy community. In this case, the policy arena is dominated by, and largely serves the interests of, those who have most to lose from action to improve the welfare of farm animals. The dominance of agribusiness interests is apparent in both the executive and legislative branches and the impotence of those groups who seek to promote the welfare of farm animals is equally apparent.

HISTORICAL ORIGINS AND DEVELOPMENT OF THE AGRICULTURAL POLICY COMMUNITY

The agricultural policy community or sub-government in the United States derives from the Agricultural Adjustment Act of 1933 which, as part of Roosevelt's New Deal settlement, created a series of commodity programmes supporting the prices of agricultural produce.[1] This introduced guaranteed prices through deficiency payments being made to make up any difference between an agreed target price laid down by Congress and the going market price. This immediately encouraged intensification and the production of surpluses since the higher the yields the greater the deficiency payment.[2] It also precipitated the development of powerful general farming organizations as well as specific commodity groups who 'became an integral part of the institutional apparatus of the state'.[3] The policy community, therefore, was born.[4]

One American academic, William P. Browne, has challenged the view that US agriculture still remains a closed, tight-knit policy community.[5] Browne documents the proliferation of active lobbying groups concerned with agricultural issues (amounting to over 200 and including animal protection and environmental groups), many formed since the 1970s, together with the expanding number of institutions concerned with agricultural policy-making. As a result, he suggests that most interests tend to focus on an extremely narrow set of agricultural issues which are of little or no interest to other organizations, and that within these so-called 'issue niches' many groups tend to be successful in achieving at least some of their policy preferences. As a consequence, he concludes: 'It appears beyond the capacity of any single interest to dominate policy-making in a single issue area as it can do in the corporatist states of Europe'.[6]

Though it may be true that issue niches have proliferated, and that a larger number of groups with more specialized interests are now able to influence agricultural policy-making,[7] farm animal welfare politics surely does not fit this pattern. Rather, as we shall see below, the dominance of Congressional agricultural committees and USDA in the making (or, to be more accurate, non-making) of farm animal welfare policy provides a classic example of a sub-government from which animal protection groups and other governmental agencies are largely excluded.

Farm animal welfare does not fit the pattern Browne identifies because, whatever else farming and agribusiness interests have conflicting interests on, and whatever agreements they may have with, or concessions they are prepared to make to, other public interest groups, they are almost universally united against measures designed to restrict the scope of factory farming. Thus, as we saw in Chapter 2, animal advocates face a lobbying coalition designed to defend intensive agriculture. Browne documents the various provisions in the 1985 Farm Act to show how many different interests got something of what they wanted. Interestingly, he cites the passing of the amendment to the Animal Welfare Act as an example.[8] Crucially, though, this, of course, did not challenge agribusiness interests and there was no chance of a reform to factory farming being included in the legislation.

Browne's analysis, however, does have important implications for possible future developments. What it reveals is that in issue areas where significant public concern has been expressed – on, for instance, the health and environmental implications of intensive agriculture – it has been more difficult for the subgovernment to retain control of the policy agenda. This offers the future possibility that a similar pattern could occur in the case of farm animal welfare. Indeed, it might be suggested that this has already occurred in Britain.

CONGRESSIONAL COMMITTEES AND FARM ANIMAL WELFARE

Of crucial importance in explaining how the agribusiness community is able to exercise so much influence is the Congressional committee system. As we saw earlier, the fragmentation of Congress has traditionally been mitigated by a powerful committee system which decides the measures to be debated on the floor of both Houses. In the case of farm animal welfare, proposed bills go before the agricultural committees in the House and Senate and, in the former, are delegated to the livestock, dairy and poultry sub-committee.

Members of congressional agriculture committees are usually hostile to measures designed to improve the welfare of farm animals and such measures usually fail at the committee hurdle.

Indeed, it is undoubtedly the case that one of the key reasons for the paucity of such measures is the reputation for power which the committees have, an illustration of non-decision-making. This hostility and inaction can be contrasted with the urgency by which the House Agriculture Committee (and particularly Charles Stenholm Democrat–Texas), drafted and reported a bill to make it a federal crime to trespass or commit other illegal acts against farms and animal research laboratories.

There have been very few committee hearings on farm animal welfare issues and this itself is indicative of the lack of interest displayed by agriculture committees. Another way of illustrating the attitude of committee members is to examine their response to outsider groups who put forward their point of view at the few committee hearings on farm animal welfare that have been held. Reading these hearings reveals an – at the least – unresponsive, and – at the most – antagonistic response to the demands of animal protection witnesses. In 1994, for example, the hearing of the livestock sub-committee of the agriculture committee began with Harold Volkmer, the chairman, admitting to not supporting the Downed Animal Protection Bill nor the Humane Methods of Poultry Slaughter Bill.[9] The bills stood no chance of being reported but the hearing still served a useful purpose, as a means of giving the impression that public concern is being taken into account and providing a safety valve for discontent.

It is instructive here to examine the record of committee members on all animal issues in general, and farm animal welfare in particular. Of the 21 members of the House livestock, dairy and poultry sub-committee in the 103rd Congress, for instance, eight members did not, at any time between 1985 and 1994, sponsor or co-sponsor a bill or resolution designed to promote the well-being of animals or their conservation.[10] A further five only co-sponsored a handful of bills or resolutions dealing with wildlife conservation and six supported measures dealing with the welfare of laboratory or domesticated animals. Only two, Steve Gunderson (Republican–Wisconsin) and Charlie Rose (Democrat–North Carolina) sponsored measures dealing with the welfare of farm animals, the former co-sponsoring the obscure Livestock Protection From Stray Voltage Act in the 100th Congress and the latter co-sponsoring a resolution in the 99th Congress calling for a stop to the hot iron branding of cattle.[11]

It is not surprising that there is general hostility towards animal welfare measures in Congressional agriculture committees. Both of the main committees, and all of the sub-committees, are dominated by members, from Midwestern and Southern states, with significant agricultural interests. Thus, in the early 1990s, only one member out of 44 in the House agriculture committee and one member out of 18 in the Senate agriculture committee represented Eastern states. In addition, agriculture committee members are assigned to sub-committees dealing with commodities of particular concern to their constituents. As Tweeten points out then: 'The configuration usually assures that any bill reported out of the committee will not place animals' welfare above farmers' welfare'.[12] Congressional agriculture committee members behave in this way because a considerable proportion of their electorates are involved in agriculture, a fact regularly drawn to their attention by organized farming interests who provide a great deal of the campaign finance received by committee members. Significantly, organizations promoting animal experimentation do not have the same focused constituency appeal.

The history of campaign finance in the United States is complex and can only be briefly sketched here. In 1907 direct corporate gifts to candidates for federal office were prohibited but this did not stop wealthy individuals from donating what they wanted. Concern over the increasing amount of money solicited by candidates, as elections in a media-dominated age became ever more expensive, led to reforms in the 1970s. Legislation in 1971 and 1974 made compulsory the disclosure of donations and expenditure by each candidate, limited the amount individuals and groups could contribute to each candidate, and removed the limitations on the ability of corporations to form PACs. As a result, there was a major expansion of corporate PACs. In addition to PACs and private individual contributions, which are restricted in how much can be given to any one candidate's election campaign, there is no limitation on the amount of money a corporation can use to support a particular candidate providing that money is not given directly to the candidate's campaign organization.[13]

Those organizations with a vested interest in the exploitation of food animals have not been reticent about giving PAC money to Congressional members, and particularly members of the agriculture committees. Indeed, some of these organizations have been amongst the most generous contributors. The dairy industry, in particular, is legendary in this respect. The National Milk Producers' Federation, for instance, ranked second only to the American Medical Association in donations to Congressional campaigns in 1976. Another dairy organization, Associated Milk Producers Inc. (AMPI), was even involved in the Watergate scandal after a $100 000 illegal donation to Nixon's campaign in 1969 was part of the impeachment case against the President. AMPI was fined $35 000.[14]

In the 1991–2 period, of the $188.5 million given by PACs, 8 per cent came from the agriculture sector.[15] The leading agricultural contributor was AMPI who gave a total of $877 000 to 356 candidates. Following not far behind were Mid-American Dairymen ($343 371 to 209 candidates), Con Agra Inc. ($300 038 to 127 candidates), the National Cattlemens' Association ($297 670 to 258), the National Broiler Council ($183 750 to 147), the National Pork Producers' Council ($155 031 to 162) the Texas Cattle Feeders' Association ($121 700 to 124) and the American Meat Institute ($105 629 to 109). In total, the dairy industry gave $2 107 911 and the livestock and poultry sector gave $1 476 005. In addition, a further amount of about $2.5 million was given by other relevant organizations involved in the production of agricultural chemicals, machinery and feed and in food processing.

These contributions are targeted as far as possible to members of Congressional agriculture committees. On average, each member of the House agriculture committee received $76 000 from agricultural interests in 1991–2, and in almost all cases, this represented the largest contribution these Representatives received from any one sector. Animal agriculture interests, not surprisingly, particularly targeted members of the House livestock, dairy and poultry sub-committee. Charles Stenholm (Democrat–Texas), the sub-committee chairman possessing a great deal of influence on the fate of farm animal welfare bills, for instance, received a total of $412 408, of which $144 303 came from the agricultural sector. Of this, $18 000 was provided by the dairy sector, $11 000 from the poultry and eggs sector and $19 450 from the livestock sector.

There is a widely-held assumption, of course, that money does buy influence, as in the old-adage that 'he who pays the piper calls the tune'. In reality, however, the connection between money and influence is difficult to determine.[16] In order to show that it plays a significant role, we have to demonstrate that contributions play an important role in achieving the election of one candidate over another and, in addition, demonstrate that, once elected, campaign contributions can influence the way a member of Congress behaves. On the first point, it is clear that money is more important for challengers than incumbents since the former need it to get recognized, something which the latter do not have to worry about so much. What happens in practice, however, is that most contributions tend to go to incumbents presumably because of the likelihood that they will win. This in turn suggests that the main purpose of contributing is to facilitate access to members of Congress rather than to help determine who wins.[17] Thus, it is noticeable that members of the House Agriculture Committee first elected in 1992 received far fewer campaign contributions than incumbents. Scotty Baesler (Democrat–Kentucky) and Tom Barlow (Democrat–Kentucky), for instance received only $13 502 and $8750 respectively from agricultural interests compared to the average donation of over $70 000. An important conclusion to draw here is that as election results become less predictable (as they have done in the past decade or so), it will become more and more difficult for organizations to identify and target winners.

The second factor we need to examine concerns the relationship between contributions and Congressional behaviour. Here, academic opinion is divided.[18] At least two important factors are relevant. In the first place, it is difficult to untangle cause and effect. Thus, it might be argued that the distribution of campaign contributions are an effect of past voting behaviour as opposed to being a cause of future voting behaviour. The concentration on incumbents with established voting records would seem to confirm this view. Secondly, in order to demonstrate influence, we have to control for other variables which may affect the voting habits of members of Congress. One crucial variable is the interests of a member's electorate. Thus, it is not enough merely to show that a member of Congress voted in accordance with the wishes of his or her major financial backers since this behaviour may simply correspond to the member's desire to represent the interests of his or her constituents, not least because of a desire to be re-elected. Only if a member behaves in a manner at odds with the interests of his constituents do we begin to get a strong inkling of money talking and even then we have not proved it conclusively.

In terms of members of agricultural committees in Congress, we cannot say without reservation that support for agricultural interests reflects the nature of campaign contributions precisely because many voters also regard these policies as being in their interests (as employees in the industry or as beneficiaries of the economic climate produced by a thriving agricultural sector, for example, or as consumers of cheap food). Of course, we can then question whether the promotion of intensive agriculture, with its environmental and health consequences and its poor working conditions, is really in the voter's interests. The problem here though is it takes us into the murky waters of false consciousness, a notoriously difficult concept to operationalize.

CONGRESS, USDA AND FARM ANIMALS

Having established the role of Congressional committees, it is important to ask why they are able to exercise so much influence in the making of agricultural policy. After all, those involved in agriculture committees constitute a small proportion of the total membership of Congress, and Congress as a whole is not dominated by members with agricultural constituencies. Indeed, by the 1970s, rural districts comprised only 60 per cent of an absolute majority in the House of Representatives (down from 83 per cent in 1966).[19] Furthermore, Congress itself is only one branch of a fragmented federal system of government.

There are a number of answers to this. In the first place, USDA – the executive agency responsible for agricultural policy – has not promoted the issue of farm animal welfare to any great extent. Indeed, it has traditionally (like MAFF in the UK) been regarded as a defender of agricultural interests. At the very least, it has sought not to get involved in debates about animal welfare issues.[20] Agriculture Secretaries usually have links with the industry. Richard Lyng, USDA Assistant Secretary between 1969 and 1973, for instance, became President of the American Meat Institute upon leaving office.[21] A former insider's view is provided by Carol Tucker Foreman, a former USDA Assistant Secretary, who comments, in the context of food safety, that 'USDA is too close to the industry to respond appropriately'.[22]

USDA's attitude is not altogether surprising. Not only does the agribusiness lobby have considerable influence within the department, but even if it was tempted to alter its stance Congress can exercise a considerable degree of power over USDA not just because of its legislative role but also through its general oversight role and, most importantly, through its ability to cut off or reduce funds in the authorization and appropriations process. This was exactly the form of the threat in the early 1980s when USDA published a brochure 'Nutrition and Your Health: Dietary Guidelines for Americans'[23] which warned against a fat-rich diet, although, for reasons explored below, in this issue area USDA has shifted its ground despite the opposition of Congressional agricultural interests.

An additional reason why the agricultural committees are able to maintain control of the political agenda is that other members of Congress are unwilling to make farm animal welfare an issue. There is a provision that enables members of Congress to prevent committees fom pigeon-holing bills they would prefer not to have debated. It is instructive to examine why this device is rarely used. The first reason is that alliances between the declining number of legislators representing agricultural constituencies and urban legislators are common because the latter can gain by cheap supplies of food and food stamp programmes which agriculture committee members can win for them.[24] Secondly, the American public still has a very positive image of farmers and farming so that non-farming legislators have little incentive to oppose decisions made by the agriculture committees. Coupled with this is the fact that public concern for the welfare of farm animals has not been salient enough to persuade Congress to act against the wishes of the committee system. Thus, after his bill to improve the conditions of veal calves was rejected by the House Agriculture Committee, Representative Charles Bennett (Democrat–Florida) sought to include its provisions as an amendment to the 1990 Omnibus Farm Bill, but the attempt was defeated on a voice vote.[25] This failure can be contrasted with the pressure that was exerted in the area of animal research in the 1980s which did produce Congressional action, despite the fact that reforming bills were rejected by committees (see Chapter 10).

Another interesting contrast here is between farm animal welfare and the issue of diet. Not surprisingly, USDA has traditionally promoted a fat-laden diet since its major concern is to further the interests of agribusiness interests. As in Britain, USDA's role is explicitly to promote the consumption of dairy and meat products and there are few means for the representation of consumer interests. There is evidence, however, that USDA's attitude has changed, however marginally, in the last two decades or so as the department has, despite enormous pressure from the food industry, made the health implications of a high-fat diet increasingly clear.[26] As Wyn Grant points out in the context of the dairy industry, 'If there is one area in which the exclusivity of the agricultural policy community has been breached in recent years it is in relation to food safety issues'.[27] The reason for this changing approach is clear. To a much greater degree than farm animal welfare, the issue of diet has become a salient political issue. This, of course, is because of the power of both the message, that *human* health suffers through a fat-laden diet, and the messengers, such as highly respected medical organizations, the increasingly visible consumer lobby and the federal Food and Drug Administration.

It is worth while asking why farm animal welfare has not been such a salient issue. It is impossible to demonstrate conclusively that were Americans fully aware of the consequences for animal welfare of factory farming methods they would be more likely to support calls for reform. Nevertheless, it is extremely likely that the lack of political saliency of farm animal welfare is a product of the myths that still exist about the conditions in which animals are kept and the nutritional value of animal proteins. As Michael Fox points out: 'What the consumer doesn't see, he doesn't grieve'.[28] A crucial factor contributing to the longevity of these myths is undoubtedly the vast amount of resources ploughed into promoting agribusiness concerns.[29] Thus, to give a few examples, the National Dairy Council 'remains the biggest supplier of nutrition educational materials for schools'.[30] Likewise, 40 per cent of the National Broiler Council's budget is allocated to the promotion of chicken in the media[31] and the National Livestock and Meat Board and the National Pork Council play a similar function. In the case of the former, its own literature points to the need to 'reach the children of the land at an early age' and 'prepare them for a lifetime of meat-eating'. As Robins points out: 'None of these "educational materials" allow a child to ever guess anything resembling the truth about how animals are kept today in the factory farms'.[32]

It is also instructive here to consider the key difference between the issues of farm and laboratory animal welfare. Agricultural interests do not have to even admit that farm animals suffer. They can, and do, maintain the myth of good lives, or at least not bad ones, and painless deaths. Researchers, on the other hand, do have to admit that pain is inflicted and, in addition, what they do is more open to public scrutiny because much of it is funded directly from the public purse.

A BRIGHTER FUTURE FOR FARM ANIMAL WELFARE?

Despite the rather gloomy prognosis for animal welfare sketched above, there is some evidence that there has been an, albeit slow, move towards a greater concern for farm animal welfare among decision-makers in the USA. A campaign by the organization Farm Sanctuary on the 'downer' animal problem, for instance, roused the public and so embarrassed members of the Agriculture Committee that hearings were held and industry groups promised to put their house in order. USDA, too, has shown a greater interest in the issue over the past three years or so. The department decided, for instance, to conduct an internal audit on the treatment of animals from the farm to the abattoir in 1996 and there have been rumours about the existence of an advisory committee on farm animal welfare within the department. More significantly, agricultural groups were not consulted on these initiatives and sought meetings with USDA officials for reassurance.[33]

One important catalyst for the changing attitude of USDA seems to have been Henry Spira, who in recent years has turned his attention from research animal issues to farm animal welfare.[34] Adopting his traditional carrot and stick approach, whereby institutions are approached about a particular problem and berated if they do not act and congratulated if they do, has already produced results. He has, for instance, persuaded parts of the meat industry to adopt more humane practices. In particular, Spira ran full-page advertisements in the *New York Times* and *Washington Post* among other newspapers publicizing the issue of the face branding of cattle imported from Mexico and USDA agreed to abolish the practice (and later to prohibit the face branding of domestic cattle) at least partly because of the number of protest letters and telephone calls (over 12 000) they received from members of the public. As Spira remarked:

> USDA did not lose sight of the fact that much of the protest against face branding originated with ordinary citizens who had no previous involvement with animal protection issues. Moreover, it seemed that the public's concern was shared by significant sectors of USDA's leadership and staff. Our campaign ads were displayed on some USDA office walls, and we heard that a petition of support was circulated in a USDA field office.[35]

The dominance of agricultural interests within Congressional committees remains, as indicated, the key obstacle to reform. Even here, though, the decline in the agricultural population, coupled with the relatively low status of the committee which makes it regularly difficult to fill the places, has meant that there are now more members on agriculture committees who do not have to represent substantial farming interests. Agribusiness lobbyists are well aware of these developments and, coupled with the increasing public concern for animal welfare, recognize that they will have to adapt to changing circumstances.[36] An encouraging sign for animal advocates is that this response has so far tended to focus on the need for industry to draw up its own codes of conduct, thereby avoiding legislative redress. As we shall see in the next chapter, the British case indicates that such self-imposed codes of practice were the forerunners of legislative and regulatory intervention. Whether a similar development will occur in the USA is still open to question. The impressive structural advantages still possessed by agribusiness interests and the present Republican dominance of Congress suggests that it will be a long haul.

8 The Politics of Farm Animal Welfare in Britain

The policy arenas concerned with farm animals in Britain and the United States have remarkably similar origins and characters. As in the United States, the relationship between agribusiness interests (more specifically, the NFU) and the state in Britain is regarded as the classic example of a policy community.[1] The incorporation of farmers occurred immediately after the Second World War, when the NFU's privileged position was enshrined in the 1947 Agriculture Act which introduced a system of guaranteed prices for agricultural products and provided a statutory right for the NFU to be consulted by MAFF on policies affecting its interests.

The ideological glue holding this cosy relationship together centred around a belief that agricultural intensification was desirable for its ability to provide a reliable, cheap and plentiful supply of food. An acceptance of factory farming, as one of the means to this goal, was a central part of the ideology. Any groups challenging this dominant ideology centring around agricultural expansionism (whether consumers, environmentalists or animal protectionists) were routinely excluded from the centre of influence. Thus, the 1947 Act facilitated the publication of Annual Reviews setting targets for increases in production levels and this emphasis on expansionism continued at least until the 1980s.[2] This was confirmed in stark fashion by two White Papers (*Food from Our Own Resources* and *Farming and the Nation*) published in the 1970s, both of which talked in terms of long-term expansionist plans and both of which mentioned the environment in passing and animal welfare not at all.[3]

There are two possible interpretations of these events.[4] One view is that the primary actors were the farmers themselves whose resources – in terms of the NFU's high density membership, considerable finances and so forth – were such that the state had no option but to provide them with a privileged position. An alternative, and arguably more persuasive, interpretation emphasizes the proactive role played by government. Here, rather than passively reacting to the NFU's status within the pressure group community, the government sought out the co-operation of the farmers in order to achieve its major policy goal which was an efficient farming sector providing a plentiful supply of cheap food. According to this second interpretation, then, the policy followed was not *caused* by the NFU's privileged position in the policy community. Rather, the policy community came about as a *result* of the pre-existing policy goals of government. This distinction is important because of what it reveals about the power relationships within the policy community, the rationale for its existence and the possibilities of change.

THE CHALLENGE OF ANIMAL WELFARE

In the 1940s and 1950s, there was little challenge to the view that intensive methods were an acceptable means to the achievement of post-war agricultural objectives. Since the 1960s, however, this ideological consensus has come under increasing attack from environmentalists, consumer groups and the animal protection movement. There is no doubt that, in terms of animal welfare, there has been a response, but it is not entirely clear how it should be interpreted.

Rising concern for the welfare of farm animals was evident in the 1950s and 1960s. Government responses of sorts were made as a result. Thus, public concern over the live export trade, which had begun in the mid-1950s originally as a response to the needs of American servicemen stationed in Europe, resulted in the appointment of the Balfour committee which reported in 1957.[5] Husbandry practices came under the spotlight in the early 1960s partly as a result of Ruth Harrison's ferocious denunciation of factory farming.[6] The government's response was the setting up of a committee under the chairmanship of the zoologist Frederick Brambell in 1964 and a year later the committee published its report.[7]

The Brambell report was a landmark in the sense that it was the first formal recognition by an official body that intensive animal agriculture raised animal welfare problems. It accepted that animals can suffer substantially, that suffering amounts to more than pain (a recognition which it thought should be included in legislation), that it should become an offence to 'cause, or permit to continue, avoidable suffering' and that it is an 'over-simplified and incomplete view' to regard an animal's productivity as the only viable determinant of suffering.[8] In principle, the report recommended that: 'An animal should at least have sufficient freedom of movement to be able without difficulty, to turn around, groom itself, get up, lie down and stretch its limbs'.[9]

This general principle translated into a number of specific recommendations. 'With some reluctance' the committee was not able to recommend the abolition of the battery cage.[10] Nevertheless, Brambell did recommend the abolition of some practices, such as the beak-trimming of battery hens and broilers, the tail docking of pigs and the use of sow stalls and tethers for pregnant sows. In addition, the close tethering of veal calves was to be prohibited and provision made for an adequate diet and a minimum size for their pens which would allow the animals to turn round and groom. Other regulations were also recommended, relating, in particular, to the size, stocking density and design of the battery and broiler systems. Finally, Brambell recognized the need for a general primary statute, so that it would be 'possible to modify any standards laid down without the necessity for constantly amending the main legislative instrument',[11] and the creation of a body which could advise ministers on animal welfare matters.

Brambell's recommendations set the agenda for the subsequent period of reform and, as Radford points out, 'one could do worse than use it as a benchmark against which to compare current practice and legal protection'.[12] What follows below are two possible interpretations of the political response to Brambell.

A DAMAGE LIMITATION EXERCISE?

One interpretation of the political response to rising concern about the welfare of farm animals is the argument that it represents an attempt by the policy community to maintain control of the agenda by offering minimal concessions aimed at 'buying-off' the more moderate animal welfare organizations and muting public concern. This represents, therefore, a classic policy community response to the politicization of issues it would rather keep off the political agenda. As Mills points out: 'when politic-isation occurs we would expect... policy communities to mani-pulate the political tension between themselves and their external environments (depoliticise the issue) while retaining the core values upon which present policies were based.'[13]

The Commons agriculture committee certainly echoed this interpretation when its report on animal welfare in 1981 com-mented that 'we have a feeling that it [animal welfare] is still [for MAFF] regarded as a tiresome complication engendered by vocal sentimentalists who need to be placated at minimum cost to producers' profits'.[14] Even Douglas Hogg, later, ironically, to find himself presiding over the BSE fiasco as secretary of state for MAFF, said that his experience of sitting on the Commons agriculture committee had given him the impression that 'animal welfare was not at the forefront of the Ministry's mind.'[15]

There are a number of arguments that can be utilized to sup-port this interpretation of farm animal welfare policy-making. In the first place, we can point to successive government's inaction as a response to public concern over animal welfare issues. More often than not, an extensive period of consulta-tion is entered into and/or an investigative committee set up, before any action is taken. In the case of farm animal welfare, the appointment of the Balfour and Brambell committees (in 1957 and 1965 respectively) might be regarded in this light, as classic instances of non-decision-making, the aim being to quieten public concern by offering the prospect that something might be done in the future. Brambell reported at the end of 1965 and there followed a further seven months of delay before MAFF announced the setting up of the farm animal welfare advisory committee and a further three years before a legislative response was forthcoming. The Commons did not even get the opportunity to debate Brambell's findings. In a similar vein, one MP speaking in a 1982 debate remarked that MAFF's lack of action on the animal welfare recommendations of the new in-vestigative Commons agriculture select committee led him to wonder whether the committee might not serve as 'a means of softening public outcry, of shelving issues, of covering matters up, of keeping a tight civil service control of Departments, and of enabling the status quo to be maintained'.[16]

The setting up of committees of enquiry is coupled with the regular refrain that more research is needed into the effects of intensive husbandry systems and the development of viable alternatives. Providing conclusive proof that a particular intensive system is responsible for animal suffering is often a difficult, if not impossible, task, and MAFF's reliance upon it might be perceived as a means of avoiding reform. In addition, the definition of a 'viable' alternative here usually refers to its profitability. As a result, the burden of proof always rests with animal welfarists whereas the mere raising of doubt by animal exploiters, about either the suffering caused by a particular husbandry system or the commercial restrictions imposed by an alternative, is usually enough to win the day.

The second point that supports the concession and co-option interpretation is that when governments have acted, their responses, from an animal welfare perspective, have been inadequate. Thus, the attempts to regulate the live exports trade through the use of the so-called 'Balfour Assurances' failed to prevent the infliction of severe suffering. For a start, the arrangements, whereby exporters would only be allowed to send animals to those countries willing to give assurances about aspects of their treatment of animals, applied, until 1964, only to cattle and only covered animals destined for slaughter and not for further fattening or the veal trade. More importantly, the Balfour Assurances were not legally binding and obviously open to abuse.[17]

Such were the obvious scale of these abuses, revealed by the media and by campaigning organizations such as CIWF, that the Secretary of State for Agriculture suspended, in February 1973, the issuing of licences for the export of sheep. Further action followed in July when the government lost a Labour opposition motion to suspend all live animal export licenses at least until a public enquiry had reported. The committee appointed under the chairmanship of Lord O'Brien eventually reported in March 1974 recommending that the ban remain until satisfactory and enforceable conditions (including the setting up of a supervisory body, with animal welfare representation, which could advise Ministers on the trade) could be introduced.[18] Despite the report's conclusions, however, Wilson's Labour government reversed its previous opposition stance and resurrected the trade despite the absence of the controls recommended by O'Brien.[19]

When we turn our attention to animal husbandry, it becomes apparent that all of Brambell's specific recommendations were initially ignored. Instead, as we saw, the legislation introduced in

1968 did not prohibit any particular practice. In addition, the legislation did not incorporate Brambell's more elaborate definition of suffering, opting instead for a general clause prohibiting the infliction of 'unnecessary suffering'. Because the emphasis is on physical pain and because 'unnecessary', rather than 'avoidable' – as suggested by Brambell – suffering is prohibited, this has meant, in practice, that only the most obvious cases of physical cruelty have been successfully prosecuted.

The power to introduce specific regulations was delegated to the Secretary of State for Agriculture. As a consequence, the policy community, within which agribusiness interests were extremely powerful, maintained control of the policy process. Not surprisingly, MAFF initially relied exclusively upon codes of practice (written by the FAWAC and later FAWC). The problem here is that they are not legally binding and evidence suggests that farmers tend not to be aware of their provisions. An RSPCA survey of egg producers in 1981, for instance, demonstrated a staggering ignorance of the code for the welfare of domestic fowls.[20]

A number of regulations were subsequently introduced and, although their positive impact on the welfare of farm animals should not be entirely rejected, it is fair to say that most of them did little to damage the interests of farmers and were rarely opposed by the NFU. Veal crates, for instance, were banned by the Welfare of Calves Regulations introduced in 1987. By this time, however, few veal operations existed in Britain and the vast majority of those that did used the alternative, and much more acceptable, loose-house system.[21] Moreover, as the protests against live exports have graphically revealed, there is still nothing to stop farmers from exporting their surplus male calves to other EU countries where the veal crate system is still legal.[22] Indeed, in the 1990s, the export of these animals reached record levels, nearly 400 000 being exported in 1991 alone.[23] It is true that the Conservative government prohibited sow stalls and tethers, against the wishes of the NFU and the National Pig Breeders Association, through the Welfare of Pigs Regulations introduced in 1991. However, it is tempting to say that action was taken only after MAFF perceived that support for Richard Body's Pig Husbandry Bill looked likely to see it through its legislative hurdles (see Chapter 5).[24] Even then, the phase-out period in the regulations (eight years) was significantly longer than Body had originally intended, thereby reducing the damage to farming interests.

Equally importantly is what MAFF has not done. Thus, the battery cage, perhaps the ultimate symbol of factory farming, is still in place. Moreover, the practice of beak trimming of poultry is still legal despite calls from both Brambell and the 1981 Agriculture Committee report that it should be prohibited and despite the provision in the code for domestic fowls which recommends that it be used only in the last resort. Likewise, slaughtering without prior stunning on religious grounds is still allowed despite a FAWC report recommending its abolition.[25]

Consistent with a concession and co-option approach is the incorporation of animal welfare interests within government itself. This was achieved by the creation of the FAWAC (later renamed FAWC). Here it might be argued that the aim of this was to co-opt the more moderate members of the animal welfare movement giving the impression that genuine access was being granted whereas in reality FAWC is at the periphery of the MAFF policy community with little influence on the centre of power. This was certainly the initial response of the RSPCA Council who refused for some time to participate in its activities. Furthermore, representation on FAWC is skewed towards industry interests with, at any one time, only about 25 per cent of the committee's membership (of around 20) likely to be sympathetic to animal welfare. Thus, the NFU did not oppose Brambell's recommendation to set up an advisory body 'provided that intensive livestock producers were adequately represented on it'.[26] This has remained the case. A final point is that although it is true that MAFF does tend to accept most of FAWC's recommendations (although there are important exceptions here, including FAWC's opposition to religious slaughter methods, the beak trimming of poultry and fur farming), it does tend to recommend only those things which it feels have a good chance of being accepted.

The creation of the animal welfare division (AWD) within MAFF might be seen in a similar light, as a public relations exercise designed to help ministers deal with complaints from animal protection groups and the public (one of its tasks is to formulate ministerial answers to parliamentary questions and to letters from the public) and to give the impression of effective access to animal protection organizations. It is certainly the case that those who work within the AWD are appointed primarily on their administrative ability as opposed to their commitment to animal welfare and so we should not assume that they will necessarily seek to promote animal welfare above the economic interest of producers.[27] Furthermore, even if it could be seen in this light,[28] the AWD's weight within MAFF, in terms of manpower and financial resources at least, would seem to be slight. It has to compete with other divisions within MAFF, and particularly the commodity divisions within the livestock group, for the ear of ministers, and not only are the producers well represented within the livestock group, but it is also based at Whitehall Place in MAFF's headquarters as opposed to the AWD, which is based some way away in Greater London. Indeed, this geographical distance from the centre of influence, which does hinder the recruitment and maintenance of top quality staff, may be itself regarded as a symbol of its rather peripheral role in policy-making.

The evolution of European Union influence on agricultural policy in general, and farm animal welfare in particular, has not weakened the position of the NFU. Farm animal welfare policy emanating from Europe tends (because of the need to muster the necessary support) to appeal to the lowest common denominator and, given that animal welfare standards are generally very poor in Southern European countries, this position is more often than not much lower than the standards presently existing in Britain. For example, the EU directive on animal transportation introduced in 1977 provided for a maximum journey time of 24 hours without food and water, whereas the British regulation of 1975 – the Transit of Animals (Road and Rail) Order – stipulated only 12 hours before animals must be fed and watered (increased to 15 hours in 1992). Moreover, the EU has no regulatory police force and it has become very apparent that the transportation and slaughtering directives are being regularly flouted. Indeed, such was the widespread recognition that Spanish slaughterhouses do not meet the requisite humane standards imposed by the EU that the British Government up to 1993 had a special dispensation allowing it to prohibit exports of animals to that country. In 1985, the RSPCA made a complaint to the Commission that the transportation directive was not being properly implemented or enforced and this was upheld by the Commission, which filed a case in the European Court of

Justice before Britain and France agreed to make sure they complied.[29]

It is noteworthy how often MAFF and the NFU regularly invoke Britain's membership of the EU as a justification for rejecting demands for unilateral reform. This can take the form of a constitutional argument (as in the live exports issue) whereby it is claimed that restricting trade is illegal under EU law, or it can take the form of a more general economic argument (as in the abolition of particular husbandry practices) whereby it is claimed that unilateral action will provide a competitive advantage for producers in other member states. Thus, for example, in the light of a FAWC report on the welfare of broiler chickens, in which extreme concern was raised about stocking densities and the leg problems caused by the growth rates of the birds, MAFF's response was to 'endorse' FAWC's concern but then to wash its hands of any responsibility by concluding that the government: 'does not intend to make changes to the farm animal welfare legislation on a unilateral basis if those changes would significantly affect the competitive position of UK producers compared to their European competitors.'[30] Such is the regularity with which the European dimension is invoked, and the apparent verve with which it is done, one might be forgiven for thinking that it provides a convenient excuse for inaction.

As indicated in Chapter 2, national farmers' unions are represented in Europe by COPA. This organization 'is widely considered to be amongst the most influential of all pressure groups in the Community'.[31] The governing body of COPA is its assembly composed of representatives from affiliated organizations and the broad framework of policy determined by the assembly is implemented on a day-to-day basis by a 'Praesidium' comprising the presidents of affiliated organizations. In May 1995 the NFU's president, David Naish, was elected for a two-year stint as COPA president. COPA representatives have unrivalled access to DG VI, the Agriculture Committee of the European Parliament, and the Council of Agricultural Ministers, usually through the Special Committee on Agriculture, a subcommittee of the full Council consisting of permanent officials from the member states.[32] In addition, COPA also provides the personnel for committees advising the Commission and the Economic and Social Committee of the Council of Ministers.[33] COPA, therefore has a privileged status within the EU and this amounts to the existence of a supra-national policy community. As Peterson points out: 'While total agreement within the EC's agricultural policy community was rare and bitter conflict not uncommon, the notion that disagreements should be kept "in the family" and outsiders be kept isolated from the locus of policy-making became powerful norms.'[34]

A revealing contrast which tends to confirm the reality of the concession and co-option interpretation is between the Conservative government's rather supine attitude to the live exports controversy and the feverish all-action approach it adopted over the BSE crisis. In the former case, the government repeatedly (and some would say conveniently) stated it could do nothing without a European-wide agreement, despite the existence of a legal judgement which suggested that Britain could act unilaterally and ban live exports under Article 36 of the Treaty of Rome.[35] This was not the first time that MAFF had denied it could use Article 36. In the wake of the so-called 'lamb wars' in 1990, where British sheep were subject to appalling suffering at the hands of French farmers, CIWF decided to seek judicial review claiming, ultimately unsuccessfully, that the British Government was wrong to deny that it could not invoke Article 36.[36] Moreover, the O'Brien Committee reporting on the live export trade in 1974 did raise the possibility of utilizing the Article.[37] There may be strong legal doubts as to the viability of invoking Article 36, not least the fact that the issue involves an 'occupied field' where precedent must be given to relevant directives – in this case a 1991 directive on the protection of calves.[38] This was never, however, simply a legal dispute and strong political pressure from the British government could conceivably have had an impact. The fact that it chose not to exert such pressure indicates that its main priority was not the welfare of animals.

By contrast, in the BSE case MAFF and the British government have worked extremely hard to get the European ban on British beef exports lifted, or at least diluted, threatening to adopt spoiling measures in the Council of Ministers to achieve its objectives.[39] In addition, before this, it is alleged that MAFF did its utmost to suppress or belittle any evidence which hinted at the possibility of a link between BSE and CJD.[40] In this context, one could be forgiven for thinking that the government was more interested in protecting the interests of farmers than in seeking to respond both to the heart-felt opposition of many

British people to the export of live animals and, indeed, to the public health concerns over BSE.

This interpretation of the policy community's approach to the BSE crisis conforms with the oft-stated claim that MAFF exists to defend the interests of the producer and, by so doing, the consumer's interests are neglected. The relationship between the producer and the ministry has been fused by an ideological consensus which holds that what matters is the technical issues relating to the provision of adequate supplies of food and not the potential dietary, environmental or animal welfare problems caused by the food production process.[41] By contrast, it appears that the consumer is better protected in the United States (and elsewhere) where there is a powerful counterbalance to USDA, thereby facilitating greater action.

It is in food policy that the relationship between the Ministry and industry is most clearly evident. Thus, as Walker and Cannon have documented, food policy (at least since the abolition of the Ministry of Food in 1955) is largely determined within MAFF and its advisory bodies tend to be dominated by the food industry.[42] As a result, even though there is now a consensus among the medical profession that there is a link between the consumption of saturated fats (found mainly in red meat, milk, cheese, margarine and butter) and cardiovascular disease, the dominance of food producers within MAFF has prevented adequate action being taken. Likewise, at the outset of the salmonella crisis in 1988, MAFF, the NFU and egg industry representatives (the British Poultry Federation and the Egg Industry Council) delayed issuing a warning to the public as long as they could and no consumer representatives were involved in the meetings. In addition, farmers were compensated for the flocks that had to be destroyed and MAFF and the NFU sought, ultimately successfully, to secure the resignation of Edwina Currie, a junior health minister, for remarking that all production was infected with salmonella.[43] More recently, in the wake of a number of deaths caused by the *e.coli* bacteria, there were claims that the policy community deliberately withheld information criticizing the hygiene standards of abattoirs from public consumption because it would have damaged the interests of the meat industry.[44]

Inadequate enforcement of the existing law is another ground for questioning MAFF's genuine interest in animal welfare.

Enforcement is the responsibility of the State Veterinary Service. Two criticisms are most apparent. In the first place, there is the failure to provide enough inspectors for the work involved. There has been a variable number of inspections with a general upward trend. In 1974, 710 inspections were made to farms in England, Wales and Scotland and by 1979 this had increased to 1825.[45] To put this into perspective, however, MAFF itself admitted that in 1980 its inspectors visited just under 3 per cent of pig farms and one per cent of poultry units and most of these were announced visits.[46] Secondly, there is the problem of inspectors 'going native' and having too cosy a relationship with the regulated. One problem here is that the State Veterinary Service was originally set up as a disease monitoring service, with an animal welfare function tacked on at a later date. The RSPCA, for one, has regularly sought the creation of an independent and specialized animal welfare inspectorate.[47] One outcome that might be the result of these enforcement weaknesses is the limited number of prosecutions undertaken. Up to September 1980, there had only been 14 prosecutions, compared to 25 taken without MAFF's assistance.[48] Evidence provided by witnesses to the Commons agriculture committee hearings in the early 1980s was such that the committee's report concluded that 'inspection directed to animal welfare is neither so frequent or so rigorous as to ensure that abuses do not go undetected'.[49]

A GENUINE ATTEMPT TO BALANCE INTERESTS?

The arguments presented above may seem so powerful that it is difficult to see how there could be an alternative interpretation of the evidence. Nevertheless, there are, I think, grounds for saying that such an alternative does exist. This would see the reforms of the last three decades or so not as some sort of conspiratorial damage limitation exercise but rather as representing a genuine attempt by governments to respond to animal welfare problems, and to balance the interests of animal welfarists with those of the producers. It may not have got the balance right yet, and it is certainly true that what has been achieved so far would satisfy only the most moderate animal welfare advocates. Nevertheless, the argument might continue, the process has by no means yet come to an end. In particular, the continuation and intensification of pressure for reform, spearheaded by the animal protection movement, might persuade the government that the balance needs to be struck even further in favour of farm animals.

There are a number of arguments that might be employed in support of this second interpretation. In the first place, it is important that, when assessing governmental responses to demands for farm animal welfare reforms, we do not distort the analysis by adopting the wrong criteria. It was suggested earlier in this book that there is a strong moral case for the abolition of many current practices endured by farm animals. From a pluralist perspective, however, this is not the benchmark, at least at present, that should be adopted. Confirmation of a pluralist view requires the balancing of interests. For our purposes, then, the benchmark for judging governmental action is not the complete abolition of factory farming, let alone the ending of all animal agriculture, but the extent to which animal welfare demands have been balanced against those with a vested interest in the continuation of intensive animal agriculture.

Seen in this context, there is evidence of significant change. MAFF's literature and organizational structure now, for instance, takes much more account of animal welfare and broader environmental concerns. In recent years, for the first time, the protection of farm animals has become one of MAFF's stated aims – along with protecting the public, enhancing the rural and marine environment, and improving the economic performance of the agriculture, food and fishing industries – and the ministry estimates that about one per cent of its expenditure (amounting to about £13 million) is spent on animal welfare, not an insignificant amount given MAFF's varied responsibilities.[50] Earlier, we pointed to the policy community's use of consultation and the appointment of investigative committees which might be seen as devices to quieten public concern. They might equally be seen, however, as genuine attempts at 'bureaucratic accommodation' whereby as many interests as possible are incorporated into the decision-making arena and where policy necessarily progresses slowly and incrementally (see Conclusion for more on this point).

The NFU, too, has had to adapt to a political environment much more sympathetic to the welfare of animals. Thus, as early as 1978, the NFU set up a 'Concern for Animals Group' as a result of the 'various developments on animal welfare'. Consisting of representatives from the various NFU committees, the terms of reference of this new body were to:

> review the state of developments in the treatment of animals and to examine the opinions of organizations concerned for animals; to prepare material setting out the Union's views and attitudes on the main issues in question; and to guide and co-ordinate as necessary all activities of the Union which affect animal welfare.[51]

In a similar vein, the NFU's Animal Health committee, which had existed for many years, was renamed the Animal Health and Welfare committee in 1987.[52] Yet again, in 1991, the NFU sought to develop an 'all-inclusive' position on animal welfare on the grounds, in the words of David Naish, the NFU President, that it is 'time for us to enter constructively into a debate which in the past we have left too much to others'.[53] As a result, in particular, of the live exports issue and the 'recognition that much closer public attention will be paid to animal welfare issues generally' the Council established an Animal Welfare Working Group 'to review comprehensively' the NFU's welfare policy as outlined in October 1991.[54] The initial report of this working group, not surprisingly, was largely – with one or two exceptions such as some hostility to religious slaughter methods – an attempt to justify present practices. Thus, rather than suggesting welfare reforms, the report emphasizes that the 'onus is on the industry to explain what it does and why'.[55]

In addition to the attempts to demonstrate farmers' concern for animal welfare, the NFU has begun in recent years to engage in public campaigns to promote farming and farmers. In 1994, for instance, the NFU launched its so-called 'living classrooms' scheme which encouraged 'educational' farm visits and, following on from this a year later, the organization's first national advertising campaign 'to win the hearts and minds of the British public' was undertaken.[56] Whether or not one regards this greater recognition by the NFU of the need to paint farmers, on animal welfare and other grounds, in a more favourable light, as mere window dressing is, to some degree, beside the point. What it does demonstrate is a recognition, by both MAFF and the NFU, that farmers and farming are under attack as never before and that the issue of farm animal welfare in particular can no longer be confined safely within the policy community.

It might also be suggested that the creation of the AWD and the FAWC was a positive step in that the existence of both is at least consistent with a pluralist interpretation. Throughout my interview with the head of the AWD, for instance, he emphasized the importance of balancing the competing interests involved, and it is undoubtedly the case that balance within MAFF is furthered by the existence of the agency.[57] Likewise, the FAWC provides a forum whereby interests on both sides of the debate can meet, and the fact that industry interests are represented too gives its conclusions added legitimacy in the eyes of the government. In the debate on Richard Body's PMB to prohibit the use of sow stalls and tethers, for instance, much was made of the fact that FAWC had recommended the ending of this practice.[58] It is true that those with an interest in animal welfare have never constituted a majority but it would be equally wrong to claim that those who have been appointed are either second-rate or do not have an impressive record in campaigning for reform. FAWC members over the years have included noted campaigners Clive Hollands and Ruth Harrison in addition to sympathetic academics such as Marian Stamp Dawkins, John Webster and Donald Broom. Furthermore, since 1979, FAWC has had a statutory basis (and a wider remit, unlike its predecessor, covering all aspects of the process from birth to slaughter) so that its reports are in the public domain. This is how we know, for instance, that the government rejected its call for a ban on religious slaughter, and every time the government does reject a FAWC proposal it has to defend it in public.[59] This is at least part of the reason why relatively few FAWC recommendations are rejected.

If we look at substantive policy reforms, it becomes apparent that, with the glaring exception of battery cages, many of the specific recommendations originally made by Brambell have been fulfilled. It is true that 'unnecessary' suffering rather than the 'avoidable' suffering advocated by Brambell was used and that, on animal welfare grounds, the latter is infinitely preferable. On the other hand, the use of avoidable suffering would have put intensive husbandry systems in greater legal doubt and it is really inconceivable that MAFF would have accepted that, and, more to the point, questionable, at least at the time, whether a pluralistic balancing of interests would have justified it. Where the 1968 statute did conform to Brambell was in the provision that regulations might be introduced as more knowledge about the nature of animal welfare became available and as the public climate changed. Fred Peart, the Labour Secretary of State for Agriculture recommended the 1968 Bill to the Commons 'as a fair, pragmatic approach to a difficult problem. We strike, I suggest, a fair balance'.[60] In some ways, all things being equal, the Bill does, in retrospect, look suspiciously like a classic compromise. Thus, some MPs on both sides of the issue criticized it for being too vague but for very different reasons. On the one hand, it was criticized for not prohibiting particular practices whilst on the other it was criticized precisely because at some point in the future it might. In this latter category, one MP stated:

> I am not wholly satisfied about the safeguards that there will be against the arbitrary use of that [regulatory] power, because he [the Secretary of State] is proposing regulations which could, under this Clause, be very wide and could have the most sweeping effect on producers'.[61]

The concern of the farming community at the wide powers given to MAFF arose again at the committee stage of the bill. Here, it became clear that the NFU was worried too. One MP in committee, for example, quoted from an NFU memo which read that: 'The scope of the matters which could be covered in these mandatory regulations is alarming',[62] and the NFU's own publication described the powers as 'excessive'.[63] Indeed, such was the concern that Peart accepted an amendment at the report stage which required regulations made under the authority of the bill to be subject to the affirmative resolution procedure (where MPs would have to approve them before they became operational) rather than the negative resolution procedure (where regulations would go through automatically provided that sufficient MPs did not object).[64]

MAFF did initially rely exclusively on codes of conduct in the years immediately after the 1968 Act. Nevertheless, despite their weaknesses, some of them have proved to be precursors of formal regulations. Before the introduction of regulations prohibiting veal crates and sow stalls and tethers, for instance, codes of practice had recommended these practices be phased out. Indeed, the cattle code was utilized in a court case in 1976 when the National Society Against Factory Farming took legal action against Quantock Veal and, although the verdict was inconclusive, the case was instrumental in persuading veal producers to discard the crate system.[65]

Now, there is a much greater emphasis on formal regulations. It is the case too, that some of these have been opposed by the NFU and commodity groups. Thus, the NFU and the National Pig Breeders Association fought tooth and nail against the Bill to ban the use of sow stalls and tethers and still complained – mainly about the cost – when MAFF took over the Body Bill and extended the phase-out period (an extension which, in actual fact, MPs had already accepted in the bill's standing committee). Indeed, even the phase-out period of eight years finally decided upon was a compromise, the NFU wanting ten years and Body five.[66] Subsequently, MAFF refused to accede to the NFU's demand and offer compensation for the economic costs of the reform.[67] There is no doubt too that public pressure played a significant role in MAFF's decision to take action here. The junior agriculture minister, David Maclean, for instance, remarked that he had received more letters on this issue than on the Gulf War[68] and that, although there would be economic consequences for pig producers as a result of the ban, MAFF had decided to put 'welfare considerations first'.[69] Maclean himself played a positive role in achieving reform here, demonstrating that individuals can have an impact on public policy. As one industry lobbyist pointed out to me, he was, unlike many of his predecessors, a minister they 'didn't trust'.[70]

It should also be noted here that the NFU did not oppose the use of veal crates, even though there was by the 1980s little commercial benefit in keeping them. The reasoning behind this was probably a 'thin end of the wedge' argument in which once a regulatory precedent was set, it would be much easier for MAFF to move on to regulate more contentious practices. A particularly extreme version of this mentality was evident in the comments made by the representative of the Agricultural Supply Trade Association to the agriculture select committee. 'In theory', he began:

there is no logical 'stopping point' between the current somewhat woolly 'codes of conduct' and the end-point of vegetar-

ianism, and any further movement along this line must be regarded as a step towards the ultimate goal of the 'non-ex-
ploitation lobby'.[71]

The regulations introduced under the 1968 Act, together with
other legislation regulating the treatment of animals in transit, at
market, and in the slaughterhouse do not, of course, constitute
the progress towards vegetarianism so feared by the agribusiness
representative quoted above. Nevertheless, few would doubt
that they do represent some improvement in the welfare of farm
animals.

    In the context of the preceding few paragraphs, it is instructive
to examine the NFU's attitude to animal welfare in the 1960s.
Here, we discover that the NFU opposed virtually all of Brambell's recommendations and supported many practices which
have subsequently been regulated against.[72] They opposed, for
instance, providing minimum space for battery hens and broilers; the banning of debeaking, sow stalls and tethers and the tail
docking of pigs; they even justified the veal crate and a diet
lacking iron and roughage for calves.[73]

    There is also an alternative interpretation of Britain's role
within the European Union. Here, it might be argued that there
is no reason to think that British governments have not worked
hard to secure agreements on transportation directives and the
abolition of the veal crate. For example, Britain helped to block
a Greek package in 1994 which would have excluded a maximum journey time limit for new transport regulations, although
it should be said that this was done only after a campaign by
animal welfare groups altered the government's position.[74]
Similarly, the British government has been at the forefront of the
campaign to revise the description of animals in the Treaty of
Rome as merely agricultural products. Thus, perhaps the one
positive act of the British government in the formulation of the
Maastricht Treaty was to insist upon a declaration being added
which refers to the need to 'pay full regard to the welfare requirements of animals' in EU legislation.

    Moreover, MAFF is, to a large degree, right in its assertion
that it is preferable to seek European-wide agreements, not least
because the abolition of particular husbandry systems in Britain
alone would not help those animals kept in worse conditions in
other member states and would probably not prevent imports of

animal products reared under these very same systems. Seen in this way, whether or not Britain could act unilaterally to ban the export of live animals becomes irrelevant. As David Maclean, a MAFF minister pointed out in a Commons debate in 1989:

> The importers concerned need live animals and would simply go elsewhere for their supplies, perhaps even to Eastern Europe. So it would be absolutely pointless for us to take a British unilateral stand only for the markets we have refused to supply to be taken up by animals imported from even further away, where welfare standards may be lower.[75]

On the question of enforcement inadequacies, it might be pointed out firstly that there can never be enough inspectors. Nevertheless, a significant number of farm visits are made and it is impossible anyway for British inspectors to follow animals exported abroad. In addition, the criticism that few prosecutions are undertaken is to some degree misplaced. It assumes that farmers are deliberately flouting the regulations or deliberately mistreating animals. There are some cases which fit into this category but the biggest problem is probably ignorance. Given this, the SVS regards it as more appropriate to offer advice and information, coupled with follow-up visits, rather than taking legal action. One final point is that inspectors have to work within the existing law and, while intensive husbandry systems are still legal, inspectors cannot, whatever their own personal views, do anything about the suffering, short of obvious cases of actual physical pain, they might suspect is taking place in such systems.

A POLICY COMMUNITY UNDER SIEGE

It is difficult to come to a firm conclusion about the validity of these respective interpretations. What should be said initially is that a thorough assessment should not just focus on what has been done up to now, but also what might happen in the future. Public concern for the welfare of farm animals is a relatively recent phenomenon as is governmental response to these concerns. As a result, it is probably true to say that we need to wait and see how much further the reforming process goes before a firm conclusion can be reached. The concession and co-option interpretation is clearly most appropriate if it can be shown that agribusiness interests have retained their central role in the policy-making process. Thus, if the institutional dominance of the existing policy community actors continues, reform will also continue to be limited. Alternatively, if governmental responses to the problem of farm animal welfare have resulted from the waning of agribusiness influence, then the potential for further reforms benefiting animals would seem to be more pronounced.

Whichever interpretation is adopted, however, the key development has been the politicization of agricultural issues. A central characteristic of a policy community is its ability to depoliticize issues through the maintenance of an ideological hegemony. There is substantial evidence now that the ideological consensus, based around an acceptance of intensive agriculture and the goals of a cheap and plentiful supply of food, which has enabled MAFF to depoliticize agricultural issues for 40 or so years, has begun to decline. Public knowledge of, and its growing reluctance to accept, the environmental, health and animal welfare implications of factory farming have kept the issue on the political agenda to the extent that MAFF often finds itself at the centre of national political debate. What we can say at the very least, then, is that there is an emerging and growing issue network operating at the periphery of the policy community and that, as a consequence, MAFF's priorities have had to change.

One interpretation of MAFF's changing priorities, as we have seen, is the view that the department has genuinely changed, relegating agricultural interests and taking more account of previously excluded ones. This interpretation is consistent with the state autonomy explanation for the creation of the policy community described above. Thus, if agricultural interests were invited to play a central role in formulating policy as a result of prior governmental objectives, it is logical to assume that as soon as government priorities change, the structure of decision-making will be transformed too. Seen in this way, the food problem which led to the creation of the policy community in the first place has now been solved and new problems caused by the original solution have emerged. Those very interests representing intensive agriculture, then, have, in many ways, become the problem whereas other interests – environmentalists, animal advocates and consumers – offer potential solutions.

It is by no means clear that the influence of agribusiness interests has substantially declined. It is the case that MAFF does, as a matter of course, engage in extensive consultation with a wide range of interests on all sides of the issue. In this sense, no one is excluded. The AWD, for instance, maintains a list of something like 600 organizations with whom it consults on FAWC reports.[76] Of course, merely being consulted is different from having regular access to decision-makers and consultation by itself does not imply influence. There is little doubt that agribusiness interests still have unrivalled access to MAFF. Senior officials of the NFU are establishment figures (witness the knighthood given to David Naish, the current President, in 1994) and are treated with considerable respect within the ministry. There is also evidence of the 'revolving-door' phenomenon whereby former officials within MAFF become lobbyists for agricultural interest groups. One illuminating illustration of this emerged from an interview I conducted with the chief lobbyist for a major commodity organization. After denying that his organization had any greater influence than major animal welfare groups, it transpired that before taking on his current position he had worked as a senior official in the relevant commodity division within MAFF. Not surprisingly, he then described his contacts with MAFF officials (as well as European Commissioners) as 'routine and extensive'![77]

Having said all of this, there is some evidence that the privileged position given to agricultural interests has begun to erode. Interviews with lobbyists for a number of the larger animal protection organizations revealed a surprising consensus on this. Both the RSPCA and RSPB, for instance, indicate that they now have regular and formalized access to the Secretary of State. In the case of the former, the Director General, Peter Davies, has a meeting every three months and these become more regular if an issue of concern to either side is particularly prominent. He described his meetings with the minister as 'very healthy' with a great deal of 'mutual respect' in evidence. Indeed, Davies makes an interesting contrast with the Home Secretary, with whom the RSPCA does not usually have meetings. This is put down partly to the fact that the Home Office has a long-standing opposition to a dog registration scheme (see Chapter 5) and has clashed with the RSPCA on this issue, and partly because the Home Office, where animal issues constitute only a fraction of its activities, does not have a 'genuine feel' for animal welfare in the same way that MAFF does.[78] Even CIWF, a much smaller – and more radical – organization has occasional meetings with senior civil servants and ministers.[79] This access is a product of the growing saliency of farm animal welfare and the growing reputation of CIWF as a responsible and respected organization which provides well-researched information and does not make unrealistic demands.

The RSPB's links with MAFF have been extensive for some time. They were the only conservation group, for instance, to be consulted over the Wildlife and Countryside Bill in the early 1980s,[80] and they continue to have much greater and more effective access than other conservation and animal protection groups. The RSPB are, of course, not an animal protection group and their conservation focus and moderate image has enabled them to attract a very large membership (approaching one million), factors which make the granting of insider status an attractive proposition for MAFF. There is also a general feeling amongst RSPB staff that the influence of the NFU within MAFF has declined as environmental issues have come to the fore.[81]

Even if the policy community has not changed to any great extent, it is the case that it faces new challenges now as a result of public pressure. This pressure can result in challenges to the agricultural policy community from other governmental arenas or in a sustained and centralized governmental response. One instance of the former was the role performed by the Department of Health during the salmonella crisis in the late 1980s. As North and Gorman have argued, MAFF 'embarked on a series of measures against egg producers', including the cruel and sometimes farcical destruction of many entire flocks, under 'what was clearly pressure from the Department of Health spurred on by leaks from the Communicable Disease Surveillance Centre'.[82] Thus, the Department of Health was more interested in the health issues than in protecting the industry, and the effect of this difference of outlook, and the conflict generated by Currie's statement and ultimate resignation, was to politicize the issue. As a result, MAFF lost control of the issue agenda.[83]

More generally, MAFF, in the same way that it recognized animal welfare concerns, has increasingly, although perhaps reluctantly, accepted the need to represent the consumer interest. Thus, in 1989 a new Food and Safety Directorate was created within MAFF, incorporating the Animal Welfare Division and the State Veterinary Service, with a staff of almost 700.[84] More recently still, after a decade of one food crisis after another, the Conservative government before its fall from power announced plans to create an independent food standards adviser, and, at the time of writing, the present Labour government intends to create a new food standards agency.[85] What we can say, therefore, is that, whatever its motivations, MAFF has increasingly alienated the NFU. The ministry's reluctance to offer full compensation to those farmers whose flocks had to be destroyed in the salmonella outbreak, for instance, annoyed the NFU to the point where they were calling for resignations.[86]

For animal advocates, the important point to note here is that the animal welfare, environmental and public health implications of factory farming are intimately related. As Richard Lacey, the well-known microbiologist, has consistently argued, the 'salmonella problem in eggs is almost certainly partly related to intensive farming and the BSE epidemic entirely so'.[87] Food producers have denied this, of course, but in a sense that is not the point.[88] What matters is the public's *perception*[89] of reality, and forging links between the various consequences of factory farming so that benefits to animals are linked with human benefits, is clearly a profitable strategy for animal advocates.

Another dimension to the pressure for more humane farming practices concerns the role of retailers. The large retailing chains have to be responsive to public demands, for healthy, environmentally friendly and humanely produced foods, and, as a result, do not necessarily have a vested interest in intensive forms of animal agriculture. There is no evidence that retailers have lobbied in farm animal welfare decision-making arenas, but there has been a shift in their marketing strategies as demand for 'free range' agricultural produce increases.[90] As a result, most large retailers now make available a greater variety of vegetarian and vegan food products and, in an innovative scheme, a number of them participate in the RSPCA's 'Freedom Foods' scheme whereby humanely produced meat products carry an RSPCA label of approval. This remains a relatively small-scale scheme, and, of course, it is not acceptable to animal rights advocates.[91] Nevertheless, it does reflect an important shift in consumer attitudes as well as contributing to greater public awareness of farm animal welfare.

There are also other potential or actual conflicts in the agricultural community which have the potential to facilitate change. Small, and particularly organic, farmers would not seem to have a great deal in common, for instance, with capital-dominated agribusiness.[92] In Britain, for example, a separate United Kingdom Egg Producers' Association representing smaller producers and retailers exists to rival the mainstream British Egg Industry Council and there is little love lost between them.[93] One particular example of a conflict between agribusiness and farmers which has an animal welfare dimension is the use of bovine somatotropin (BST), a hormone which has the ability substantially to increase milk yields. In Britain, the rest of Europe and the United States, farmers, already burdened by milk surpluses, have opposed its use with some success, despite the obvious benefits for very large producers and the agrichemical companies who market BST.[94]

Finally, a clear conflict of interests emerged in the British live exports controversy, between, on the one hand, farmers concerned with maximizing their incomes through exporting animals live and, on the other, British slaughterhouses and the animal by-products industry that stand to gain financial benefits from greater home slaughter.[95] So, while the NFU has been at the forefront of the campaign to maintain the live export trade, to the point of threatening legal action against port authorities that decided to have nothing more to do with it, the meat trade has been deeply concerned about the rapidly expanding live export trade. The president of the National Federation of Meat Traders, for instance, has commented that 'jobs, profits and businesses throughout the meat trade in this country are in jeopardy' as a result of it.[96]

Whether or not the agricultural policy community is in decline, there is enough evidence to suggest that British governments may go much further than they have at present in improving the welfare of farm animals. For this to happen, public pressure has to be maintained and the consequences of intensive agriculture have to become more apparent. Already, public pressure has resulted in a weakening in the sectorized nature of policy-making in this area. While in 'normal' times the evidence still broadly supports a policy community interpretation, it was noticeable that in the cases of the salmonella, BSE and – to a lesser extent – the live exports crisis, the political centrality of the issue necessitated a centralized governmental response. As a result, the issues could no longer be quietly resolved within the policy community. Whether these crises are a precursor for the permanent reshaping of the policy community or merely a blip after which things will return to normal, is difficult to predict.

9 The Politics of Animal Research in Britain

Though there are doubts about the appropriateness of applying the pluralist label in the case of British farm animal welfare policy making, these doubts become less pronounced if we turn our attention to decision-making relating to animal research in Britain. Although it would be absurd to overlook both the influence of the animal research lobby and the inadequacies of the present legislative and administrative framework designed to protect animals used for research, it would be equally inaccurate to deny the genuineness of the governmental response to public concern and the importance of the role played by a section of the animal protection movement in bringing about legislative reform.

ORIGINS OF THE ANIMAL RESEARCH POLICY NETWORK

Animal research became an issue of public concern in nineteenth-century Britain as a result not so much of what British scientists were doing but because of the activities of foreign vivisectionists. Thus, the work of two French physiologists, François Magendie and Claude Bernard, caused particular public outrage as did the repeated cutting procedures carried out by veterinary students at Alfort, near Paris, in the 1840s. The gradually rising public hostility to the use of animals in medical research and the nuisance value of the newly formed anti-vivisection movement resulted in the setting up of a Royal Commission in 1876 and the eventual passage of the 1876 Cruelty to Animals Act.[1]

The significance of the legislative and administrative framework created by the 1876 Cruelty to Animals Act lies in the fact that it was devised specifically for the purpose of protecting animals used for research. The Home Office had no prior interest in this issue. There is a marked contrast here with the farm animal policy arena. As we have seen, responsibility for farm animal welfare lies with a policy community, within which actors with a vested interest in utilizing animals for agricultural purposes have a highly influential role, that already had responsibility for the fate of farm animals prior to the modern concern for their welfare. New institutions and procedures dealing with farm animal welfare were simply grafted on to an existing structure.

To repeat, it is not being claimed here that the research community was not, and is not, an extremely influential lobby. We saw in Chapter 2, for instance, that the Association for the Advancement of Medicine by Research developed extremely close ties with the Home Office, acting as the department's unofficial adviser on the working of the 1876 legislation.[2] Having said this, research interests did not have from the outset the kind of structural advantages that the British farming community had. As a result, it seems safe to conclude that governments have been more able to respond to rising concern about the use of animals in the laboratory and thereby more able to exercise the balancing of interests required by pluralist theory. Thus, while the 1876 Act had its serious shortcomings, it did have some impact on the activities of animal researchers, preventing outright abuses and probably discouraging some animal research which might otherwise have been done.[3]

From the end of the nineteenth century, the issue of animal experimentation largely disappeared from the political agenda. A second Royal Commission was appointed in 1906 and in the six years it deliberated a number of reforms were proposed and acted upon. The most important were the appointment of full-time inspectors, the attachment of a 'pain condition' – which required the experimenter 'to cause the painless death of any animal which in his opinion is suffering severe pain that is likely to endure' – and the creation of an advisory body selected from persons nominated by the Royal Society and the Royal Colleges of Physicians and Surgeons.[4]

LITTLEWOOD TO MELLOR

Growing disquiet about the use of animals in research began to emerge again in the 1960s. This was generated not just by the changing moral climate but also by the changing nature of animal research itself. The original 1876 legislation was introduced at a time when animal research was small-scale, mainly involving surgical techniques designed to increase knowledge of bodily functions. In 1877, only 23 licences were granted and only about 200 experiments performed. Even by 1912 there were only 94 registered premises.[5] In the twentieth century, the character of animal research has changed out of all recognition. New branches of science – such as bacteriology, immunology, chemotherapy, virology, endocrinology and genetics – have been developed, requiring the use of animals as a central part of their study. Moreover, the increasing volume of medicinal and non-medicinal products on the market, and a greater concern for public safety, has resulted in the regular use of animals for toxicity testing. As a result, by 1991, under the new legislative framework, a total of 4383 project licences were held, along with 17 879 personal licences and animal experimentation was conducted in 341 designated sites.[6]

In the late 1950s and early 1960s, the RSPCA regularly petitioned the Home Secretary to set up a committee of enquiry and in 1962 he eventually formed such a committee under Sir Stanley Littlewood with the remit 'to consider the present control over experiments on living animals, and to consider whether, and if so what, changes are desirable in the law or its administration'.[7] The publication of the Littlewood Report in April 1965 was followed by a decade of inertia. Despite repeated requests from MPs, successive ministers – including Frank Soskie, Roy Jenkins and David Ennals – refused to be drawn on their intentions. Over three years later, Merlyn Rees, a junior Home Office minister, was still repeating the familiar refrain, 'I am not in a position' to make any statement.[8] In 1969, minor administrative changes, such as an increase in the number of inspectors, were made, but it was not until March 1971 that the Commons got the chance to debate the issue – and even this was an adjournment debate initiated by a backbencher[9] – and not until June 1971 that a full-scale debate, lasting for about four hours, was held on the failure to act upon the Littlewood Report. Even then, some six years after the report, and with Littlewood himself no longer alive, the Conservative Home Secretary (Mark Carlisle) was heard to say that 'the Government have not yet finalised their attitude to the Report in the sense of assuming a commitment to legislation'.[10]

This inertia was at least partly a product of the Littlewood Report's conclusions themselves. While recognizing that the 1876 legislation was seriously out of date, the report announced that the committee was satisfied that the Home Office had adapted its administrative procedures to take account of the radically different character of animal research.[11] Equally significantly, it found no evidence of extensive public demands for reform, let alone pressure which might be electorally significant.[12] Given these conclusions, it is not surprising that Labour and Conservative governments during this period, with many pressing problems on their plates and no one within their ranks who was particularly concerned with the issue of animal research, were reluctant to commit themselves to legislative reform which would not only take up valuable parliamentary time but would also incur inevitable controversy. Thus, Mark Carlisle, for one, used both arguments – the lack of public interest and the report's conclusion that there was nothing fundamentally wrong with the existing law – as reasons for inaction.[13]

In the 1970s, it was less easy for governments to ignore demands for reform. The public's consciousness of the use of animals in research was raised by a reinvigorated and radicalized animal protection movement and a popular press which was prepared to sensationalize aspects of the issue. A number of initiatives by the animal protection movement in the 1970s were both causes and effects of this changing political climate. The organization of an Animal Welfare Year in the mid-1970s helped to facilitate the creation of an ad hoc group of individuals later, in March 1977, to be christened the Committee for the Reform of Animal Experimentation (CRAE). This group submitted a paper calling for reform (popularly labelled as the Houghton–Platt Memorandum after two of its best known signatories) to the Home Office.[14] As a result of this memo, and under Houghton's patronage, Hollands and his colleagues in CRAE were granted access to the Home Office, where they put their case. As Ryder notes:

> Houghton taught us that...it is *governments* which introduce legislation and that without government support no Bill is likely to succeed. Moreover, Houghton managed to effect several meetings with old colleagues who were again in office after the Labour election victories of 1974.[15]

As a consequence of the focus on the executive and the animal protection movement's campaigns in the mid to late-1970s (organized by the General Election Co-ordinating Committee for Animal Protection under the 'Putting Animals into Politics' slogan) directed particularly at reform of the 1876 Act, the Home Office became sufficiently convinced of the political importance of animal research that it felt granting access to animal advocates on a regular basis was a worthwhile exercise. In addition, the advisory committee was extended in 1977 by the appointment of four 'non-scientific' members and for the first time the committee was asked to examine the general principles relating to a specific animal research issue, the justifiability of the LD50 test. By the end of the 1970s all of the major parties had included a commitment to legislate for a replacement to the 1876 Act in their 1979 election manifestos.[16]

Despite the renewed interest in the issue apparent in the 1970s, reforms to the existing legislative framework were never going to be a priority for any government, and the period between the early 1970s and the appearance of the Conservative government's initial White Paper in 1983 was a frustrating time for animal advocates. Richard Ryder notes, for instance, how the initial contacts between CRAE and Home Office Ministers were frosty. Moreover, the Houghton–Platt proposals were rejected in an astonishing public attack by the recently retired Chief Inspector.[17] A Home Office minister (Brynmor-John), replying to an adjournment debate in January 1977, trotted out the familiar line, that 'we have no plans to introduce legislation' of the kind suggested by the Houghton–Platt memorandum.[18] Even as late as 1985 there were some doubts as to whether the bill was going to be in the Queen's Speech (the government believing the bill to be too contentious and time-consuming) and it took numerous meetings between CRAE and the Home Office before the government agreed to include it.[19]

Nevertheless, the links with the executive forged by CRAE were to prove invaluable and this period also witnessed signs that the influence of the research community was waning. Evidence for this is the government's attitude to the private members bill introduced by Lord Halsbury, a former President of the RDS, in 1979. From the 1960s onwards, the research community had denied the need for reform claiming that there was nothing fundamentally wrong with the existing legislation. By the late

1970s, however, it realized reform of some kind was inevitable, given the growing public pressure which the government was finding it increasingly difficult to deflect, and to pre-empt a more stringent government bill it lent its support to Halsbury's bill.

Halsbury's Laboratory Animals Protection Bill sought, as far as possible, to maintain the status quo.[20] Ministers rejected it ostensibly on the grounds of a lack of parliamentary time and a desire to wait for the conclusion of European Convention deliberations on the issue. An additional, and probably more important factor, however, was the government's desire to avoid alienating the animal protection movement, or at least those parts of it that might be persuaded to support them if a more stringent bill was introduced. It was Houghton, here, who was instrumental in warning the government of the consequences of supporting the Halsbury bill. Thus, he pointed out to the Lords' committee that the bill did not have the support of any animal welfare society and that there has to be a wider degree of support, a 'closing of the gap' or a 'biggest common denominator'.[21]

A private members' bill – the Protection of Animals (Scientific Purposes) Bill – introduced by the Conservative backbencher Peter Fry and sponsored by the RSPCA, was going through the House of Commons virtually simultaneously. This was more radical than the Halsbury bill, and indeed the eventual Act passed in 1986, seeking, among other things, to prohibit animal testing that was not relevant to human health and to specify how animals were to be cared for in the laboratory environment. The Home Office opposed the bill on the same grounds as they had done with the Halsbury bill, that, in the words of Timothy Raison, a junior Home Office minister, 'it does not... achieve a balance that would be generally acceptable'.[22]

As a result of the Halsbury bill's failure (it passed all of its stages in the Lords but time ran out before it could be considered in the Commons), reform was still on the agenda but the RDS appears to have found itself increasingly marginalized, arguably paying the price of failing to reach consensus with the government on a bill which would be accepted by the widest number of participants. As a result, it was the CRAE which became the reasonable party, willing to negotiate and find a consensus. By contrast, as the backbencher Hugh Jenkins pointed out in the Commons in 1977, the RDS had become 'hostile and not constructive'. Those who sought to defend the status quo, he continued: 'with astonishing passion, even virulence – who pretend that closer supervision of what is going on in some fields constitutes a total rejection of all research – seem to me to be verging on the irrational'.[23] It would take until 1983 for the government to issue a White Paper on the subject and even then this fell by the wayside because of the general election. It was not until Mellor was given responsibility for legislation that reform was assured, and only then after a supplementary White Paper was issued in May 1985.[24]

1986 ANIMALS (SCIENTIFIC PROCEDURES) ACT

The long-awaited reform finally reached the statute book, as the Animals (Scientific Procedures) Act, in 1986 and by the summer of 1989 all scientific procedures were covered by project licences issued under the Act. The key differences from the 1876 Cruelty to Animals Act are discussed in more detail below but, in brief, the Act introduced a dual licensing system whereby researchers would have to apply for a personal licence (reviewed every five years) and a project licence permitting particular procedures. In addition, the legislation created a statutory Animal Procedures Committee (APC), previously recommended by Littlewood in the 1960s, with provision for the representation of animal advocates. Finally, as had also been suggested by Littlewood, animal breeders and suppliers were, by 1 January 1990, to register and be subject to inspection under the legislation.

There are a number of points worth making about the nature of this statute and the process which brought it about. In the first place, the more moderate sections of the animal protection movement played a central role in the formulation and passage of the legislation. If one criterion for judging the success of a challenging group is the degree to which it is accepted as 'a valid spokesman for a legitimate set of interests' involving consultation, negotiations, formal recognition and inclusion,[25] then it is clear success had been achieved by the mid-1980s. In the first place, many of the proposals which formed the basis of the bill were modelled on the recommendations of the advice given to the Home Secretary by the advisory committee, part of the membership of which – including Clive Hollands, Michael Balls (FRAME), T. Field-Fisher (legal adviser to the RSPCA) and Judith Hampson (RSPCA) – was drawn from the animal welfare community. Moreover, an Alliance of CRAE, FRAME and the BVA built upon its initial forays into high politics. Thus the CRAE Alliance published, in March 1983, proposals for new legislation which, the initial White Paper acknowledged, played an important role in the government proposals.[26] As Lord Houghton pointed out, then, 'some of us have had special privileges in consulting with the Home Secretary and his Ministers on the structure of this Bill'.[27]

It is obviously not being claimed here that the research community had no influence in the drawing up of the proposals. No acknowledgement was given to scientific bodies in the first White Paper although in the Supplementary White Paper it was stated that: 'We have also kept in close touch with . . . the Research Defence Society and a large number of other bodies in the scientific community'.[28] Furthermore, the Supplementary White Paper included, unlike the first, a section on the scientific and medical benefits of animal experimentation and granted two important concessions, introducing a proposal to apply legal sanctions against unlawful disclosure of information made available during the administration of the legislation (section 24 in the 1986 Act) and making provision for representation against the refusal or revocation of a personal or project licence (section 12).[29]

Despite these concessions to the research community, there is no question that a great effort was made to ensure that a balancing of interests took place throughout the process. To this end, during the formulation and passage of the bill, the CRAE Alliance was granted considerable access to the Home Office. Indeed, the evidence suggests that David Mellor, the junior Minister responsible for piloting the legislation through the Commons, was particularly reliant on the advice of the Alliance, principally Houghton, Hollands, Balls and David Morton.[30] Significantly, the bill sailed through its parliamentary stages virtually unscathed. During the committee stage in the Commons, the main opposition came from those MPs who did not think the bill had gone far enough.[31] Before the start of each committee session, Mellor consulted with CRAE representatives to discuss amendments and their position on them.[32]

Another crucial point to make here is Mellor's own commitment to reforming the law, without which the animal protection

movement might have been more disappointed than it subsequently was. A cynic might say that his commitment to getting
the measure on the statute book was more to do with advancing
his career than his interest in animal welfare. This might be
somewhat disingenuous. He had, for instance, shown some
concern earlier when, as a backbencher in 1979, he had criticized his own government for delaying the introduction of a
reforming measure. Moreover, Mellor openly supported Fry's
bill, not least as a means of influencing the outcome of European
deliberations.[33] Whatever his motives, however, Mellor's central
role is not in dispute and was commented upon by others. Janet
Fookes, the Conservative MP and a senior member of the
RSPCA Council, for instance, commented during the second
reading debate in 1986 that: 'I suspect that had it not been for the
personal commitment and drive of the Under-Secretary of State
we should not be debating the Second Reading tonight.'[34] Similarly, Lord Glenarthur, the Home Office minister responsible
for piloting the bill through the Lords, described Mellor as the
'vital catalyst for change'.[35]

Secondly, what is striking about the government's pronouncements on the legislation is their perpetual search for
balance and consensus. CRAE, of course, was granted access in
the first place because of its recognition that the Home Office
had to reach consensus with conflicting interests. Mellor himself
went out of his way in the Commons to praise the CRAE Alliance's contribution and particularly Clive Hollands 'for whom I
have a great admiration'. Despite being an anti-vivisectionist,
Mellor continued, Hollands 'has been brave in recognizing that
the best should never be the enemy of the good, and who ... has
striven to make the bill achieve the consensus that it has
achieved'.[36] The incorporation of animal protection interests
was symbolized by the granting to Hollands of an OBE some
years later in the 1995 honours list.

Involving a part of the animal protection movement in the
formulation of the bill was essential if consensus was to be
achieved. Richard Ryder recalls how Mellor, in the light of the
RSPCA's hostility to the government's proposals, took the 'unprecedented [and ultimately unsuccessful] step' of attending the
organization's Council meeting in order to try to get their consent.[37] Nevertheless, if the co-operation of the moderates he already had on board was to be guaranteed and maintained, the

Government had to pay some price in terms of policy concessions.[38] The dangers of losing this good-will was ever present.
One illustration of this concerned the issue of re-using animals
already subject to a procedure. The first White Paper allowed re-
use but this was subsequently omitted from the Supplementary
White Paper as a result of pressure from CRAE and attacks from
the anti-vivisection movement. In the report stage in the Lords,[39]
the government, at the behest of peers supporting the research
community, introduced an amendment allowing re-use. Houghton was furious, not least because he had received an undertaking from Home Office ministers that no such amendment
would be introduced, and threatened to remove CRAE's support
from the legislation, or, at the very least, force a vote on the
issue.[40] As a result, the government, recognizing that it had to
keep CRAE on board, withdrew the amendment.

The issue arose again during the committee stage of the bill in
the Commons. A similar amendment permitting re-use was introduced by MPs supportive of the research community. As with
the government spokesman in the Lords, Mellor was anxious
that if the concern expressed by 'my closest advisers', and in
particular Clive Hollands, was not listened to, it would damage
the consensus reached.[41] Patrick Nicholls, a Conservative
member of the committee spelt this out clearly:

> People [meaning animal rights groups that opposed the bill]
> have said that the BVA, the CRAE and FRAME are either
> dupes or are co-operating with the Government in some kind
> of conspiracy. We have been able to repel those allegations so
> far. What concerns me is whether we would still be able to do
> so if we passed the amendment.[42]

In the event, Mellor abstained on the vote, which was passed by
nine votes to seven (a vote which was confirmed at third reading)
and he gave an assurance that re-use would only be allowed by
the express consent of the secretary of state, who would insist
upon rigorous conditions – relating, for instance, to the time
allowed between the first and second procedure – being applied.[43]

Two particular clauses in the Act represented a significant
improvement on its predecessor and it seems likely that both
came about as concessions to the CRAE Alliance. The first

concerned the creation of a new statutory Animal Procedures
Committee (APC) to replace the advisory committee. Unlike its
predecessor, the reports of the APC are in the public domain,
providing for the greater accountability of those responsible for
administering the legislation. In the first White Paper there was
no specific requirement that animal welfare interests should be
represented on the APC nor was there any limitation on the
number of members who could hold licenses under the Act.
Instead, it was merely stated that the APC will consist 'of a
Chairman and not more than 12 members, two-thirds of whom
will be drawn from medicine, veterinary science and other bio-
logical sciences'.[44] In the Supplementary White Paper one of the
above weaknesses, from an animal protection perspective, was
dealt with when an additional clause was added requiring not
more than half of the APC's members to be current or recent
licence holders.[45] The second weakness was partly dealt with
when a government amendment was added at the report stage
(Section 19, clause 3 of the Act) stating that 'in making ap-
pointments to the Committee the Secretary of State shall have
regard to the desirability of ensuring that the interests of animal
welfare are adequately represented' (see below for a more detailed examination of the APC's role).

The second clause in the legislation which appears to have
been a concession to the animal protection movement concerns
the use of severity bandings and a cost–benefit clause. This was
included in the Supplementary White Paper with specific reference to its advocacy by the CRAE Alliance in their comments
on the initial White Paper.[46] When making an application for a
project licence, each researcher has to provide information on
the level of suffering – either mild, moderate or substantial – that
a particular procedure is intending to inflict. Together with information on the proposed benefits of the research, the Home
Office inspectorate are supposed to weigh up the costs and
benefits of each application before deciding whether to grant a
licence. Section 5, sub-section 4 of the Act spells this out:

> In determining whether and on what terms to grant a project
> licence the Secretary of State shall weigh the likely adverse
> effects on the animals concerned against the benefit likely to
> accrue as a result of the programme to be specified in the li-
> cence.

This cost–benefit clause represents a compromise, a half-way house between a complete prohibition on the infliction of pain – the position of the RSPCA and, ultimately, what CRAE would have liked – and no restriction on the suffering that can be inflicted – a position realised by the granting of a certificate under the 1876 legislation (although, in practice, since the 1920s, Home Office inspectors have, following the adoption of the 1906–12 Royal Commission recommendation, imposed the so-called 'pain condition' whereby severe and enduring pain had to be alleviated, at least if the main result of the enquiry had been attained). Even though Home Office inspectors could have (and claimed that they had) denied certificates required under the 1876 Act on the grounds that the benefits of the research did not justify the suffering that researchers intended to inflict, the Littlewood Report suggested otherwise when it commented that the Home Office was not 'concerned to assess the potential value of proposed research or the results of past research' but was only concerned to make sure the right certificates were being applied for.[47]

TEN YEARS ON – HAVE THE ANIMALS BENEFITED?

It is over 10 years since the Animals (Scientific Procedures) Act received its Royal Assent and it is worth while asking, with the benefit of some hindsight, how far, if at all, research animals have benefited from the legislation. The first point that needs making here is that, while this chapter has emphasized the growing importance of the animal protection movement as an accepted participant in the political process, it is true that this participation was conditional upon working within an ideological consensus which was still basically pro-animal research. Thus, at no time did the government give the impression that it thought animal research in general, or indeed particular types of animal research, should cease. Those animal rights groups that disputed that position were effectively excluded from the decision-making arena, and, on the whole, wished to be so excluded.

An aspect of this ideological consensus which should be emphasized is that one way of viewing the 1986 legislation, and its predecessor, is its role in protecting animal researchers and allowing for the continuation of animal research. Thus, without some legislative framework permitting painful procedures to be carried out on laboratory animals, researchers would be liable to prosecution under general anti-cruelty statutes. This was recognized by the House of Lords select committee examining the Halsbury bill when it pointed out that legislation in this area 'provided the means of warranting, in law and public policy, the doing of things which would, or might, otherwise be punishable as cruelty'.[48] The research community supported legislative controls precisely because of this.[49]

Nevertheless, even though the importance of this ideological consensus as a form of power benefiting those with a vested interest in continuing to use animals should not be ignored, it should also be recognized that there are signs that the dominance of the pro-vivisection ideology has shown signs of weakening. The fact that many welfare issues concerning the use of animals in research have been raised at the centre of the policy arena is an indication of this. Significantly, these welfare issues include abolitionist themes. Thus, prohibiting the use of animals for testing the toxicity of cosmetic products and in military research are very much on the political agenda on the grounds that they are unnecessary. In addition, even though medical research is still generally regarded as necessary because of the human benefits allegedly accruing, there is now a greater reluctance to accept the need for, particularly severe, suffering to be inflicted on animals and a greater scepticism about the efficacy of animal research. In this context, it should be noted that much of the campaigning of the modern anti-vivisection movement consists not so much in challenging the morality of animal research but in trying to show either that it does not produce the benefits claimed for it or that such work would be redundant if human lifestyles and environments changed.[50] Mary Ann Elston, for one, has argued that it was this relatively recent challenge to the utility of animal research which was especially worrying to the scientific community and precipitated the public campaigns they began to promote in the 1980s (see Chapter 2).[51]

At this point, the work of the APC is worth commenting upon in more detail. It is true that, as with the FAWC and the IACUCs in the United States, those who are not prepared to accept, even for the sake of negotiation, that some animal research would have to be allowed, have been excluded from the committee. It is also true, as we have seen, that the research community is well represented on the APC.[52] Typically, only about 20 per cent (4 out of 20 or so) of APC members can be regarded as animal welfarists with, perhaps, one or two others with animal welfare sympathies (see Table 9.1).

Nevertheless, as with the FAWC, the animal advocates on the committee have been figures of real stature and, in some cases, they can be regarded as radicals too. We have already had cause to comment on Clive Hollands. Worth mentioning too are Tony Suckling, the Scientific Director of the RSPCA and with the added credibility of someone with a science background, and Cindy Milburn, a lobbyist for WSPA and a well-known campaigner. It should be pointed out here, too, that animal welfare representation was by no means assured. As late as the 1970s, for instance, the British Pharmacological Society was arguing that the members of the advisory committee should be chosen from a list of people nominated by scientific bodies.[53] Seen in this context, the addition of a specific statutory requirement effectively guaranteeing the representation of animal welfare interests should be regarded as a victory for animal advocates and another example of the government's desire to reach a consensus.

Of course, the APC, even in its short existence, has not been standing still. Important changes to the regulations have come about as a result of APC recommendations and, because the committee's reports are in the public domain, it is much more difficult for the Home Secretary to reject them (see below). Important administrative changes not requiring legislation have involved the APC taking on extra responsibilities. In particular, not only does the committee examine all cosmetic and tobacco project applications but it also now receives information on all new project licences which allow for the use of non-human primates, and all project applications requiring the use of wild-caught, non-human primates must be referred to the APC before a decision is taken. Moreover, it is also consulted about all licence applications involving procedures of substantial severity before a decision is taken.[54] Worth mentioning here too is the introduction, from 1 April 1994, of a mandatory training programme for those holding, or intending to hold, personal licences. Interestingly, the training course does not just include technical material on animal husbandry, but also involves modules on the historical background to legislation, the

Table 9.1   Animal Procedures Committee: membership as at 31
December 1994

Professor Margaret Brazier (Chairman), Professor of Law, University
of Manchester

Professor Ronald S. Anderson, Professor of Animal Husbandry,
University of Liverpool

Professor Michael Balls, Head of the European Centre for the
Validation of Alternative Methods; Chairman of the Trustees of the
Fund for the Replacement of Animals in Medical Experiments

Edward Bernard, Chairman, Seotec Ltd

Professor Margaret Boden, Professor of Philosophy and Psychology,
University of Sussex

Professor Barry Bridges, formerly Director, Medical Research Unit,
Queen's University, Belfast

Professor Fiona Broughton Pipkin, Professor of Perinatal Physiology,
University of Nottingham

Dr David Christopher, Director of Laboratory Sciences, Huntingdon
Research Centre

Dr Yvonne Cripps, Reader and Director of Studies in Law, Emmanuel
College, Cambridge

Professor Anthony Dayan, Professor of Toxicology, St Bartholomew's
Hospital Medical College, London

Roger Ewbank, Director of the Universities Federation for Animal
Welfare

Dr John Flack, Director of Pharmaceutical Sciences, Corning
Hazleton, Harrogate

Dr Paul Flecknell, Director, Comparative Biology Centre, the Medical
School, University of Newcastle

Clive Hollands, Secretary to the Committee for the Reform of Animal
Experimentation

Sir Andrew Huxley, formerly President of the Royal Society and
Professor of Physiology at University College, London

Professor Susan Iversen, Professor and Head of Department of
Experimental Psychology, Oxford University

Judy Macarthur Clark, recent past President, Royal College of
Veterinary Surgeons

Dr Iain Purchase, Director Central Toxicology Laboratories, Zeneca

Professor Lord Soulsby, formerly Professor of Animal Pathology,
University of Cambridge

Professor Michael Spyer, Professor of Physiology, University College,
London

Dr Anthony Suckling, Director of Scientific Affairs, RSPCA

Source: *Report of the Animal Procedures Committee for 1994*, pp. iv–v.

requirements of the 1986 Act and, most importantly of all, ethical aspects of animal use.[55]

Recently, moreover, there is evidence that, under the present chairmanship of Margaret Brazier – a law professor at Manchester University – the APC has begun to adopt a much more pro-animal point of view (see below for more on this). This could have a significant effect on the general drift of the animal research debate. Unlike its predecessor, the APC is a statutory body whose opinions are a matter of public record. Furthermore, it is much closer to the centre of decision-making than the FAWC has been. As such, it provides a very useful contact point for the animal protection movement. As Houghton commented in 1980, the lack of an adequate vehicle for the complaints and grievances of animal advocates had forced:

> animal welfare organizations into propaganda, into lobbying and, some of them, into violence because there had been nowhere for them to go, no repository for their sense of frustration. This is highly emotive and has a profound significance for the point of view of social contentment...Shut these people out and they will bang at the gates.[56]

Now, they do not need to 'bang at the gates'. As the APC report for 1994 revealed: 'We received regular reports of campaigns mounted by anti-vivisectionist groups, together with copies of reports prepared by these groups about particular aspects of research'[57] (see below for the response of the APC and the regulatory system in general to particular campaigns mounted by anti-vivisection organizations).

In assessing the impact of the legislative and administrative framework deriving from the 1986 Act in general, it should be said initially that not even the moderates in the animal protection movement would claim that the legislation and its enforcement cannot be improved. Critics of the legislation point to the fact that even the research community has generally supported it. The RDS, for instance, has regularly made the claim that the legislation would not stop researchers from doing anything they already did.[58] It is true that the legislation does not prohibit any particular procedure and this, it might be argued, gives too much power to the Home Office inspectorate who themselves are generally sympathetic to the use of animals in research. Equally importantly, the secrecy surrounding the administrative machinery makes it very difficult, as we shall see below, to assess the effectiveness of the legislation.

To a certain extent, on the other hand, we should not take the research community's response at face value. No group likes to lose a battle, and there is no question that the RDS, as previously stated, did find itself somewhat marginalized in the 1980s. Moreover, although the Act does not prohibit any particular procedures, an element of public accountability has been introduced through the work of the APC. Indeed, it is public knowledge that the APC has rejected some applications seeking to use animals for tobacco and cosmetic tests (see below). Furthermore, the RDS did lobby its supporters in parliament to raise objections about the cost-benefit clause but they quickly realised that the government was not going to change its mind. The same applied to amendments, introduced by Lord Adrian – the RDS spokesman in the Lords – to exclude decerebrated animals from coverage under the Act; to include secondary schools as possible holders of licences; and to prevent those who are opposed to animal research from being members of the APC.[59]

Unlike the farm animal welfare policy network in Britain, the division of influence within the policy arena dealing with animal research is much more balanced, and, because of this, Home Office Ministers are much more likely to be influenced by the demands of the animal protection movement than their colleagues in MAFF are. This point was eloquently noted by Houghton who, in one of the closing speeches on the bill in the Lords, said:

> although the Bill prohibits little, it controls everything. How that control is to be exercised is in the Bill; the criteria to be observed in permitting what is to be done are in the Bill, too. What is not prohibited by law under the Bill may nevertheless be curbed, curtailed or even stopped if the Home Secretary decides to use his powers under the Bill.[60]

THE THREE Rs

In attempting to assess how far research animals have benefited so far from the new legislative framework, it is useful to utilize the 'three Rs' approach first suggested in the 1950s.[61] This allows us to make judgements in terms of whether fewer animals are now used (reduction), whether the severity of procedures has been, on average, reduced (refinement), and, finally, the degree to which the development of alternatives to the use of animals have been encouraged (replacement).

Reduction and Refinement

It is true, firstly, that, as Table 9.2 reveals, the number of animals used in scientific procedures has gradually decreased in Britain. In 1987, 3.6 million scientific procedures were started which represented the 11th successive annual fall. Indeed, this figure represents just over half of the number of procedures started a decade earlier. Between 1987 and 1994, there has been a more moderate drop in the number of animals used and the figure now stands at below three million. It is impossible to determine accurately how far the legislation is responsible for this, however, since no details of specific licence applications, and the decisions made on them, exist. Clive Hollands, an insider who served on the APC during the initial years of the new legislation, does argue that 'a major factor' in this decline 'has been, without doubt, a more careful appraisal of project licence applications by the Home Office'.[62] Against this, there are plenty of explana-

Table 9.2   Scientific procedures, 1987–94

	No. of procedures (m.)	No. of project licences	Designated places
1987	3.6	1293	–
1988	3.5	2132	375
1989	3.3	991	375
1990	3.2	4427	381*
1991	3.2	716	363
1992	2.9	1312	358
1993	2.8	1477	345
1994	2.8	1024	338

* The statistics from 1990 include breeding and supply establishments.
Source: *Statistics of Scientific Procedures on Living Animals* (HMSO, 1987–94).

tions, not related to the legislation – the decline in research funds, the expense of buying animals, economic recession and so forth – why the number of procedures has gone down.

In a sense, the raw figures on the number of animals used may not be the best criteria to adopt in an assessment of the present state of animal research. At least two additional factors need to be added to the equation, both of which relate to the refinement of animal experimentation. The first of these concerns what is done to animals in the laboratory and the second concerns the species used. Utilizing many more animals in procedures which either cause little pain, discomfort or stress, or for painful procedures where anaesthetics are used throughout, is clearly preferable to using fewer animals where a great deal of suffering is inflicted. Likewise, in terms of species, using non-human primates raises far more serious welfare, and therefore ethical, problems than, say, rats or mice.

The 1986 Act now provides us with some information on the severity of the procedures carried out, since all licence applicants have to document whether the procedures they intend conducting are likely to cause mild, moderate or substantial suffering. This information, for those applications authorized, is provided in Table 9.3. These figures reveal that substantial suffering is only involved in a relatively small number of procedures although there is a worryingly large number which are classified as moderate. In addition, there is no evidence of a downward trend in the most severe procedures which does not suggest that such research is being more critically examined by the inspectorate.

In reality, there are some severe problems with interpreting this information because determining what level of suffering is involved is, to some degree, a subjective exercise and, in addition, any individual project licence may involve the infliction of varying levels of suffering. The Home Office's procedure for assessing the severity banding within which each project licence should be placed is based upon the number of animals used, the proportion of these animals which may be expected to be exposed to the upper limit of severity and the duration of these adverse effects upon the animals. The consequence of this is that a project which is assessed overall as being in the mild or moderate category may involve some procedures which are assessed as being in the severe category. Likewise, a project clas-

Table 9.3   Animal suffering in UK scientific procedures, 1987–93

	Mild	Moderate	Substantial
1987	570	629	23
1988	864	1087	47
1989	451	456	16
1990*	1832	2155	103
1991	349	317	15
1992	563	642	36
1993	629	758	21

* The figures for 1990 include the total project licences in force in that year rather, as with the other figures, those project licences issued during the year. The figures for 1994 were not available.
Source: *Reports of the Animal Procedures Committee, 1987–93.*

sified overall as severe may involve some procedures which are mild or moderate. In general, a project is assessed as of substantial severity if a third or more of the animals seem likely to suffer such effects.[63]

In terms of the species used, the APC has again had an impact. In 1992, for instance, the committee recommended that the octopus be included within the terms of the Act and this was accepted by the Home Secretary.[64] More significantly, two years later the APC recommended that researchers intending to use non-human primates should have to provide special justification and that the use of wild-caught, non-human primates be banned 'except where a project licence applicant can establish exceptional and specific justification'. This, again, has now been put into practice along with the provision that all applications seeking such an exception be referred to the APC.[65]

Another essential ingredient of an animal research regulatory body is, of course, the purpose for which animals are being used. Questions relating to the degree of suffering inflicted and the species used, therefore, should be examined in conjunction with the purported aim of the 1986 Act to balance the costs of animal research against the benefits likely to accrue. There have clearly been problems with operationalizing the cost–benefit clause in the 1986 Act and the consensus seems to be that the Home Office has not yet arrived at an adequate criteria for so doing. As a result, 'there are many cases where the burden of suffering borne by the animals is far too great in comparison with the likely benefits of the research'.[66]

It is the case too that, to some degree, a version of cost–benefit analysis has always, it seems, been utilized by those administering the law, whether under the 1876 or 1986 legislation. A Home Office official giving evidence to the House of Lords committee on the Halsbury bill, for instance, pointed out that the inspectorate and the advisory committee did turn down applications on the grounds that they were not considered to be worth while or involved too much pain (although the Littlewood Report did suggest that this was not the primary function of inspectors – see above).[67] Even if such a cost–benefit analysis had been used prior to 1986, however, it is useful for this requirement to be enshrined in law, not least because it focuses the minds of those responsible for licensing project applications.

The most controversial area of animal use is for those purposes – military research and the testing of household products and cosmetics – deemed by many to be trivial and unnecessary. As we saw, opponents of the 1986 Act were particularly critical of its failure to prohibit such procedures. As a compromise, it was decided that all applications relating to cosmetics testing and research involving tobacco would be referred to the APC. The annual reports of the APC reveal that relatively few such applications have been received (one or two a year). Indeed, at any one time, few project licences are held for these purposes, six, for instance, being held in 1989 authorizing the testing of cosmetics on animals. Most, but not all, applications have been authorized but usually only after substantial modifications were made. The reports do make clear that some members of the Committee (presumably from amongst the animal welfare representatives) were opposed to all applications involving tobacco and cosmetics, and sometimes their views have prevailed. In the 1988 report, for instance, it was revealed that one application for a project licence involving tobacco was referred to the Independent Committee on Smoking and Health within the Department of Health before being 'subsequently withdrawn'.[68] It should also be pointed out that examining the APC's response to specific applications, of course, may not give us a total picture because what we do not know is to what extent potential applicants may have been deterred from applying because they suspected they would be denied authorization.

There is some evidence, as noted above, that Margaret Brazier's term as Chairman of the APC is producing a more hardhitting approach. The 1994 report contains an interesting introductory section in which Brazier contemplates whether, in determining the necessity of a particular procedure, more attention should be placed upon the need society has for the product being tested. Seemingly answering the rhetorical question in the affirmative, she concludes by saying that: 'We recognize that the Committee ... exists to reflect public opinion on the proper boundaries of animal research'.[69]

Replacement

The development of alternatives to the use of animals in scientific procedures is perhaps the area where least has been achieved. From its inception, the APC was made responsible for allocating research money but it has regularly complained about the Home Office's failure to provide enough funds. Indeed, for at least one member of the APC this almost became a resignation issue. Thus, in 1988, 124 applications for funding were received but only £70 000 was allocated and only four proposals were chosen for funding.[70] By 1990, the money available had increased, to £122 000, but this was later in the year cut back as a result of general Home Office financial stringency. This led the APC to write a letter to the Home Secretary expressing 'grave concern' about the limited funds. 'Failure to make adequate funds available', the letter continued: 'inevitably casts doubt over the Government's commitment to the fundamental principle of the Act that non-animal alternatives are to be preferred to the use of living animals.'[71] This strongly worded letter seems to have had some impact as the funding made available was subsequently increased, to £215 000 in 1991, £253 000 in 1992 and £273 000 in 1994.

The prospects for alternatives to animal use do not, of course, stand or fall by the funding available from the Home Office. At the European level, for instance ECVAM or the European Centre for the Validation of Alternative Methods was created for this specific function and many individual academics are involved in the search for alternatives. As FRAME have argued, however, 'the Act itself has rarely been used as the stimulus for such research [and] we are left with the feeling that the main effect of the Act has often been to permit the continuation of what was done before, albeit with higher standards of experimental work and of animal care'.[72]

ENFORCEMENT

A final, and crucial, issue we need to touch upon is that of enforcement. As with farm animal welfare, the enforcement mechanism designed to police the 1986 Act has been regularly criticized by animal advocates. These criticisms tend to focus on the inadequate number of inspectors and the alleged pro-animal research bias of those who conduct them.[73] The first of these is more straightforward. The size of the inspectorate, as revealed in Table 9.4, has gradually increased (three to four in the inter-war years, eight by 1964, 14 by 1973, 16 by 1979) and, at around 20, is greater now than it has ever been. This growth has not, however, kept pace with the increasing number of animals used nor the number of designated sites. The Littlewood Report concluded that the inspectorate had been 'undermanned' and that the 'establishment of twenty-one inspectors is the minimum required whether or not the law is reformed as we suggest'.[74] If this is an accurate assessment then the present position is barely adequate.

The size of the inspectorate can be related to the second criticism mentioned above. In the wake of the Medical Research Council's findings in the Feldburg case (see below) which resulted in blame being attached to the Home Office, the Home Office declared that the aim of the inspectorate is not to police the Act but to offer advice and information.[75] This may explain why the number of site visits declined significantly between 1987 and 1994 (see Table 9.4). While advice and information is obviously crucial, and the creation and maintenance of a viable working relationship between the regulated and the regulator is hindered by too much coercion, the implication – that all researchers will automatically conform to the legislation and the specific conditions of their licences – is not backed up by the evidence. Indeed, the APC has regularly berated licence-holders for their failure to understand the system of controls created by the legislation. In the 1991 report, for instance, the committee relayed their 'continuing cause for concern' about researchers' 'singular

Table 9.4   Enforcement under the 1986 Animals (Scientific Procedures) Act, 1987–94

	Infringements	Licences revoked	Inspectorate	Visits
1987	9	1	19	8302
1988	20	2	19	7640
1989	14	1	18	6681
1990	14	4	19	2829
1991	13	22	19	2933
1992	11	4	21	3299
1993	12	1	20	2984
1994	13	13	19	2726

Sources: *Statistics of Scientific Procedures on Living Animals*, (HMSO, 1987–94); *Reports of the Animal Procedures Committee, 1987–94.*

lack of understanding of the importance of the controls'. A symbol of this has been the regular failure of many licence-holders to ensure their returns, detailing what they had done in the previous year, were sent on time or even at all. Thus, in 1991, no less than 20 project licences were revoked as a result of the non-appearance of the holder's returns. This reflected, according to the APC, 'a disturbing disregard . . . for the condition attached to the project licence'.[76] This problem was clearly still evident three years later when the 1993 statistics were not published until January 1995 partly because of the late arrival of some returns.

Another apparent illustration of the effects of undermanning and an ideology of self-policing are the serious infringements of the legislation which the inspectorate have not picked up. Four cases, in particular – involving Professor Wilhelm Feldberg, a 70-year-old researcher working at the Medical Research Council's Institute for Medical research, Shamrock (Great Britain) Ltd, Hazleton UK, and Wickham Research Laboratories – revealed illegal animal abuse, and yet were all drawn to the attention of the regulators by animal protection organizations that had mounted investigations of their own.

In one sense, these cases illustrated the value of the new system in that, once informed, the Home Office did take action against the parties who had infringed the law and the APC played a full role in the response. In the Feldberg case, for instance, the APC recommended that holders of personal licences over retirement age should be scrutinized very closely and Feldberg's licence was revoked.[77] Likewise, in the Wickham case, the APC 'welcomed the decision by the Home Office to discuss some of the issues raised fully with representatives of the BUAV'.[78] Indeed, the BUAV had their first formal meeting with Home Office officials as a result of the Shamrock and Wickham cases.[79] There is no reason why animal advocates should not continue to play a full role in the administration of the legislation and the Home Office's willingness to treat their representations in a positive manner can only be regarded as a positive development, even if the department's response to allegations by anti-vivisection groups is not always regarded in a favourable light by the complainants.[80]

Against this, however, is the obvious point that concern should be expressed that the documented abuses were not uncovered by the Home Office inspectorate. This can only lead to suspicions that some have gone, and will continue to go, unchecked. This is clearly not acceptable. Furthermore, there is also doubt about the adequacy of the penalties imposed for infringements of the legislation. As far as I am aware, only one case since 1986 – involving a commercial rabbit breeder who sold animals for scientific procedures despite not being a designated establishment – has resulted in a successful prosecution, and there have been very few other cases where papers were passed to the Director of Public Prosecutions, who then decided not to act. The usual Home Office response is to remove licences or demand changes in facilities where infringements have been identified. While, in some cases, this is appropriate, and it should be remembered that the removal of licences can have a severe impact on a researcher's career, the failure to take legal action in some cases does give the impression that the Home Office, and, indeed, society itself, does not take animal abuse in the laboratory seriously enough. The APC has, from time to time, expressed disappointment that more serious action was not taken against infringements of the law and, in 1991, made the general point that it was 'increasingly of the view that those who [even inadvertently] breach these controls should expect to be more harshly dealt with'.[81]

We have seen in this chapter how the animal protection movement came from nowhere to play a central role in the formulation, passage and administration of the 1986 Animals (Scientific Procedures) Act. The response of governmental actors to growing public concern about animal experimentation and the privileged position granted to a section of the animal protection movement, tends to reveal that the policy community model is not applicable to this policy arena. The subsequent working of the new legislation has left a great deal to be desired but far and away the most positive development has been the greater accountability facilitated, in particular, by the work of the APC. The responsiveness of the policy network means that public pressure may well lead to further restrictions on animal research in the future.

10 The Politics of Animal Research in the United States

In many ways, the animal research policy arena in the United States is the most difficult to describe and evaluate. It is clearly the case that since the 1960s Congress has responded to intermittent bouts of public pressure and that, superficially at least, the legislative protection afforded to research animals is better than it was. The range of institutions and actors involved in the animal research decision-making process would also suggest the existence of a pluralistic issue network rather than a closed policy community. What this chapter will seek to show, however, is that this very pluralistic structure has appeared, more often than not, to blunt the edges of reform thereby thwarting the will of Congress and a concerned public.

PUBLIC PRESSURE AND CONGRESSIONAL ACTION

The animal protection debate in the United States has tended to centre on the issue of animal research. The sheer volume of animals used, the sometimes severe suffering inflicted and, at least in contrast to animal agriculture, the ease with which animal advocates are able to provide information for public consumption, has ensured the issue a greater prominence than it has achieved anywhere else.[1] Significantly, Congressional action, in passing the original Laboratory Animal Welfare Act in 1966 and its subsequent amendments, has followed periods of heightened public concern.

LABORATORY ANIMAL WELFARE ACT 1966

As in Britain, anti-vivisection organizations in the USA emerged in the nineteenth century, but there was never the same level of public protest or chance of governmental action as had occurred on the other side of the Atlantic. Instead, despite the opposition of the powerful Hearst press, animal research was regarded, at least by those who bothered to think about it at all, as an essential part of scientific research which developed enormous prestige in the twentieth century.[2]

The first federal legislation affecting the use of animals in research was passed in 1966. This statute, designed to control the trade in laboratory animals, came about as a result of unprecedented public pressure following media stories (one of which was featured as the cover story of *Life* magazine in February 1966) revealing the deplorable conditions in which some dealers were keeping animals destined to be sold to research laboratories. The fact that there was also evidence that some animals sold to laboratories were stolen pets added to the public uproar. Indeed, it was said that members of Congress received more mail on this issue than on civil rights or the Vietnam War.[3] The two Congressional committees concerned with the issue (House Agriculture, Senate Commerce) received 80 000 letters between them on this issue between July 1965 and July 1966.[4] As we saw in Chapter 1, the legislation passed did not, in effect, regulate the use or even the care of animals in the laboratory but primarily the process whereby animals arrived in laboratories.

What was significant about the success of the legislation was that it was won in the teeth of opposition from the research community. From the early 1960s, a number of bills were introduced, largely at the behest of Christine Stevens. Most of these sought to control the conduct of scientific procedures, using the British legislation as a model. All of them failed to get beyond the committee stage. The US research community opposed them all as unnecessary and damaging, and the participation of British scientists in Congressional hearings supporting reform along the lines of the 1876 Act only served to bring an element of jingoism into the deliberations with American researchers pointing out that the great scientific advances had come from the USA and not from Britain.[5] At one sub-committee hearing in 1965, the vice-president of the British Royal College of Surgeons commented that: 'We do not commit the atrocities which are reported from time to time in some other countries', after which the chairman of the committee – to whom, as Christine Stevens pointed out, 'a word from NIH was law' – decided to cancel the hearing and refuse to allow the proceedings up to that point to be published.[6]

The public uproar caused by media coverage of the behaviour of some dealers and the animal suffering which resulted from it led to the introduction of numerous bills (the first by Representative Joseph Resnick in 1965) and the holding of a number of Congressional hearings. Thus, the hearing held in March 1966 lists no less than 31 bills on the topic. While the research community did not oppose attempts to deal with the problem of pet theft, they did want all references to research facilities removed so that they did not have to be registered or keep records on the origins of the animals used. Not surprisingly, too, they opposed USDA being given responsibility for regulation. The National Society for Medical Research argued that:

> It would seem contrary to public policy to have two federal executive agencies charged with duplicating the same functions. Since the Department of Health, Education and Welfare [now Health and Human Services] is more concerned than is Agriculture with support of research and teaching that involves the use of most laboratory animals it would appear that HEW would be the more appropriate agency to determine systems of inspection and accreditation, and to promulgate appropriate standards.[7]

Such was the perceived influence of the research community that Helen Jones, then the President of the National Catholic Society for Animal Welfare and later the founder of the International Society for Animal Rights, urged, along with the leaders of HSUS and the AHA, the exclusion of laboratory registration on the grounds that it was necessary to 'report a bill with teeth that can begin the reform of dealers and not to weaken that effort by attempting, but failing, to regulate laboratories at the same time'.[8] Her pessimism proved to be misplaced.

Indeed, the final bill, far from being the least the animal protection movement could get, was something of a compromise. The bill that passed the House sought merely to license dealers and prescribe humane standards governing their treatment of the animals. The bill in the Senate – sponsored by Mike Monroney (Democrat–Oklahoma) not only sought to extend the coverage to other species but also contained a provision requiring the humane treatment of animals in research facilities before and after experimental procedures. The eventual statute did allow for the registration of research facilities but, as we saw, removed any effective means of regulating the care of animals in the laboratory. Documenting the passage of the bill at the time the *Congressional Quarterly Almanac* remarked that the research community and the, initially hostile, Johnson administration accepted the bill in the 'hope that enactment... would reduce public and Congressional interest in the subject and thus blunt... attempts by animal welfare groups to obtain much stronger legislation'.[9]

As a result of the 1966 legislation, a precedent had been set, that researchers working with animals could be subject to regulatory control. The very fact that the research community was being forced to argue its case was a significant development. The familiar argument, that legislation was unnecessary, became more difficult to maintain. In 1965, as a last desperate attempt to avoid it, an organization called the American Association for Accreditation of Laboratory Animal Care was set up by the NSMR and the AMA in order to show that animal welfare was being voluntarily upheld. The 1966 Act, then, was the essential forerunner to further controls established by subsequent amendments.

IMPROVED STANDARDS FOR LABORATORY ANIMALS ACT 1985

The 1985 amendment to the Animal Welfare Act represented the culmination of almost five years of general animal protection campaigning. It was the impact of two particular 'moral shocks', however, which graphically illustrated the need for reform. The first of these was the well-documented case involving the abuse of monkeys in Edward Taub's Silver Spring laboratory.[10] The abuse publicized by Alex Pacheco's undercover investigation came to light in 1981 and revealed, among other things, the failure of USDA's inspection programme. The affair drifted on for several years afterwards through Taub's conviction and his – successful – appeal, investigations by USDA and NIH, a Congressional hearing[11] (at which Alex Pacheco was invited to give evidence) and the long-drawn out process whereby the animal protection movement vied – unsuccessfully – with NIH for custody of the surviving monkeys. The affair was not only the catalyst for the growth of PETA but also received widespread publicity raising the care of laboratory animals as an issue of national prominence. NIH alone, for instance, was flooded with letters on this issue as were George and Barbara Bush.

Even worse was to follow for the research community in the shape of revelations of the mistreatment of baboons being used in Thomas Gennerelli's head-injury laboratory at the University of Pennsylvania.[12] In 1985, an ALF raid produced shocking video evidence of researchers mocking injured animals, using unsterilized equipment and even smoking while carrying out procedures. From the masses of video evidence collected, the most damning scenes were included on a 20-minute video called 'Unnecessary Fuss' (ironically described as the Watergate Tapes of the animal rights movement) which was shown in a special viewing to members of Congress[13] and repeatedly on network television. As the official journal of the American Association for the Advancement of Science commented, 'from a public relations standpoint' the effects of the video 'range from embarrassing to disastrous'.[14] The immediate repercussion was the intervention of Margaret Heckler, Secretary of the Department of Health and Human Services, who – only, it should be added, after a petition from members of Congress and a sit-in by animal advocates at NIH headquarters intensified the publicity (both the Washington Post and the New York Times supported the activists) and the government's embarrassment – ordered that the research funding for the research facility be suspended. The facility was eventually ordered to pay a $4000 fine.

In the long term, as a result of these two cases and the general increase in public consciousness of the issue,[15] the research community found itself on the defensive and it became extremely difficult to counter the demands for further legislative controls.[16] These cases did, however, force scientists out into the open. Their lobbying arm, as we saw in Chapter 2, was reorganized and individual scientists were encouraged to defend animal experimentation in the media, at public meetings and, from time to time, in court. The intensification of the research community's activities was not enough to prevent Congressional action. This occurred in the form of two Acts carried in 1985, the Health Research Extension Act relating to NIH's responsibilities and reforms to USDA's responsibilities under the Animal

Welfare Act in the form of the Improved Standards for Laboratory Animals Act.

There are a number of significant points about the passage of this legislation. In the first place, the research community fought it tooth and nail. The origins of the 1985 Act derive, in particular, from ideas developed by several animal advocates in Colorado and various reforming bills were introduced in Congress from the late 1970s onwards.[17] The research community opposed all of them and this played a significant part in the decision of a succession of committees to pigeon-hole them. In 1983, for instance, the research community was unhappy about several aspects of the bill – such as the provision to allow for lay representation on IACUCs – introduced by Senator John Melcher and their tactic was to suggest an alternative proposed by Senators Hatch and Kennedy (the Animal Welfare in Research Study Act of 1983) which, by proposing further study of the issues, was basically a delaying measure.[18]

Reform eventually came about as a result of an amendment to the 1985 Farm Bill introduced by Robert Dole, the Senate Majority Leader, on the Senate floor. Thus, the reforms constitute a tiny section (about six pages) of the Food Security Act, which ran to over 600 pages. The patronage of Dole here, along with the assistance of House Majority Whip, Tom Foley, at the Conference stage and Senator Melcher – who tabled an amendment in the Senate on the psychological well-being of primates – was crucial.[19] Equally important were the links that Christine Stevens had forged with Dole over a number of years.

Absolutely crucial, however, was the willingness of Congress as a whole to override the continued failure of Congressional committees to report out similar bills and support Dole's amendment. In the House, it is customary for a committee's decision not to report a bill to be respected by the chamber as a whole.[20] In the Senate, however, the rules permit legislation blocked in committee to be considered on the floor, although it is rare for this to happen. On this occasion, the willingness of Senate to consider Dole and Melcher's amendments, coupled with the success of the amendments at the conference stage, despite strong lobbying against them by the research community, was a product of the public concern for this issue, a concern which has not expressed itself with the same magnitude in the case of farm animal welfare issues.

PET THEFT ACT 1990

The latest amendment to the Animal Welfare Act, passed in 1990, was concerned with the thorny issue of pet theft. The issues raised by pound seizure and pet theft have been, for many years, an important component of the debate about animal research in the United States. This issue does not arise in Britain and many other European countries where only purpose-bred animals are allowed to be used for animal research. In Britain, for instance, the use of companion animals for medical research was prohibited by the Dogs Act in 1906. A number of scientific organizations in the 1960s did ask for the use of stray animals but this was opposed not only by animal welfare organizations but also by the police. As a result, the Littlewood Committee recommended no change in the legislation and since then the issue has not been a significant one.[21]

In the United States, however, research facilities are entitled to obtain so-called 'random source' animals from dealers[22] and, where pound seizure still exists, from animal shelters. The issue of using strays, many of whom would be destroyed anyway, raises one set of issues.[23] Much more contentious is the possibility that companion animals may end their lives suffering in a hostile laboratory environment. This is linked to the pound seizure issue because of the possibility that shelters may be forced to hand over animals to research institutions before their owners have had a chance to claim them. In addition, there has been disturbing evidence that a proportion of the animals bought by research institutions from dealers are stolen pets.[24]

In the 1940s and 1950s, the issues of pet theft and pound seizure reawakened interest in the animal research issue. As previous chapters have illustrated, the issue was instrumental in reviving lobbies on both sides. In the 1940s, demonstrating the strength of the research lobby, many states passed laws requiring pound seizure whereby animal shelters were legally obliged to hand over their animals to researchers. As the animal protection movement gained strength in the 1970s, some states (14 by 1991) prohibited pound seizure, and there have been attempts to introduce bills at the federal level to prohibit it nationally. As we saw, too, the original Laboratory Animal Welfare Act was precipitated by public concern over pet theft.

Rising concern over pet theft cases revealed in the media and by animal advocacy campaigns resulted in a number of bills being introduced in the late 1980s. One of these (introduced by Senator Wendell Ford) was approved by the Senate on 10 August 1988. This bill made it an offence for Class B dealers to get 'random source' cats and dogs from sources other than publicly operated shelters or humane societies or individuals who have bred and raised animals on their own premises. Further, in order to deal with the possibility that shelters might inadvertently be handing over unclaimed pets, the bill dictated that pounds and shelters must hold cats and dogs for at least seven days before handing them over to dealers. The major effect of the bill, therefore, was to regulate where dealers got their animals from and to prohibit registered dealers from trading with each other and trading with unlicensed 'bunchers'. This was designed to eliminate, in particular, the sale of animals at auctions, the prime means, it seems, for disposing of stolen pets.[25]

Ford's bill failed to be reported by the House agriculture committee. There were two main reasons for this. In the first place, the research community opposed the key provisions of the legislation. They argued that prohibiting dealers selling to other dealers would make it much more difficult to get hold of animals, particularly in those states where pound seizure laws had been repealed.[26] The committee remained generally 'supportive' of the bill but a key factor in their reticence seems to have been the splits in the animal protection movement. In particular, the ASPCA strongly opposed the bill on the (apparently erroneous) grounds that it would encourage pound seizure.[27] In the event, a very much diluted form of Ford's original bill was added in the Senate to the 1990 Food, Agriculture, Conservation and Trade Act. The Senate version included the major provisions of Ford's bill but this was gutted at the conference stage. A holding period for shelters was maintained but restrictions on dealer's sources of animals were removed.[28]

WHAT HAS CONGRESS ACHIEVED?

The legislative framework for the protection of research animals created by Congress is less stringent than the British version. Firstly, some (probably several thousand) research institutions are excluded from coverage under federal legislation because they do not receive federal funding (and are not, therefore, subject to NIH rules) and they use species (rats, mice and birds) which are exempt from USDA regulations.[29] Moreover, the influence of the research community has been able to prevent Congress from interfering in all but a peripheral way with the actual procedures carried out on animals in the laboratory. The 1985 amendments explicitly state, for instance, that 'nothing in the Act shall be construed as authorizing the Secretary [of Agriculture] to promulgate rules, regulations, or orders with regard to the design, outlines, or guidelines of actual research or experimentation by a research facility or Federal research facility'.[30] Thus, even though the 1985 amendments require that procedures involve the minimum discomfort, distress and pain, the use of anaesthetics and a consideration of the use of alternatives, researchers are given the autonomy to decide that the scientific value of the work necessitates overriding all of these factors.

The NIH has since the 1960s, as Chapter 1 revealed, drawn up guidelines on the treatment of animals, some of which were given statutory authority in 1985, and the agency could theoretically remove federal funding from any institution not complying. Moreover, NIH is also mandated by the 1985 legislation to establish plans for research into methods of experimentation which 'do not require the use of animals, which are likely to reduce the number of animals used, or which would produce less pain and distress than methods currently in use', and NIH has allocated some funding ($1 million in 1987) to achieve these objectives.[31] In addition, the scientific merit of research proposals is assessed before funding is granted by the Public Health Service. However, these provisions only cover federally funded research. More importantly, NIH's role is essentially one of self-regulation since a system of peer-group assessment is operated whereby scientists comment upon each other's research proposals. The NIH, in any case, is hardly a neutral arbiter, as the Home Office inspectorate claims to be in Britain, since it seeks to promote the use of animals in bio-medical research (see below).

A major feature of the legislation was the requirement that all institutions conducting animal research create an institutional animal care and use committee (IACUC) to consider the ways in which they utilize animals through assessing research proposals, visiting laboratories and reporting deficiencies to USDA. In actual fact, such committees already existed in some shape or form in most institutions prior to being made a statutory requirement under the 1985 legislation. An initial point to note in an assessment of these committees is that there has been a suspicion that they are designed not primarily to benefit animals but merely to give the *impression* that this is the case in order to shield researchers from further criticism. Indeed, the Act itself does refer to the importance of meeting 'the public concern for laboratory animal care and treatment' so that 'research will continue and progress'.[32]

In so far as these committees are designed to benefit animals, a number of problems are evident. In the first place, some argue that they do not have the authority to judge the scientific merits of a particular proposal, only the treatment of animals during procedures and their general husbandry. If this is so, a coherent view of the moral acceptability of a proposal cannot be undertaken.[33] Certainly, as indicated above, the 1985 amendment to the Animal Welfare Act does explicitly state that the legislation should not interfere with the actual conduct of scientific work. It is difficult to see, however, how IACUCs can avoid touching upon the scientific merit of research proposals since this has an important bearing, in a cost-benefit analysis, upon what level of suffering is regarded as acceptable in any particular procedure.[34] There does seem, in addition, some contradictory evidence as to their purpose. The 1986 PHS policy, for instance, states that when undertaking protocol review, IACUCs should ensure that: 'procedures involving animals should be designed and performed with due consideration of their relevance to human or animal health, the advancement of knowledge, or the good of society.' And again, in a guidebook to IACUCs issued by NIH in 1992, it is stated that 'The higher the level of the anticipated distress the stronger must be the justification of the value of the research'.[35]

It might be argued in any case that the above discussion is irrelevant because the composition of the committees undermines their purpose. NIH policy requires that each committee should have a minimum of five members including only one member unaffiliated to the institution and one member who is not a scientist. It is obvious, then, that voices critical of animal research, or even those with an open mind, are unlikely to constitute a significant force. In practice, too, it is extremely rare for abolitionists to be chosen as the unaffiliated member and quite rare for a representative of any animal advocacy group.[36] The justifications for this – that abolitionists will be obstructive and will have little to contribute to the committee's deliberations – are similar to the ones employed in the context of the British APC, and similar objections can be raised. In the first place, it is difficult to see how abolitionists can be obstructive, since they will be outnumbered. Secondly, given this fact, abolitionists will have to attempt to engage in constructive dialogue otherwise they will be marginalized. Above all, as Finsen points out:

> To those who fail to see its built-in bias, the misleading impression may be created that the institutions who have IACUCs have engaged in a full and open discussion of the ethical acceptability of their research programs, when in fact certain points of view have probably been excluded from consideration from the start.[37]

The existence of local review committees, however, is in some ways preferable to the British system of central control and the RSPCA, for one, has advocated their creation in British institutions using animals for research.[38] As Rollin points out, in such committees researchers have to consider openly the ethical dimensions of their work[39] and this 'might help to sensitize some who would not otherwise concern themselves with the ethical issues'.[40] Likewise, discussing a particular research programme may be of some benefit in terms of the adoption of methods leading to a reduction in animal suffering. Further, at least one member must represent community concerns and cannot be affiliated to the committee's institution. This requires researchers to explain their work in a non-specialist way.[41]

Finally, even though few opportunities exist for animal advocates to participate directly in committee deliberations, they do provide an additional means whereby animal advocates can get information on the nature of animal use in the laboratory which, together with greater freedom of information, can be contrasted with the inherent secretiveness of the British system.[42] In some cases, there is no doubt that public pressure has influenced committees or the funding decisions of the NIH. Deborah Blum, for instance, documents the case of a researcher working at the University of Washington who wanted to conduct a version of the isolation experiments perfected by the now infamous Harry Harlow in the 1950s. The proposal was discussed by the University's IACUC and eventually accepted by ten votes to seven. The animal protection movement then mounted a campaign against the work and the NIH eventually turned down an application for funding. The NIH denied this had anything to do with the campaign but it was undoubtedly a factor. Blum, for one, quotes a scientist involved in the process who claims that 'NIH was afraid to approve it'.[43] The use of so-called 'sunshine' laws – those federal and state laws that require public access to certain records and meetings – in the context of IACUCs has become something of a battleground with animal advocates attempting to gain access to meetings and research institutions seeking to prevent them. Court cases brought by animal advocates to force openness have met with mixed results. So far, it has been established that Sunshine Laws apply to IACUCs in six states and do not apply in five with the law in other states, where IACUCs remain closed to animal advocates, having not been tested.[44]

As might be expected, research suggests that the work of IACUC's varies from place to place and there is a clear need for more central control of their activities.[45] It is rare, it would seem, for committees to recommend a reduction in the number of animals used and rarer still for research protocols to be rejected or stopped once under way but refinements are regularly suggested and sometimes insisted upon.[46] Orlans reports the work of a conscientious IACUC, for instance, which insisted that a researcher, despite his objections, stop using water deprivation to induce primates to perform tasks.[47] Likewise, the attitudes of scientists to lay members varied widely with some treated either dismissively or with hostility and others accorded respect and every effort made to involve them in the committee's work. Continuing on this theme of decentralization and variety, local and state authorities have a good deal of autonomy in determining how animal research is to be regulated in their areas. Sanders and Jasper, for instance, document the creation of a city ordinance in Cambridge, Mass. which sets guidelines for the regulation of research laboratories.[48]

Despite the regional and institutional variations, it remains the case that there are few formal controls on what researchers may do to animals in the conduct of procedures, and this is a serious weakness with the American legislation. If public opinion is to be assuaged, more will have to be done in this area. Having said that, we should not belittle the attempts to eradicate the obvious cases of animal abuse (seen in the Taub and Gennerelli cases) nor the attempts to improve the general environment for laboratory animals, and particularly for non-human primates. As we shall see below, however, there are serious doubts as to whether Congress's intentions here have been carried out.

EXECUTIVE AGENCIES AND ANIMAL TESTING

A sub-sector of the policy network surrounding animal research relates to the safety testing of products. This network involves a diverse range of actors. As we saw in Chapter 1, many federal agencies either conduct animal toxicity testing themselves or require data that derives from animal testing. No legislation has emanated from Congress on this issue although bills have been introduced. In 1990, for instance, Representative Barbara Boxer (Democrat–California) and Senator Harry Reid (Democrat–Nevada) introduced bills into their respective houses which would have made LD50 test results redundant as well as requiring federal agencies to specify non-animal tests for product testing. In this issue area, animal advocates have to compete with the expressed interests of consumer and environmental groups who, while not necessarily overtly supportive of animal testing, are nevertheless concerned about product safety.

As a result of campaigns by animal advocates, most notably those mounted by Henry Spira in the 1970s, industry has been forced to confront this issue. A succession of US companies in the 1970s and 1980s announced an end to product testing on animals and, in addition, some have put money into developing alternatives to animal testing.[49] The centre-piece has been the creation of the Center for Alternatives to Animal Testing situated at John Hopkins University in Baltimore. Most of the funding for this centre is directed through the Cosmetics, Toiletry and Fragrance Association. Between 1981 and 1985, for instance, this organization contributed $1 316 000 out of a total budget of $1.8 million.[50] Federal agencies involved in animal testing have also been conscious of the growing political saliency of the issue. In 1984, for instance, the FDA established a steering committee on animal welfare issues and a number of agencies have collaborated in drawing up guidelines worked out in the Interagency Research Animal Committee.[51]

Reducing the need for animal test results, however, has been frustratingly slow. This is partly because the biomedical research community has been equally hostile to reforms in product testing regulations as it has been in the use of animals for medical research. Presumably, this is primarily because it regards product testing reform as the 'thin end of the wedge', whereby if animal advocates are successful in this area the next step would be medical research. Thus, in hearings on Boxer's Consumer Products Safe Testing Bill, which was not relevant to medical research at all, a representative for the Department of Health and Human Services remarked, quite erroneously, that the effect of the bill would be that 'research and testing on the causes, treatment and prevention of cancer would be crippled'.[52]

It is true, in addition, that a genuine Catch-22 situation exists.[53] No law requires, for instance, the use of animals for testing of cosmetics and household products and the FDA has said it would accept data acquired from non-animal tests (for non-pharmaceutical products at least) when the industry validates such tests. The problem is that industry has no incentive to do so until the FDA recognizes the tests as acceptable. At present, most companies still regard animal testing as their ultimate defence in a lawsuit and also see it as the most likely means of receiving permission to market a product. Progress is being made, however. The Department of Transport, for example, became the first federal agency to approve, in 1993, an *in vitro* alternative to animal testing.[54]

THE ISSUE NETWORK AND REGULATORY OBSTRUCTION

Whatever the strengths and weaknesses of the Congressional legislation considered above, the crucial point to note about animal research decision-making in the United States is that even the limited intentions of Congress have been seriously weakened during the implementation and enforcement stages following the passage of the primary legislation. In Britain, it is less easy to distinguish separate legislative and regulatory stages. In the case of animal research, the primary legislation (in 1876 and 1986) was formulated by the executive who then guided it through the legislature before creating and amending the regulatory machinery to put it into effect. In the United States, by contrast, no such centralized control has existed. Thus, once legislation leaves Congress, it is subject to scrutiny by a network of institutions within the executive and judicial branches. This arena has in turn provided, eagerly taken, opportunities for the research lobby to continue fighting to ensure the legislation damages their interests as little as possible.

Central to the regulatory system, as we have seen, is the role of the NIH and the USDA and it is worth considering the nature of these two agencies. NIH is quite clearly not a neutral player but is actively concerned to promote the use of animals in biomedical research. Active animal researchers play a central role in its activities with an on-going interaction between the agency and the research community. There is a revolving door policy, for instance, with active animal researchers employed in key NIH posts. The most notable case of this was the decision by the Alcohol, Drug Abuse and Mental Health Administration (part of NIH) in July 1991 to hire Professor Adrian Morrison, a noted proponent of animal research and a major opponent of the animal protection movement, as its first director of the Office of Animal Research Issues.[55] In the other direction, James Wyngaarden, formerly director of NIH, became Chief Officer for the Duke University Medical Center.

Likewise, in the 1980s, NIH led the discussions on how to respond to the challenge of the animal rights movement.[56] A classic example of its bias occurred in 1990, on the eve of the first March for the Animals in Washington DC, when Louis Sullivan, the then Secretary of Health and Human Services, sought to discredit the animal rights movement by indiscriminately labelling it as terrorist and anti-science.[57] Similarly, Frederick Goodwin, during his time as administrator of HHS's Alcohol, Drug Abuse and Mental Health Administration, spoke and wrote about the 'dangers' to scientific research of the animal protection movement's objectives and his agency has responded with glossy literature, some of which is designed for school children, defending animal research.[58] It was Goodwin who was responsible for appointing Morrison justifying it in the following way:

I believe that it would be a dereliction of duty were I, as head of a major health agency and as a physician, not to help make the public aware of the true nature of the animal rights movement and to educate them to the health benefits that accrue to them as a consequence of responsible animal research.[59]

No doubt some or even most Home Office officials responsible for administering animal experimentation law in Britain would concur with Goodwin's comments but neither they, nor the ministers they serve, would ever be so blatantly hostile to the animal protection movement. Still less would they appoint someone who has such a high-profile status as an animal experimenter as an official spokesman on the issue. This would be the equivalent of appointing someone such as Professor Colin Blakemore, the Oxford physiologist and noted critic of the animal rights movement. Such a move would be inconceivable.

As has been regularly noted by observers, the debate about animal research in the United States has been exceedingly polarized, although less so now than in the past.[60] Generating a consensus has proved difficult; you are either, it seems, on one side or the other. NIH has been no exception. Faced with a hostile and reinvigorated animal protection movement, it has defended animal research – as, in the words of a senior official, 'both a legislative mandate and a moral imperative'[61] – vigorously and sometimes to extremes. In the Silver Spring monkey incident, for instance, it refused to accede to animal advocate's (and Congress') repeated requests to allow the surviving monkeys from Edward Taub's laboratory to live out their lives in peace at a primate sanctuary, since this would be 'giving in' to the animal protection movement.[62] Furthermore, it is widely suspected that its funding decisions are not 'blind to animal research politics' in the sense that, whatever the value of the proposal, funding tends to be denied to those who have raised, however moderately, problems with animal research.[63]

The values and attitudes of USDA are somewhat more difficult to evaluate. It was chosen as the agency responsible for regulating animal research precisely because of its independence from organized interests on both sides of the issue. This was clearly preferable to giving the NIH responsibility, which was the preferred option of the research community. As a result, as we saw in Chapter 2, the animal research lobby did have to work hard to create links with USDA. It would be grossly inaccurate to suggest that USDA always sides with the research community. The consultative machinery, for instance, allows for considerable input from animal advocates, often through concerned members of Congress, with REAC operating an 'open door' policy to pressure groups.[64] Thus, no less than a record 7800 comments were received on USDA's initial regulations following the 1985 Act.[65] Agriculture Secretary Richard Lyng also criticized the Office of Management and Budget for its delay in considering regulations required to implement the 1985 amendments to the Animal Welfare Act. USDA also opposed the 1990 Farm Animal and Research Facilities Protection Bill, eventually passed in 1992, which sought to impose severe federal penalties for laboratory and factory farm break-ins. The agency wanted nothing to do with its enforcement on the totally justifiable grounds that: 'We question the advisability of placing regulatory officials in the position of protecting the entities they regulate'.[66]

To say the least, however, USDA does not give the impression that it has taken on board its new responsibilities with any great enthusiasm (see below on enforcement weaknesses). Thus, while not objecting to the passage of the Animal Welfare Act in 1966, the agency did not see why it should be given responsibility for enforcing it. Since then, it has regularly opposed reforms to the initial statute. Thus, it opposed the 1976 amendments and most of the reforms which were incorporated in the 1985 amendments,[67] and it opposed the Pet Theft Act in 1988. As a result, while it would be wrong to claim that USDA deliberately serves the interests of the research community, the agency has failed to implement fully its legislative responsibilities and has proved to be no match for other members of the policy network who seek to promote the animal research community's agenda.[68]

One example of the failure of USDA to implement the Animal Welfare Act effectively is the department's continued insistence upon excluding rats, mice, birds and farm animals from coverage under the Act. The consequence of so doing becomes apparent when it is realised that these species constitute about 85 per cent of the animals used in scientific procedures! Such an exclusion is clearly in defiance of the 1970 amendment to the

Animal Welfare Act which mandates that all 'warm-blooded' animals be covered. Even the NIH *does* include these animals and NABR does not seem to have any problem with this clause. After a petition from the Animal Legal Defense Fund, a federal court in January 1992 found that the exclusion was 'arbitrary and capricious' and ordered USDA to establish regulations incorporating the excluded species.[69]

The case which best illustrates how the issue network can undermine the intentions of Congress concerns the fate of the 1985 amendments to the Animal Welfare Act. As we saw in an earlier chapter, USDA was instructed to draw up regulations setting minimum standards for the humane handling, housing, care, treatment and transportation of laboratory animals, and in particular, the legislation sought to ensure that research facilities provided for the 'psychological well-being' of non-human primates as well as adequate exercise for dogs. After consulting widely with interested parties, including the NIH and individual scientists, USDA drew up a set of regulations laying down what it perceived to be a reasonable interpretation of Congress' intent. These regulations were based upon the use of so-called 'engineering standards' whereby specific requirements were laid down to which research institutions must adhere. For example, the proposed regulations stated that laboratory dogs should be exercised for 30 minutes a day as 'a reasonable minimum for maintenance of a dog's health and well-being'.

It was at this point that the issue network came into play. The regulations were sent (in 1989) to the Office of Information and Regulatory Affairs (OIRA) in the President's Office of Management and Budget. Under President Reagan, as part of his programme of financial stringency, the OMB became much more active in monitoring the regulations emanating from agencies. To this end, the OIRA was set up in 1980 and Executive Order 12291 issued in 1981 required agencies to undertake a cost-benefit analysis of its regulations whereby it has to be shown how their benefits to society outweighs their costs.[70]

The proposed regulations languished for nearly eight months at the OIRA. In the meantime in March 1989, the Animal Legal Defense Fund filed a complaint in the US District Court for the District of Columbia against the OMB and others for what they claimed was an illegal delay in introducing the regulations. Significantly, the complaint claimed that OMB's actions violated the Constitution's separation of powers by blocking 'the express delegation of rule making authority...to the Secretary of Agriculture'. Suitably chastened by the court action, OIRA returned the regulations to USDA in April 1989 but with the request that USDA change the basis of them from engineering standards to so-called 'performance standards' whereby the desired performance is described and each institution must determine their own way of complying. In the meantime, NABR had filed an 118-page legal brief criticizing USDA's regulations on the grounds that the cost involved was not justified by, what the organization saw as, the minimal improvements to animal welfare that would result.[71] As a result of this pressure, USDA backed down and its final regulations published in 1991 did adopt performance, rather than engineering, standards and the previous specific requirements were abandoned.

Interpreting these events requires initially an assessment of the extent to which the change from engineering to performance standards represent a denial of the original Act's intentions. Here, it should be noted firstly that the research community itself preferred the latter, but, unless we add the assumption that researchers are not interested in improving the welfare of laboratory animals, this does not necessarily tell us very much. Indeed, there are some grounds for saying that engineering standards are inappropriate in this case. It is, in particular, a difficult task to draw up specific standards which may have to vary for different species and which may prevent inspectors from exercising their discretion.[72]

Despite the positive features of performance standards, however, there is nevertheless a, not unjustified, suspicion that USDA's adoption of performance standards represents a weakening of the protection provided for laboratory animals and therefore a victory for the research community. This was certainly the verdict of the court which was petitioned by the Animal Legal Defense Fund and the Society for Animal Protective Legislation after the final regulations were published. The Ritchie judgement issued on 25 February 1993 argued that the regulations were 'arbitrary and capricious' failing to carry out the will of Congress and therefore USDA should go back and try again. Ritchie was also critical of the delay in promulgating regulations. In a significant passage, Ritchie argued that the courts:

were not created by our founding fathers to rubber stamp such failures to act over indefinite periods while bloated bureaucrats contend with each other and the special interest groups who transfer their efforts from the Legislative Branch to the Executive Branch, after a bill has passed.[73]

The way that the regulations have subsequently operated has given cause for concern too. Under the regulations, scientists are required to provide a plan detailing how they are ensuring the psychological well-being of primates. Such researchers, however, have generally refused to send these reports to USDA because by doing so they are available to public inspection. By keeping these reports at the institutions within which the work is being carried out, particularly if the institution is a private university, the public has no right of access. It is impossible, therefore, for animal advocates to monitor the working of the regulations.[74]

Now, USDA inspectors do get to see and comment on the reports but this is not entirely satisfactory from an animal protection point of view. In the first place, as we shall see below, USDA has been regularly criticized for its failure to effectively enforce the Animal Welfare Act. Furthermore, animal advocates have no idea what USDA inspectors think is an appropriate environment to ensure the psychological well-being of primates. There is a suspicion, however, that their definition is very limited and justifies what many would regard as unacceptable.[75]

On the positive side, however, there is also evidence that by having to consider, like never before, the environmental enrichment of laboratory animals, inspectors and researchers have had to focus on animal welfare to an unprecedented degree and, as a consequence, the standards of animal care may be rising. USDA inspectors, for instance, will not accept single-housed primates or restraining devices unless there is a very good justification for it.[76] Furthermore, as Andrew Rowan has pointed out: 'these performance-based standards stimulated considerable research into environmental enrichment for primates and dogs that have improved housing conditions for the animals'.[77] Likewise Martin Stephens, vice-president for animal research issues at the HSUS commented in general terms in late 1996 that: 'Many observers of the vivisection scene have a vague sense that the situation is changing for the better: that animal use is indeed dropping, that alternative approaches are gaining in popularity, that housing conditions are improving, etc.'[78] The difficulty of accurately assessing the validity of this 'vague sense' is almost entirely due to the research community's apparent desire to keep the public in the dark about what goes on in laboratories. In so doing, they are not helping their cause.

If we turn to look at the process by which USDA's draft regulations were overturned, it becomes apparent that there was a concerted attempt by members of the issue network to destroy the aims of the legislation. This came about partly because of the general anti-regulatory climate of the Reagan era and partly because of the influence of those, inside and outside of government, who sought to limit the effects of the regulations on the grounds that they represented an unwarranted intrusion into the activities of animal researchers. The desire to scupper the regulations is apparent not only by OIRA's delay in responding to USDA's draft regulations, but also by its eventual response.[79] For, in asking USDA to improve its cost–benefit analysis, OIRA made its own ideological preferences in favour of animal research abundantly clear. Thus, it asked USDA to 'list the contributions of biomedical research to human health safety that have resulted from animal research and describe the potential losses to society when research costs are increased by the regulations'. It did not, on the other hand, ask for information on the potential benefits of the regulations – in terms, say, of the gain to society of knowing that laboratory animals are treated humanely – or the possible costs of animal research – in terms, say, of the dangers of extrapolating from animal to human models. It seems fair to say, then, that OIRA's preference for performance standards was caused less by the technical problems associated with applying them but by a general desire to minimize the effects on the research community.

It is not surprising that USDA found itself faced with hostile voices within the executive branch. In the first place, the research community was extremely active in lobbying governmental bodies. The American Council on Education, representing the nation's research universities, for instance, hired Michael Harowitz – a former counsel for OMB – to lobby against the regulations. NABR, too, was unremitting in its attempts to influence the participants and, when USDA finally adopted regulations to the research community's liking, NABR was also instrumental in persuading USDA, clearly uncertain as to what it should do, to appeal against the Ritchie court ruling.[80] On 20 May 1994, the US Court of Appeals for the District of Columbia reversed the Ritchie decision on the grounds that the plaintiffs lacked 'standing' to sue. As Christine Stevens pointed out, NABR 'just pushed and nagged and pushed until the government had to do something'.[81]

Governmental participants, too, were active in opposing the regulations. We have seen that OIRA was generally indisposed to further regulatory controls, but its opposition to these particular regulations was undoubtedly intensified by the extensive consultation it engaged in with NIH, an institution, as we have revealed, not favourably inclined towards further restrictions on researcher's autonomy. Finally, the former head of NIH, James Wyngaarden, was at this time a senior figure in the President's Office of Science and Technology Policy, providing another importantly placed voice opposed to the regulations.[82]

ENFORCEMENT FAILURES

Whatever regulations prescribe is immaterial, of course, if they are not properly enforced. This responsibility lies almost entirely with USDA. NIH has, as we saw, its own guidelines for federally funded research but it does little to enforce these guidelines. Indeed, before 1982 (when NIH began a programme of site visits as a consequence of the Silver Spring monkey affair) it did nothing at all. As Rollin points out, for instance, even though NIH regulations prohibited repeated use of animals in surgery tuition, 'this rule was ignored virtually everywhere'.[83] From 1985 onwards, in the wake of the Gennerelli case, NIH did allocate further funding for unannounced inspections, usually undertaken in the wake of complaints, and closer co-operation between NIH and USDA was forged to allow information on violations to be shared. Even now, though, NIH would not claim to operate a comprehensive regulatory function.

The main enforcement responsibility, then, lies with USDA (or, to be more accurate, the Investigative and Enforcement Services branch of APHIS) and here, given the agency's rather luke-warm attitude towards its regulatory responsibilities and the federal government's general anathema – at least under the

Reagan and Bush presidencies – to regulations,[84] it is not surprising to learn that there are serious doubts as to the effectiveness of the agency's enforcement mechanisms. What makes
these criticisms particularly apposite is they have been confirmed by internal governmental enquires.[85]

Reports have regularly shown that many facilities are not
being inspected in accordance with the regulations, and that in
many cases follow-up visits are not being made to institutions
where violations of the regulations have been uncovered. Thus,
a damming report in 1992 by USDA's own Office of Inspector
General revealed that, in the case of animal dealers: 'Our audit
concludes that APHIS cannot insure the humanitarian care and
treatment of animals ... as required by the act'. The report also
revealed that in 1991 over 16 per cent (46 out of 284) of research
facilities had not received an annual inspection, which is required by law. Moreover, of those that did receive such an inspection, 156 were cited for violations but 126 of these did not
receive a follow-up visit within the 30 days required by USDA's
regulations.[86]

These enforcement failures have been caused by a chronic
lack of funding. One author has claimed that USDA's lack of
interest is a product of indifference and even corruption on the
part of USDA officials more interested in career advancement
and financial gain than the protection of animals and the rooting
out of those who violate the regulations.[87] There is little evidence, however, that a deliberate strategy of non-enforcement for
these reasons has occurred and such a view is certainly not
supported by the animal protection community. Adele Douglass,
the legislative director of the AHA who was centrally involved in
lobbying for pet theft legislation remarks, for instance, that:

> The problem was not a conspiracy, but rather a lack of will on
> the part of the US government to deem animal issues im-
> portant. The material she used was all outdated, material that
> came from newspaper reports that I submitted to the Congress
> several years before publication of her book. Frankly, I had no
> idea that all I had to do to make money was to take the
> hearing transcript and assume a conspiracy theory.[88]

That there has been underfunding is an unquestionable and
long-running fact. In 1984, for instance, APHIS was given about

$279 million for its entire operation, of which about $4.8 million was devoted to enforcing the Animal Welfare Act. To put this into perspective, the total budget for agricultural programmes in that year was $34 billion. The appropriations for APHIS in 1991 ($450 million out of a total budget of $52.5 billion) and 1994 ($450 million out of $69 billion) did not reveal any change in emphasis,[89] although by 1996 REAC had been allocated a slightly bigger share of $9 million. As early as the mid-1970s, an APHIS spokesperson honestly revealed to a Congressional hearing that 'we just do not have enough money to cover the present scope of the act'.[90] Even research advocacy groups and the NIH concede that the level of funding is inadequate and, in a rare show of consensus, they have joined forces with animal advocates to call for more money to be appropriated.[91]

As we have pointed out, USDA is only part of the policy network surrounding animal research and to a large degree it is not in control of the budget it can allocate to APHIS. As a consequence, the public pronouncements of APHIS officials have had to follow the Department's line which, in turn, is determined by more general budgetary priorities decided elsewhere, in the legislative and executive branches. Notwithstanding the comment above, therefore, APHIS officials have usually sought to deny that they do not have enough resources to fulfil their responsibilities under the Animal Welfare Act. Indeed, in the 1980s, USDA requested a reduction in funding, which Congress refused to accept.

Whatever the reason, the lack of funds has prevented the agency from employing an adequate number of inspectors. In 1992, for example, 87 inspectors were responsible for regulating 4400 animal dealers, 1470 research facilities and over 1486 animal exhibitors. As Adele Douglass scathingly pointed out: 'You don't have to be a mathematical genius to figure that 90 inspectors can't do a good job' reviewing so many inspection sites.[92] We cannot know for certain what the consequences of these enforcement failures are. The animal protection movement claims that widespread abuses are allowed to continue.[93] More significantly, an NABR lobbyist has admitted that whilst the picture is nowhere near as bad as the one painted by the animal protection movement, it is not as good as the one painted by NABR.[94]

While these criticisms remain valid, it is also important to point out that it is unrealistic to expect that enough inspectors will ever be appointed to ensure a day-to-day scrutiny of research facilities. Because of this, as in the case of the British regulatory regime, it has been pointed out by government officials that APHIS does rely to a certain degree on animal advocates themselves revealing problems in research laboratories and it encourages such participation.[95] It might be added that this is somewhat disingenuous in the light of ever increasing security which prevents the public from finding out what is going on inside the windowless buildings within which animals are kept. An additional point here is that the creation of REAC in 1989 was a move in the right direction, since it is specifically concerned with animal welfare whereas the Veterinary Services section which used to enforce the Animal Welfare Act had a greater specialism in disease control. As a result of REAC's creation, animal welfare inspectors were treated with greater respect by individual researchers and by NIH.[96]

Funding is also not the only problem. It was not lack of funding, for instance, that resulted in the abuses of the Silver Spring monkeys falling through the net, since Taub's laboratory was inspected by APHIS officials just two months before the scandal broke. Why the inspection did not uncover serious problems remains something of a mystery, but if it happened then, there must be concern that it is still happening now. Christine Stevens argued in Congressional hearings on the Taub case that the inspectorate is not qualified enough, a criticism related at least in part to lack of finance, and that this, coupled with the decentralized nature of the regulatory regime whereby critical reports can remain on file without action being taken, ensured that the animal suffering in the Silver Spring case was not averted.[97] There is little evidence that this situation has since been remedied. A final point is that it might also be argued that the penalties for non-compliance are not rigorous enough. Thus, as in the British case, prosecutions are rare and very much the last resort with APHIS usually dealing with problems through so-called 'Cease and Desist' orders whereby a facility is asked to put any infringements right before a follow-up visit. Even if a follow-up visit (if it is made at all) reveals a failure to correct the deficiencies, the inspector has to send the paperwork to head office who will then decide whether to proceed further. This process can be very time-consuming and animals may be suffering as a consequence.

There is some cause for greater optimism. At a USDA public meeting which I attended in April 1996, Mike Dunn, the assistant secretary of agriculture responsible for APHIS did admit that the hierarchy of the department in the past 'didn't give a hoot' about the Animal Welfare Act but that this was going to change under the new agriculture secretary, Dan Glickman.[98] Whether or not improvements have occurred is difficult to say. In the autumn of 1996 REAC was reorganized (see Chapter 1) and there is some evidence that operational changes are being introduced. Thus, a national training programme for Animal Care employees was held for the first time which will aid uniformity of enforcement. Further, the agency said it was going to focus more of its resources on institutions who had poor records of compliance, introduce a merit programme to reward those institutions for 'consistently exceeding the AWA requirements', and prioritize the prosecution of violations so that the worst and regular offenders are dealt with more quickly.[99]

As this chapter has repeatedly stated, the legislative and administrative controls on animal research in the United States are weaker than those existing in Britain and a number of other European countries. This is partly to do with the influence of the research community but, unlike the policy network surrounding decision-making affecting the welfare of farm animals in the United States, this influence has been exercised in an increasingly complex and open policy network which has allowed the intentions of Congress, and therefore public opinion, to be thwarted. This concurs with Kitschelt's account of 'political opportunity structures' where a social movement's chances of success are dependent, not just upon the quality or volume of protest, but upon the political input and output structures they face.[100] Thus, while the US animal research arena is reasonably open, with an independent and fragmented legislature, the output structures are weak, with the absence of a centralized executive to aggregate demands. As a consequence, stalemate, and a good deal of frustration on the part of challenging groups, is reached.

Despite the current weaknesses, however, it is, I think, possible to end this chapter on an up-beat note for animal advocates. The crucial point here is that the animal research issue has been politicized over the last two decades or so. Those who use animals in their research have, like never before, had to justify their activities to an increasingly sceptical public. This in itself presages a huge, albeit subtle, shift in the attitude of the research community.

Those who criticize the existing legislative framework usually do so on the grounds that it does not prohibit researchers from conducting some, or all, research on animals. In some ways, though, this is the wrong benchmark for judging the progress that has been made. The starting point we should adopt is the long-standing ideological consensus of the scientific community in the United States which denied the moral significance of animal suffering or, worse still, the very existence of animal suffering. As Rollin suggests, the fact that this old ideology has been challenged and, to a large extent, successfully overcome represents a seismic shift in the debate.[101] Because the ethics of animal use are now out in the open and because Congress, at least before the Republicans gained control in the 1990s, has begun to reflect this changing environment, it may well prove difficult to counter pressure for more adequate implementation of the current law as well as further reforms in the way laboratory animals are treated.

Conclusion: Animal Protection and Pluralist Politics

This study set out to examine the nature of decision-making in policy areas affecting the welfare of animals. The organizing theme was the utilization of policy network theory which provides the means to engage in meaningful comparisons between two very different political systems. The key finding of this analysis is that the political systems of Britain and the United States have played a significant role in determining the nature of policy outcomes. To explore further how we have arrived at this conclusion it is necessary to consider four questions. Firstly, how far is animal protection policy-making sectorized? Secondly, what is the balance of power between the respective participants of policy networks? Thirdly, how far can policy outcomes be determined by the structure of policy networks and fourthly, how do we explain change within policy networks?

THE DEGREE OF POLICY SECTORIZATION

We need to consider firstly, then, to what extent the concept of a policy network is a useful tool in helping us to understand policy-making. With important exceptions we can answer this question in the affirmative. Thus, decisions relating to animal welfare, during normal times at least, are taken in distinctive policy networks with a relatively small number of actors. There are, however, important exceptions to this broadly accurate conclusion. We saw in the USA, for instance, that there was a much greater unity of purpose between the various organizations with a vested interest in continuing to use animals in the laboratory and for food and that this unity of purpose involved considerable cross-sectoral lobbying. This, in turn, was partly a product of a greater recognition than in Britain of a common

229

enemy and partly to do with overlapping institutional responsibilities whereby Congressional agricultural committees and
USDA occupy central positions in both the farm and laboratory
animal networks.

What this study has also revealed is that at times of crisis or
heightened political activity, the boundaries of policy networks
become blurred and such is the openness of the policy arena at
these times that it is not even clear that we can talk sensibly
about sectorized policy-making at all. During the passage of the
1985 amendments to the Animal Welfare Act, for instance, a
wide range of institutions – the executive, legislative and judicial
branches of the federal government, a large number of interest
and cause groups, and the media – were involved. In Britain,
likewise, the live exports crisis necessitated a governmental
response and the cosy, insulated world of MAFF was broken
apart by an issue which generated huge public interest and
concern.

POWER STRUCTURES WITHIN NETWORKS

This study also reveals that the power structures within particular animal protection networks differ significantly. More specifically, whereas the British and American farm animal networks
are more akin to closed, insulated and consensual policy communities, the laboratory animal networks are closer to the issue
network end of the continuum. In the United States, decisions
relating to farm animals are taken by a small group of actors
operating with an ideological consensus opposed to significant
restrictions on their activities. As we saw in Chapter 8, there is
some evidence to suggest that the influence of the NFU has
begun to decline in the agricultural policy community in Britain
and that animal advocates are able to gain more effective access
than they used to. The extent to which the policy community has
begun to break up is difficult to determine. What we can say is
that, even if the institutional dominance of the agricultural
community remains firm, it has become increasingly difficult for
the policy community actors to depoliticize farm animal welfare
issues.

The decision-making structures concerned with the welfare of
laboratory animals in Britain and the USA are not as closed and

consensual as farm animal decision-making structures. In the British case, this would seem to be at least partly explained by the circumstances in which the network evolved. Thus, administrative and enforcement structures were set up specifically to deal with laboratory animal use which, at the end of the nineteenth century, was still in its infancy. Unlike farm animal welfare decision-making structures in both countries, no prior network existed. In the United States, this was not the case, since animals were being used for experimental purposes long before the first federal legislation regulating the practice was passed in 1966, and the research community had developed extremely strong ties with NIH. The key differences, however, were that primary regulatory responsibility was given to an agency (the APHIS branch of USDA) with no prior responsibility for the issue and Congressional committees with responsibility for laboratory animal use have never been dominated by the research community in the way that agricultural interests dominate agriculture committees. Because the research community faced disadvantages in having to gain access to a new institutional structure and because they could never guarantee the support of Congressional committees, the decision-making structure has been more fluid and responsive to the animal protection movement.

THE RELATIONSHIP BETWEEN STRUCTURE AND OUTCOME

The assumption of policy network theory is that policy outcomes will be determined by the nature of the structure. Thus, a balancing of interests will only be possible in a network which is open and conflictual whereas a closed and consensual policy community will benefit only those who have a privileged place within it. In two of the networks identified in this book the relationship between outcome and structure is relatively clear cut. Thus, in the USA farm animal policy community, the privileged position of agribusiness interests has prevented any significant farm animal welfare reforms. In the British laboratory animal network, by contrast, the relative openness of the system allowed for the participation of the, more moderate, elements of the animal protection movement. The resulting legislative framework created by the passage of the 1986 Act did at least try to balance the interests of the participants.

In the other two networks identified, the relationship between structure and outcome is more problematic. In the case of the structure surrounding British farm animal welfare, there is some evidence that the policy community has begun to break up and, insofar as this is the case, it is possible to explain welfare reforms in terms of the greater influence of animal advocates. As we saw, however, agricultural interests are still very influential and an alternative explanation is that the policy community has remained intact by managing change – offering policy concessions and trying to co-opt the moderate elements of the animal protection movement. If correct, the implication here is that, albeit limited, policy changes can occur without a change in the basic structure. But even here it might be suggested that because the policy community's ideological hegemony has disappeared because of its failure to depoliticize the issue of farm animal welfare, it is not entirely true to say that the policy community has remained intact.

To the extent that the British government has responded positively to the rise of concern for the welfare of farm animals, it concurs with a 'policy style' called 'bureaucratic accommodation' which some scholars see as characteristic of British policymaking. This policy style involves the avoidance 'of electoral politics and public conflict in order to reach consensus or "accommodation" in the labyrinth of consultative machinery which has developed'.[1] Thus, in response to the rise of public concern for animal welfare, governmental actors sought to incorporate the major interests within the state machinery through the creation of formal bodies such as the FAWC and the APC and in informal consultation exercises. Balance and consensus, the characteristic features of pluralist politics, are, according to this view, part of the 'standard operating procedure' of British decision-makers. It goes without saying, however, that keeping all sides happy is a difficult task and there are times – such as the period when the campaign against the live export of animals was at its height – when governmental actors are unable to institutionalize and regularize conflict. It is during such periods that the greatest opportunity for fundamental reform occurs.

Whether or not this is an accurate depiction of the British approach to animal protection policy-making, it is certainly not applicable to the United States. Indeed, a characteristic feature of US animal experimentation policy is the lack of central direction which has prevented managed change through accommodation and consensus. Thus, a wide array of actors are involved but change benefiting animals has been slow and patchy because, in the absence of a central authority, defenders of animal research have been able to obstruct change by using the very plurality of the network. This leads us to the conclusion that far from being a cause of dynamic and unpredictable change, issue networks can in fact benefit the status quo.

Another factor we need to consider is the nature of regulatory activity. A constant theme in Chapters 7–10 was that, although many regulations designed to protect animals do exist, serious doubts have been raised as to their effective enforcement. One explanation for this failure is the view that regulations soon come, if that was not their original intention, to serve the interests of the regulated.[2] Without an additional argument, however, it is not clear why regulators will inevitably acquiesce to the regulated.[3] The policy community model of decision-making does seem to provide one additional factor to the equation which provides greater resonance to the 'capture' critique of regulatory activity. Here, it might be suggested that relying on policy community actors to effectively enforce regulations they are not too keen on having in the first place, is doomed to failure.

Some patterns of animal protection decision-making do not, as we have seen, accord with the policy community model, yet similar problems with regulatory enforcement occur across the board. In addition, to assume that officials, whether working within a policy community or not, will always seek to take the side of the regulated is to belittle their professionalism and genuine intent on doing their job as effectively as possible. If this stands, we may have to look elsewhere for an explanation for regulatory failures, such as the view that state regulations can never realise their goals because it is an intrinsically ineffective institution. One final point here is that regulatory performance can be improved as a result of public pressure. Thus, as with policy communities, politicization of the issues regulatory agencies are concerned with can highlight deficiencies and ensure improvements are made. This was the function performed, for instance, by the Taub and Gennerelli scandals in the United States. Likewise, the focus on live exports in Britain ensured that animal transportation practices were put under the microscope, not least by Labour's Elliot Morley, the opposition spokesman on animal welfare, who asked agriculture ministers numerous detailed questions on regulatory practices.

EXPLAINING CHANGE

Any case study of policy-making in a particular field would be deficient without an examining of the dynamics of change. This is particularly the case with animal welfare where, as we have seen, there has been significant policy developments in recent years. To some degree, of course, the determinants of change will vary from country to country. In Britain, for instance, the impact of party on public policy outcomes is much greater than in the USA. In actual fact, party divisions in Britain, despite their central importance in the political system, have had relatively little impact on the nature of animal welfare policy-making. This, however, could be about to change. As we saw, Labour MPs are much more likely to be supporters of animal welfare and the party's election victory in 1997 could presage important changes, and not least the banning of fur farms and hunting as well as greater pressure on the EU to reform factory farming. As we saw in Chapter 6, party is an important determinant of support for animal welfare in the USA too, although it is a faction of the Democratic Party – liberals from the North East and West – who are most heavily represented. In addition, unlike the British system, American parties do not put forward binding policy programmes which are implemented once elected.

Policy network analysis does tend to underplay the role of individuals in policy change, preferring instead to focus on broader social forces. This is, I think, broadly accurate but we should not underestimate the role of key individuals in the policy process. Indeed, this study of animal protection politics reveals that key actors have played a surprisingly important role at crucial moments. The roles played by Houghton, Mellor and Hollands in the passage of the 1986 Animals (Scientific Procedures) Act is one obvious example. Another is the role played by Robert Dole and Christine Stevens in getting reforms to the Animal Welfare Act in 1985. It is worth speculating in this context that the existence of countervailing organizations in the form of animal protection groups has enhanced state autonomy. It might be argued, for instance, that the campaigns against live exports in Britain enabled MAFF officials to act in an area where they had felt previously constrained by the NFU. Parliamentary support for Richard Body's bill to abolish pig stalls and tethers might be seen in the same light.

Equally, here, we should also emphasize the role of individual state actors in obstructing reform. The ideology of the Reagan administration, for instance, had a big impact in determining the character of the 1985 amendments to the Animal Welfare Act in the USA. Likewise, it is well known that some MAFF ministers are more sympathetic to animal welfare than others. Disinterest by state actors rather than outright hostility can be equally important. There was no one in the 1960s and 1970s, for instance, who was interested in promoting reform of animal research within Labour or Conservative governments.

This study has revealed above all, though, that it is public pressure that has led to reform. Time after time we have noted how legislative change only occurred after public concern had materialized, often as a response to a particularly well-publicized event (such as the publicity given to the shocking treatment of animals by researchers at the University of Pennsylvania) which has illustrated the need for reform. Public pressure is often mobilized and sustained by knowledge. Thus, there is no doubt that increased awareness of the public health and environmental implications of factory farming is an important lever of change, as is the awareness of both what is done to animals in the laboratory and that there may be alternatives which will produce the same or even better results. A final point here is that, as suggested earlier, public concern for animal welfare issues is more likely to be sustained if it can be shown that there are human, as well as non-human, costs of animal exploitation.

One crucial question remains to be asked. This is the degree to which the law relating to animal protection is politically legitimate. As previously stated, from an animal rights perspective the scale of animal exploitation is clearly unacceptable. There is, it was also suggested, another benchmark provided by the pluralist model of the state which suggests that what is crucial is the balancing of interests. I realise that animal rights advocates are not going to be persuaded, and rightly so, that it is morally legitimate to sacrifice the fundamental interests of animals.

Remember though, that the fundamentalist position, articulated most successfully by Gary Francione, wants to suggest that such an effective balancing of interests cannot work since, short of abolishing particular uses of animals completely, the property status of animals in our society will always mean they lose out even if the resulting human benefit is a trivial one.

I do not think anyone could deny that a great deal more balancing of human and non-human interests now goes on than it did 20 or 30 years ago. This balance may still be skewed in favour of the exploiters of animals, and there is still a long way to go, but change there has been. Of course, this generalization disguises important variations. In the USA, farm animals in particular but laboratory animals as well have not benefited to the same degree as they have in Britain, and this book has attempted to pinpoint why this has been the case.

In the case of animal research, the fragmented nature of the US system of government has played a key contributory factor in explaining weak policy outcomes. In the case of farm animals, the policy community has not, unlike its British equivalent, faced the same kind of public pressure. In this context, it is worth while discussing the relationship between pluralism and policy communities. There is an assumption that policy communities, because of their closed and exclusionary nature, are inherently anti-pluralist[4] and that those interests with a privileged position within them exercise illegitimate influence. It seems to me, however, that this is not necessarily the case. We are justified in labelling a particular policy arena as pluralist when its outcomes are broadly consistent with the strength of interests within society as a whole. If there is not a great deal of public concern for the welfare of farm animals then the dominance of agricultural interests within the political system may not be politically, as opposed to morally, illegitimate.

We can derive empirical conclusions from the preceding normative analysis. It is true that public concern for farm and, to a lesser degree, laboratory animal welfare is greater in Britain than it is in the USA, both in terms of raw numbers and in terms of the saliency of the issues. As a result, at least part of the explanation for the failure of US policy arenas to balance competing human and non-human interests effectively is to do with the failure of the animal protection movement to mobilize public opinion and politicize the issues in the way they have been in

Britain. This is quite an optimistic point at which to end this account, for this book, if nothing else, has revealed that both the British and American political systems have shown themselves to be reasonably responsive to change. The task facing the animal protection movement in both countries is to mobilize, by whatever means, a large enough constituency to make further improvements in the lives of non-human animals a reality.

Appendix I: Database Design

The database (using 'File Maker Pro' software) created for this study contains two files, the *Parliamentary Animal Welfare Database* (PAWD) and the *Congressional Animal Welfare Database* (CLAWD). Both cover legislative activity on animal welfare for the period 1985–1994.

CLAWD contains two sections and contains, at present, 839 records: details of 293 Bills and Resolutions and 546 records of Congressional members responsible for them.

PAWD is divided into four sections and contains, at present, 2440 records: 1900 Parliamentary Questions, 105 Early Day Motions, 83 Bills and petitions and the details of 352 MPs responsible for them.

The information generated from the database has been utilized in various parts of this book but the bulk of the material can be found in Chapters 5 and 6. In order to rank legislators, a scoring system was used. In terms of British MPs, each parliamentary question asked was awarded half a point, each Early Day Motion and petition introduced two points and each bill five points. For members of the House of Representatives, following a study by Jeremy and Carol Rifkin (Voting Green, p. 287), a sponsor of a bill was awarded six points and a co-sponsor three; and a sponsor of a resolution was awarded two points and a co-sponsor one.

Appendix II: Questionnaire Design

The purpose of the questionnaire used for this study was to establish the *number* of groups concerning themselves with animal welfare, *what* issues they were most concerned about, the *extent* to which they were actively involved in putting their case forward and *who* were their main targets of influence.

The questions asked of identified groups were as follows:

A   When did your organization begin lobbying?

B   How many lobbyists does your organization employ?

C   Would you describe your organization's lobbying as extensive and continual, intermittent or rare?

D   Does your organization lobby on animal welfare legislation extensively, intermittently, rarely or never? (asked of industry groups only).

E   What lobbying strategies does your organization use?

F   Which animal protection/wildlife conservation organizations do you think are most influential?

G   Why do you not lobby on animal protection legislation (for industry groups who do not lobby on animal protection issues only).

H   Respondents presented with a number of bills (for details see Table 2.3) and asked whether they lobbied on them extensively, intermittently or rarely and whether they supported, opposed or had no position on the legislation.

The answers to questions D and G facilitated the creation of a list of those groups that lobbied on animal welfare extensively and that were regarded as important by their competitors. These groups were then targeted for interviews where the respondents were asked to elaborate on the questionnaire answers. Question H was designed to discover the scope of an organization's concerns. From this information it was possible to reach conclusions about the extent of policy sectorization.

In all, about 200 questionnaires were sent out to animal welfare and industry groups in the UK and USA. The response rate was about 75%, which is high for a questionnaire-based survey. Only one or two groups, all in the United States, were hostile to the project, reflecting the paranoia of some industry groups. Most were happy to co-operate with the project, although in the case of one crucial group in the USA (the American Feed Industry Association), I was only able to gain access after the intervention of a lobbyist from the American Humane Association (a group they regard as 'respectable'), who verified my credentials.

Notes

Introduction

1. A. Heidenheimer, H. Heclo and C. Teich Adams, *Comparative Public Policy*, 3rd edn (New York: St Martin's Press, 1990) p. 3.
2. See, to name but a few, P. Singer, *Animal Liberation*, 2nd edn (London: Cape, 1990); T. Regan, *The Case for Animal Rights* (London: Routledge, 1984); B. Rollin, *Animal Rights and Human Morality* (New York: Prometheus, 1981); R. Ryder, *Victims of Science: The Use of Animals in Research* (London: Davis-Poynter, 1975).
3. R. Garner, *Animals, Politics and Morality* (Manchester University Press, 1993).
4. K. Shapiro, 'Editorial', *Society & Animals*, 3 (1995) p. 2.
5. See C. Hollands, *Compassion is the Bugler* (Edinburgh: McDonald, 1980); R. Ryder, *Animal Revolution: Changing Attitudes Towards Speciesism* (Oxford: Blackwell, 1989); I. Newkirk, *Free the Animals* (Chicago: Noble Press, 1992).
6. See D. Henshaw, *Animal Warfare: The Story of the Animal Liberation Front* (London: Fontana, 1989).
7. J. Berry, *Lobbying for the People* (Princeton University Press, 1977) pp. 110–40.
8. J. Jasper and D. Nelkin, *The Animal Rights Crusade* (New York: Free Press, 1992); S. Sperling, *Animal Liberators: Research and Morality* (Berkeley: University of California Press, 1988); L. Finsen and S. Finsen, *The Animal Rights Movement in America: From Compassion to Respect* (New York: Twayne, 1994); G. Francione, *Animals, Property and the Law* (Philadelphia: Temple University Press, 1995); For Britain see Garner, *Animals, Politics and Morality*; R. Thomas, *The Politics of Hunting* (Aldershot: Gower, 1983)
9. K. Shapiro, 'The Caring Sleuth: Portrait of an Animal Rights Activist', *Society and Animals*, 2 (1994) pp. 145–65; H. Herzog, ' "The Movement is My Life": The Psychology of Animal Rights Activism', *Journal of Social Issues*, 49 (1993) pp. 103–19; J. Jasper and J. Poulson, 'Fighting Back: Vulnerabilities, Blunders and Countermobilization by the Targets in Three Animal Rights Campaigns', *Sociological Forum*, 8 (1993) pp. 639–57.
10. See P. Bachrach and M. Baratz, 'The Two Faces of Power', *American Political Science Review*, 56 (1962) pp. 947–52.
11. Jasper and Poulson, 'Fighting Back', p. 655. See also M. Kaufman, 'Backlash: The Counter-Attack Against the Animal Rights Movement', *Animals' Agenda* (May–June 1993) pp. 14–19.
12. See Garner, *Animals, Politics and Morality*, ch. 2.
13. The basic framework for such an analysis is set out in Garner, *Animals, Politics and Morality*, pp. 230–9.
14. For a survey see P. Dunleavy and B. O'Leary, *Theories of the State* (London: Macmillan, 1987).

240

15. See in particular R. Dahl, *Who Governs?* (New Haven: Yale University Press, 1961); R. Dahl, *A Preface to Democratic Theory* (University of Chicago Press, 1956).
16. For useful summaries see A. McFarland, 'Interest Groups and Theories of Power in America, *British Journal of Political Science*, 17 (1987) pp. 136–9; W. Gamson, *The Strategy of Social Protest* (Illinois: Dorsey Press, 1975) pp. 5–7; G. Jordon and J. Richardson, *Government and Pressure Groups in Britain* (Oxford University Press, 1987) pp. 43–61.
17. For a general account of the debate see J. Berry, *The Interest Group Society*, 2nd edn (London: HarperCollins, 1989) pp. 197–99. The major texts seeking to challenge pluralism are: C. Wright Mills, *The Power Elite* (New York: Galaxy, 1959); N. Polsby, *Community Power and Political Theory* (New Haven: Yale University Press, 1963); Bachrach and Baratz, 'Two Faces of Power'; T. Lowi, *The End of Liberalism*, 2nd edn (New York: Norton, 1979).
18. S. Lukes, *Power: A Radical View* (London: Macmillan, 1974).
19. W. Grant, *Pressure Groups, Politics and Democracy in Britain*, 2nd edn (Hemel Hempstead: Harvester-Wheatsheaf, 1995) p. 34.
20. For the US origins of policy network theory see G. Jordan, Sub-Governments, Policy Communities and Networks: Refilling the Old Bottles?', *Journal of Theoretical Politics*, 2 (1990) pp. 319–24.
21. See D. Marsh and R. Rhodes (eds) *Policy Networks in British Politics* (Oxford University Press, 1992).
22. G. Jordan and J. Richardson, 'Policy Communities: The British and European Policy Style', *Policy Studies Journal*, 11 (1983) p. 607.
23. See R. Rhodes and D. Marsh, 'The Concept of Policy Networks in British Political Science: Its Development and Utility', *Talking Politics*, 8 (1996) pp. 210–22.
24. R. Ripley and G. Franklin, *Congress, the Bureaucracy and Public Policy*, 5th edn (Pacific Grove: Brooks, 1991) describe sub-governments as 'clusters of individuals that effectively make most of the routine decisions in a given substantive area of policy' (p. 10). See also R.H. Salisbury *et al.*, 'Triangles, Networks, and Hollow Cores: The Complex Geometry of Washington Interest Representation', in M. Petracca (ed.) *The Politics of Interests: Interest Groups Transformed* (Boulder: Westview, 1992) pp. 130–49 and J. Berry, *The Interest Group Society*, pp. 164–94.
25. See Jasper and Nelkin, *The Animal Rights Crusade*, pp. 12–21.
26. F. Loew, 'Turning Plowshares into Volvos: Changing American Attitudes Toward Livestock', *Journal of Agricultural and Environmental Ethics*, 1 (1993) 105–6.
27. G. Wilson, 'American Interest Groups in Comparative Perspective', in Petracca, *The Politics of Interests*, pp. 80–95.
28. See, in particular, H. Helco, 'Issue Networks and the Executive Establishment', in A. King (ed.) *The New American Political System* (Washington DC: American Enterprise Institute, 1978) and Berry, *The Interest Group Society*, p. 179.
29. G. Francione, *Animals, Property and the Law* and *Rain Without Thunder: The Ideology of the Animal Rights Movement* (Philadelphia: Temple University Press, 1996).

30. Gamson, *Strategy of Social Protest*, p. 28.
31. Ibid., p. 34.
32. W. Browne, *Private Interests, Public Policy and American Agriculture* (Lawrence: University of Kansas Press, 1988) pp. 192–3.
33. H. Moyer and T. Josling, *Agricultural Policy Reform: Politics and Process in the EC and the USA* (Hemel Hempstead: Harvester-Wheatsheaf, 1990) p. 1.

1. The Institutional Framework of Animal Protection

1. Information on the total number of bills, PQs and EDMs introduced during this period is gained from the *Sessional Information Digest* published annually by HMSO.
2. 'Early Day Motions, Factsheet', *Public Information Office*, House of Commons.
3. Figures calculated from the *Congressional Quarterly Almanac* (Washington DC).
4. See Ryder, *Animal Revolution*.
5. M. Radford, 'Partial Protection: Animal Welfare and the Law', in R. Garner (ed.) *Animal Rights: The Changing Debate* (London: Macmillan, 1996) pp. 70–5.
6. Interview with Chris Ryder, head of the AWD, 7 May 1996.
7. Ibid.
8. R. Goddard Svendsen, 'Animal Welfare and the European Union' in Garner, *Animal Rights*, pp. 143–65.
9. *Agscene* (Autumn 1996) p. 7.
10. R. French, *Antivisection and Medical Science in Victorian Society* (Princeton University Press, 1975) pp. 103–4, 114–42.
11. See Y. Rydin, *The British Planning System: An Introduction* (London: Macmillan, 1993).
12. Garner, *Animals, Politics and Morality*, p. 191.
13. There is now an extensive literature on the politics of agriculture. For an introduction see R. Garner, *Environmental Politics* (Hemel Hempstead: Harvester-Wheatsheaf, 1996) pp. 156–63. See also M. Smith, *The Politics of Agricultural Support in Britain: The Development of the Agricultural Policy Community* (Aldershot: Dartmouth, 1990).
14. Animal Welfare Institute, *Animals and Their Legal Rights* (Washington DC, 1990), p. 49.
15. *Hearing Before the Committee on Labour and Human Resources on Poultry Safety*, United States Senate, 102nd Congress, First Session, 28 June 1991, p. 81.
16. *The Animals' Agenda* (March–April 1997) pp. 22–6.
17. L. Tweeten, 'Public Policy Decisions for Farm Animal Welfare', *Journal of Agricultural and Environmental Ethics*, 1 (1993) p. 88.
18. See Francione, *Animals, Property and the Law*, pp. 142–56.
19. *The Animals' Agenda*, 14 (1994) p. 11.
20. *Animal Care Industry Report* (USDA, Spring 1997).
21. Interview with Louis Sibal, 4 April 1996.
22. F. Orlans, *In the Name of Science: Issues in Responsible Animal Experimentation* (New York: Oxford University Press, 1993) pp. 51–5.

23. *Hearing before the Research and Technology Subcommittee of the Committee on Armed Services on the Use of Animals in Research by the Department of Defense,* House of Representatives, Second Session, 13 April 1994, pp. 101, 198.
24. Francione, *Rain Without Thunder,* n. 42, p. 235.
25. *New York Times,* 28 June 1989.
26. By far the best account of the court's role in animal protection politics is Francione, *Animals, Property and the Law.*
27. Orlans, *In the Name of Science,* p. 59.
28. See Francione, *Animals, Property and the Law,* pp. 234–49.
29. *The United States Government Manual* (Washington DC: Office of the Federal Register, National Archives and Records Administration, 1987) p. 316.
30. Finsen and Finsen, *The Animal Rights Movement,* p. 15.
31. M. Corn, 'The Steel Jaw Leghold Trap: Issues and Concerns', *CRS Report for Congress,* 29 March 1993.
32. Finsen and Finsen, *The Animal Rights Movement,* p. 110.
33. *Animal People* (December 1994) p. 2.

2. The Economics and Politics of Animal Exploitation

1. See A. Rowan, 'The Use of Animals in Experimentation: An Examination of the "Technical" Arguments Used to Criticize the Practice', in Garner, (ed.) *Animal Rights,* pp. 104–22 as an example of an attempt to assess the empirical validity of using animals in laboratories.
2. See R. Garner, 'Wildlife Conservation and the Moral Status of Animals', *Environmental Politics,* 3 (1994) pp. 114–19.
3. The NRA claims 'to promote hunter safety, and to promote and defend hunting as a shooting sport and as a viable necessary method of fostering the propagation, growth, conservation, and wise use of our renewable wildlife resources'. Quoted in *Foundation for Public Affairs,* 'Public Interest Profiles 1992–3' (Washington, DC: Congressional Quarterly Inc., 1992) p. 173.
4. L. Mighetto, *Wild Animals and American Environmental Ethics* (Arizona University Press, 1991) pp. 27–41.
5. See A. Ford, *John James Audubon: A Biography* (New York: Abbeville Press, 1988).
6. R. Gottlieb, *Forcing the Spring: The Transformation of the American Environmental Movement* (London: Earthscan, 1994) pp. 157–8.
7. The Defenders of Wildlife, founded in 1947, has never had an overall position on hunting and has always been opposed to the steel-jawed leghold trap.
8. J. Rifkin and C. Grunewald Rifkin, *Voting Green* (New York: Doubleday, 1992) p. 169.
9. Rifkin and Grunewald Rifkin, *Voting Green,* p. 174.
10. Browne, *Private Interests,* pp. xi, 4.
11. J. Burns, 'A Synoptic View of the Food Industry', in J. Burns, J. McInerney and A. Swinbank (eds) *The Food Industry: Economics and Politics* (London: Heineman, 1983) p. 3.

12. S. Harris, A. Swinbank and G. Wilkinson, *The Food and Farm Policies of the European Community* (Chichester: John Wiley, 1983) p. 62.
13. J. Rifkin, *Beyond Beef: The Rise and Fall of the Cattle Culture* (Harmondsworth: Penguin, 1992) p. 154.
14. See N. Fiddes, *Meat: A Natural Symbol* (London: Routledge, 1991) pp. 26–9.
15. There is now an extensive literature on the environmental consequences of intensive agriculture. The most accessible of these publications are T. Clunies-Ross and N. Hildyard, *The Politics of Industrial Agriculture* (London: Earthscan, 1992) pp. 19–27; Fiddes, *Meat*, pp. 210–23; Rifkin, *Beyond Beef*, pp. 185–230; Johnson, *Factory Farming*, pp. 141–73.
16. On factory farming see R. Harrison, *Animal Machines: The New Factory Farming Industry* (London: Vincent Stuart, 1964); J. Mason and P. Singer, *Animal Factories* (New York: Crown, 1980); Johnson, *Factory Farming*; J. Rifkin, '*Beyond Beef*'.
17. Goodman and Redclift, *Refashioning Nature*, p. 111.
18. H. Newby, 'Living From Hand to Mouth: the Farmworker, Food and Agribusiness', in A. Murcott (ed.), *The Sociology of Food and Eating: Essays on the Sociological Significance of Food* (Aldershot: Gower, 1983) p. 38.
19. D. Goodman, B. Sorj and J. Wiljinson, *From Farming to Biotechnology: A Theory of Agro-Industrial Development* (Oxford: Basil Blackwell, 1987) p. 25.
20. MAFF, *Annual Review of Agriculture*, 1988, p. 2.
21. J. McInerney, 'A Synoptic View of Policy-Making for the Food Sector', in Burns *et al.* (eds) *The Food Industry*, p. 164.
22. Goodman *et al. From Farming to Biotechnology*, p. 163.
23. Rifkin and Grunewald Rifkin, *Voting Green*, p. 237; Goodman *et al. From Farming to Biotechnology*, p. 119.
24. See Rifkin and Grunewald Rifkin, *Voting Green*, pp. 226–42.
25. FAWC, *Report on the Welfare of Laying Hens in Colony Systems*, p. 5.
26. Goodman *et al*, *From Farming to Biotechnology*, p. 52.
27. Ibid., p. 179.
28. W. Grant, *The Dairy Industry: An International Comparison* (Aldershot: Dartmouth, 1991) p. 53.
29. *Guardian*, 24 February 1993.
30. H. Newby, 'Living From Hand to Mouth', pp. 42–3.
31. Clunies-Ross and Hildyard *Industrial Agriculture*, p. 69. Hillsdown Holdings was the subject of criticism when in 1993 it was disclosed that the company had done £2000 worth of restoration at the home of the then Minister of Agriculture John Gummer. See *Guardian*, 12 February 1993.
32. J. Rifkin, *Beyond Beef*, pp. 130–1.
33. J. Malcolm, 'Food and Farming', in Burns *et al.* (eds) *The Food Industry*, p. 73.
34. Clunies-Ross and Hildyard, *Industrial Agriculture*, p. 69.
35. J. Abraham, *Science, Politics and the Pharmaceutical Industry: Controversy and Bias in Drug Regulation* (London: UCL, 1995) pp. 38–9.
36. W. Reekie and M. Weber, *Profits, Politics and Drugs*, (New York: Holmes & Meier, 1979) pp. 1, 7.
37. R. Ballance, J. Pogamy and H. Forstner, *The World's Pharmaceutical Industries: An International Perspective*, (Aldershot: Edward Elgar, 1992) p. 3.
38. Ballance, *et al* (eds) *The World's Pharmaceutical Industries*, p. 8.

39. Ibid., 108–9.
40. Reekie and Weber, *Profits, Politics and Drugs*, pp. 7, 24.
41. W. Coleman and W. Grant, 'Business Association and Public Policy: a Comparison of Organizational Development in Britain and Canada', *Journal of Public Policy*, 4 (1990) p. 226.
42. Abrahams, *Science, Politics and the Pharmaceutical Industry*, p. 59.
43. House of Lords, *Report of the Select Committee on the Laboratory Animals Protection Bill*, vol. 1 (HMSO, 1980) pp. 240–1, 203.
44. *Report of the Select Committee on the Laboratory Animals Protection Bill*, p. 137.
45. Home Office, *Statistics of Scientific Procedures on Living Animals 1983*, Cmnd. 8883, (HMSO, 1983) p. 2.
46. R. Sharpe, *The Cruel Deception* (London: Thorsons, 1988) pp. 256–8.
47. This information is derived, for American organizations, from A. Close, *Washington Representatives* (Washington DC: Columbia), published annually, from the appearance of organizations at Congressional hearings and from interviews with participants. British organizations were identified from appearances at committee inquiries, from interviews with participants and from P. Millard, '*Trade Associations and Professional Bodies of the United Kingdom* (London: Gale Research International), published annually.
48. A major recent study of the pharmaceutical industry (Ballance et al. (eds) *The World's Pharmaceutical Industries*) has only two brief passages on the use of animals in the research process.
49. Abrahams, *Science, Politics and the Pharmaceutical Industry*, pp. 54, 58.
50. Ibid., pp. 66–75.
51. J. Greenwood and K. Ronit, 'Established and Emergent Sectors: Organised Interests at the European Level in the Pharmaceutical Industry and the New Biotechnologies', in Greenwood *et al.*, *Organized Interests and the European Union*, pp. 69–98.
52. *Report of the Select Committee on the Laboratory Animals Protection Bill*, pp. 44–56.
53. See S. Lederer, 'The Controversy over Animal Experimentation in America, 1880–1914', in N. Rupke (ed.) *Vivisection in Historical Perspective* (London: Routledge, 1987) pp. 236–58.
54. Orlans, *In the Name of Science*, pp. 44–5.
55. Ibid., p. 46.
56. See Council on Scientific Affairs, 'Animals in Research', *Journal of the American Medical Association*, (23–30 June 1989) pp. 3602–6. For the role of the Foundation for Biomedical Research see F.L. Trull, 'The Research Movement', *Lab Animal*, 23 (1994) pp. 23–6. See also M. Laufman, 'Backlash: The Counter-attack against the Animal Rights Movement', *The Animals' Agenda* (May–June 1993) pp. 14–19; J. Howard, 'The Politics of Animal Research', *The Animals' Agenda*, January–February 1997, 31–3 and Finsen, *The Animal Rights Movement*, 163–4.
57. Interview with Barbara Rich, 9 April 1996.
58. *Animal People* (March 1993) p. 12.
59. See N. Rupke, 'Pro-vivisection in England in the Early 1880s: Arguments and Motives', in N. Rupke (ed.) *Vivisection in Historical Perspective*, pp. 190–3.

246 *Notes*

60. R. Sharpe, *The Cruel Deception*, p. 251.
61. Quoted in M.A. Elston, 'The Anti-vivisectionist Movement and the Science of Medicine', in J. Gabe, D. Kelleher and G. Williams (eds) *Challenging Medicine'*, (London: Routledge, 1993) p. 173.
62. The British Egg Information Service, *The British Egg Industry Council: Some Questions and Answers* (London, 1993).
63. A. Ball and F. Millard, *Pressure Politics in Industrial Societies* (Basingstoke: Macmillan, 1986) p. 136.
64. Interview with Steve Kopperud, 8 April 1996.
65. NFU, *Annual Report and Accounts* (1992) p. 7.
66. Interview with Mark Matfield, 16 April 1996.
67. Interview with Steve Kopperud, 8 April 1996.
68. Interview with Barbara Rich, 9 April 1996.
69. Interview with Steve Kopperud, 8 April 1996.
70. *Hearing Before the Committee on Agriculture, Nutrition and Forestry, United States Senate on Improved Standards for Laboratory Animals*, Second Session, 98th Congress, 20 July 1983, p. 45.
71. W. Browne and A. Cigler, *US Agricultural Groups: Institutional Profiles* (New York: Greenwood, 1990) p. 183.
72. *RDS Annual Report* (November 1995) pp. 9–10.
73. Browne and Cigler, *Agricultural Groups*, p. 29.
74. NFU, *Annual Report and Accounts* (1993) p. 28.
75. B. Holbeche, 'Policy and Influence: MAFF and the NFU', *Public Policy and Administration*, 1 (1986) pp. 41–2.
76. Browne and Cigler, *Agricultural Groups*, pp. 28–30.
77. Mason and Singer, *Animal Factories*, pp. 175–6.
78. Information from NFU *Annual Reports and Accounts*.
79. NFU *Annual Reports and Accounts*, (1993) p. 37.
80. Ibid., p. 35.
81. *British Farmer* (March 1987).
82. *British Farmer* (July 1993).
83. Browne, *Private Interests*, pp. 99–100.

3. The Animal Protection Movement

1. see Garner, *Animals, Politics and Morality*, ch. 2.
2. Berry, *Lobbying For the People*, p. 7.
3. See D. Truman, *The Governmental Process* (New York: Alfred Knopf, 1951).
4. M. Olson, *The Logic of Collective Action* (Cambridge Mass.: Harvard University Press, 1965).
5. Olson, *Collective Action*, pp. 132–3.
6. Interview with Mike Ring, 17 August 1994.
7. McFarland, 'Interest Groups and Theories of Power in America', p. 131.
8. Kay Schlozman, 'What Accent the Heavenly Chorus? Political Equality and the American Pressure System', *Journal of Politics*, 46 (1984) p. 1013.
9. Interview, 9 April 1996.
10. This was the strategy pursued by the participants in the Great Ape Project. See P. Cavalieri and P. Singer, *The Great Ape Project* (London: Fourth

Estate, 1993). See also K. Tester, *Animals & Society: The Humanity of Animal Rights* (London: Routledge, 1991).

11. For the classic account which deliberately compares human and animal exploitation see M. Spiegel, *The Dreaded Comparison: Human and Animal Slavery* (Philadelphia: New Society, 1988).

12. The only way of squaring the circle here is to impute intrinsic value to the natural world so that it can also be classified in the same vein as exploited. This, of course, is what deep ecologists seek to do.

13. Literature discussing the relationship between animal protection and the left includes J. Sanbonnatsu, 'Animal Liberation: Should the left Care?, *Z Magazine* (October 1989) pp. 101–10; T. Benton, *Natural Relations: Ecology, Animal Rights and Social Justice* (London: Verso, 1993); A. Charlton and G. Francione, 'The American Left Should Support Animal Rights: A Manifesto', *The Animals' Agenda* (January–February 1993) pp. 28–34. Animal protectionist literature from a feminist perspective is C. Adams, *The Sexual Politics of Meat* (New York: Continuum, 1990) and *Neither Man Nor Beast: Feminism and the Defense of Animals* (New York: Continuum, 1995).

14. J. Walker, 'The Origins and Maintenance of Interest Groups in America', *American Political Science Review*, 77 (1983) p. 397.

15. R. Salisbury, 'An Exchange Theory of Interest Groups', *Midwest Journal of Political Science*, 13 (1969) p. 20.

16. *Public Interest Profiles*, p. 501.

17. J. Berry's study, *Lobbying For the People*, p. 24, confirms that the entrepreneurial model had a great deal of utility for public interest groups in general.

18. Garner, *Animals, Politics and Morality*, pp. 41–8.

19. This is described as 'commitment theory' by P.A. Sabatier, 'Interest Group Membership and Organization: Multiple Theories', in Petracca (ed.) *The Politics of Interests*, p. 109.

20. Shapiro, 'Caring Sleuth'.

21. Berry, *Lobbying For the People*, pp. 115–16.

22. J. Jasper and J. Poulson, 'Animal Rights and Anti-Nuclear Protest: Political Networks and Moral Shocks in Recruitment', paper presented at the American Sociological Association annual meeting, San Francisco, 1989, pp. 10; 28–30. See also J. Jasper, 'Recruiting Intimates, Recruiting Strangers: Building the Contemporary Animal Rights Movement', unpublished manuscript, 1992. By contrast, a study of social movements in the Netherlands revealed that there was almost a complete overlap between members of the anti-nuclear power, environmental, anti-racism and the third world movements. P. Klandermans, 'Linking the "Old" and the "New": Movement Networks in the Netherlands', in R. Dalton and M. Kuechler (eds) *Challenging the Political Order: New Social and Political Movements in Western Democracies*, (Cambridge: Polity, 1990) pp. 122–36.

23. Herzog, 'The Movement is my Life', p. 112;

24. Sperling, *Animal Liberators*, p. 117.

25. See Garner, *Animals, Politics and Morality*, pp. 63–5.

26. Jasper and Poulson, 'Animal Rights and Anti-Nuclear Protests', pp. 19–21.

248 *Notes*

27. P. Greanville and D. Moss, 'The Emerging Face of the Movement', *The Animals' Agenda* (March–April 1985) pp. 10–11, 36.
28. Sperling, *Animal Liberators*, pp. 99–102, 121.
29. On the role of post-material values see R. Inglehart, 'Values, Ideology and Cognitive Mobilization in New Social Movements', in Dalton and Kuechler (eds) *Challenging the Political Order*, pp. 43–66. On sentimental anthropormorphism see Jasper and Nelkin, *The Animal Rights Crusade*, pp. 11–24. See also J. Twigg, 'Vegetarianism and the Meaning of Meat', in Murcott, *The Sociology of Food and Eating*, pp. 18–30 and Fiddes, *Meat*, pp. 101–10.
30. W. Gamson, 'The Social Psychology of Collective Action', in A. Morris and C. Mueller (eds) *Frontiers in Social Movement Theory* (New Haven, Conn.: Yale University Press, 1992) p. 56.
31. Greanville and Moss, 'Emerging Face of the Movement'. Other surveys have confirmed the accuracy of these figures. See Jasper and Poulson, 'Animal Rights and Anti-Nuclear Protest', pp. 15–18; Jasper and Nelkin, *Animal Rights Crusade*, pp. 38–41.
32. J.L. Mansbridge, *Why We Lost the ERA* (University of Chicago Press, 1986) p. 179.
33. W. Gormley, 'Regulatory Issue Networks in a Federal System', *Polity*, 18 (1986) pp. 608–9.
34. Jasper and Nelkin, *Animal Rights Crusade*, p. 43.
35. M.A. Giannelli, 'What Do We Want? Animal Rights! When Do we Want it?: Til Ideology, Ego, or Whatever Do Us Part...' (unpublished document, 25 October, 1996).
36. *Animal People* (January/February 1993) p. 2.
37. H. Silverstein, 'Unleashing Rights: Law and the Politics of the Animal Rights Movement', PhD thesis, University of Washington, 1992, pp. 139–54.
38. Sperling, *Animal Liberators*, p. 85.
39. Francione, *Rain Without Thunder*.
40. This more conciliatory approach has not gone too well with radical activists, some of whom were on the executive committee. The conflict came to a head in 1994 when a meeting held to debate proposals to weaken the position of the radicals ended in uproar. See *Independent*, 7 November 1994.
41. Here, I would take issue with Jasper and Nelkin, *Animal Rights Crusade*, pp. 8–9, who distinguish between welfarists, pragmatists and fundamentalists. Their distinction between the latter two positions is based, incorrectly I think, upon both ideology and strategy. In ideological terms, they are wrong to claim that pragmatic animal rightists such as Henry Spira see some animal exploitation as being justified on moral grounds. Likewise, associating fundamentalism strategically with direct action and pragmatism with legality is overly simplistic.
42. Francione, *Animals, Property and the Law* and *Rain Without Thunder*.
43. Francione, *Animals, Property and the Law*, pp. 256–8; *Rain Without Thunder*, pp. 110–46.
44. Francione, *Animals, Property and the Law*, p. 4. See *Rain Without Thunder*, pp. 126–39 for a concise exposition of this view.
45. Francione, *Animals, Property and the Law*, pp. 204–5.

46. *Rain Without Thunder*, ch. 2. Those who Francione describes as 'new welfarists' include the present author as well as Peter Singer, Kim Stallwood, editor of the American animal rights magazine, *Animals' Agenda*, Don Barnes, a leading member of the American Anti-Vivisection Society, Henry Spira and Ingrid Newkirk.
47. Francione, *Rain Without Thunder*, chs. 3 and 4.
48. Ibid. pp. 62–76.
49. Giannelli, 'What Do We Want? Animal Rights! When Do we Want it?'.
50. *Animal People* (April 1996); Francione, *Rain Without Thunder*, pp. 226–9.
51. Finsen and Finsen, *The Animal Rights Movement*, pp. 146–7.
52. For a discussion of Francione's position see Finsen and Finsen, *The Animal Rights Movement*, pp. 258–64; Garner, *Animals, Politics and Morality*, pp. 246–9, Garner, *Animal Rights*, pp. 4–6.
53. Francione, *Rain Without Thunder*, chs 6–7.
54. Ibid., pp. 165–9.
55. Ibid., p. 217.
56. Some farmers have taken advantage of an EU slaughter fund which effectively means that some calves will end up in pet and baby food products. See *Guardian*, 11 January 1995.
57. T. Benton and R. Redfearn, 'The Politics of Animal Rights: Where is the Left', *New Left Review*, 215 (1996) p. 51.
58. Benton, 'Politics of Animal Rights', p. 57.
59. Francione, *Rain Without Thunder*, pp. 207–11.
60. Ibid., pp. 162–5, 192.
61. J. Berry, *The Interest Group Society*, p. 105.
62. Garner, *Animals, Politics and Morality*.
63. Francione, *Rain Without Thunder*, pp. 21–2.
64. G. Francione, 'Animal Rights: An Incremental Approach' in Garner, *Animal Rights*, pp. 43–6.
65. Orlans, *In the Name of Science*, p. 22.
66. Francione, *Rain Without Thunder*, pp. 136, 211.
67. In April 1997, the National Trust, a major private UK land owner, announced, as a result of public pressure, that it would no longer allow stag hunting on its land.
68. Francione, *Rain Without Thunder*, pp. 167–70.
69. See Rifkin, *Beyond Beef*, pp. 256–60.

4. Lobbying for Animals

1. Finsen and Finsen, *The Animal Rights Movement*, pp. 53–6.
2. For details of Henry Spira's campaigns see H. Spira, 'Animal Rights: The Frontiers of Compassion', *Peace and Democracy News* (Summer 1993) pp. 11–14; 'Fighting to Win', in P. Singer (ed.) *In Defense of Animals* (Oxford: Basil Blackwell, 1985) pp. 194–208. See also Finsen and Finsen, *The Animal Rights Movement*, pp. 58–60; Jasper and Nelkin, *Animal Rights Crusade*, pp. 26–9.
3. Interview with Alex Hershaft, 4 May 1993. See also Finsen and Finsen, *The Animal Rights Movement*, pp. 74–5 and Jasper and Nelkin, *Animal Rights Crusade*, pp. 29–31.

4. Garner, *Animals, Politics and Morality*, pp. 51–4.
5. Ibid. pp. 54–60.
6. Letter from 18 industry groups to Paul Irwin, President of HSUS, 29 October 1993.
7. 'Blood Sports, Lobby Groups and the Criminal Justice Bill: a survey of MPs' (London: Access Opinion Limited, 1994).
8. MORI, 'Attitudes of Members of Parliament' (1993).
9. This relatively low score for CIWF is related to the date of the poll. The organization's high-profile role in the live exports campaign has undoubtedly considerably increased its name recognition.
10. *Public Interest Profiles*, p. 503.
11. *Animal People* (May 1994), pp. 11–12.
12. Finsen and Finsen, *The Animal Rights Movement*, p. 80.
13. Letter to the author, 7 April 1993.
14. Quoted in C. Matlack, 'Animal Rights Furor', *The National Journal*, 23 (1991) p. 2143. This point is confirmed by others, such as Adele Douglass, Washington Director of the AHA, interview, 5 May 1993.
15. See Garner, *Animals, Politics and Morality*, pp. 182–5.
16. Matlack, 'Animal Rights Furor', p. 2146.
17. *Public Interest Profiles*, pp. 173–5.
18. Ibid., p. 176.
19. See C. Hollands, *Compassion is the Bugler*, pp. 37–87.
20. House of Commons, First Report from the Agriculture Committee. *Animal Welfare in Poultry, Pig and Veal Calf Production*, vol. 2, pp. 240–74.
21. Hollands, *Compassion is the Bugler*, pp. 38–48.
22. Interview, 8 September 1994. It is evident that the RSPB is similarly concerned about organizational maintenance. A classic illustration of the conflicts that can arise because of this emphasis occurred in the aftermath of a major oil spill in 1994. RSPCA staff told me they were annoyed that the RSPB were raising money for cleaning birds whereas it was the RSPCA who were primarily responsible for undertaking it.
23. Hollands, *Compassion is the Bugler*, p. 124.
24. Communication from Richard Ryder, 2 December 1993.
25. *Report of the Select Committee on the Laboratory Animals Protection Bill*, pp. 54–5.
26. Personal interview, 23 May 1996.
27. British Veterinary Association, *Annual Review 1993–4*, p. 1.

5. Parliament and Animal Protection

1. See P. Norton, *Does Parliament Matter?* (Hemel Hempstead: Harvester-Wheatsheaf, 1993).
2. On the NFU's view, see *British Farmer* (November 1990).
3. See R. Body, *Agriculture: The Triumph and the Shame* (London: Temple Smith, 1982).
4. For the second reading debate see *Hansard*, vol. 184, cols 563–626.
5. See *Hansard*, vol. 189, cols 1368–92.
6. Even *The Times* in an editorial on 12 January 1991 supported the Bill.

7. Thomas, *Politics of Hunting*. Note though, that, as Angela Smith, at the time the political director of the LACS, revealed (interview, 24 March 1994), for a Labour MP to vote against an anti-hunting bill would cost 20–30 votes in the Shadow Cabinet election.
8. *Wildlife Guardian* (Spring 1996) p. 2; *Guardian*, 15 November 1995.
9. R. Worcester, 'Scenting Dissent', *New Statesman and Society*, 21 April 1995, pp. 22–3.
10. P. Cowley and N. Stace, 'The Wild Mammals (Protection) Bill: A Parliamentary White Elephant?', *The Journal of Legislative Studies*, 2 (1996) p. 348.
11. *New Labour Because Britain Deserves Better* (London: Labour Party, 1997) p. 30.
12. *Observer*, 1 September 1996. The Political Animal Lobby, IFAW's lobbying arm in Britain, also provides the funds for Labour's animal welfare research assistant in addition to funding the production of a document on Labour's animal welfare commitments, 'New Life for Animals', in 1997.
13. *Guardian*, 6 May 1997.
14. See Cowley and Stace, 'Wild Mammals (Protection) Bill'.
15. *Report of the Select Committee on the Laboratory Animals Protection Bill.*
16. *Animal Welfare in Poultry, Pig and Veal Calf Production.*
17. MORI, 'Attitudes of Members of Parliament' (1993).
18. The scores allocated to MPs incorporate parliamentary activity throughout the period 1985–94 and not just in the 1987–92 period.
19. Clark, a vegetarian well known for his opposition to hunting, was minister of state at the DTI between 1986 and 1989. In a remarkable passage in his diaries, he recounts how Thatcher prevented him from introducing a fur labelling order and how he considered resigning over the issue. A. Clark, *Diaries* (London: Weidenfeld & Nicholson, 1993) pp. 213–17.
20. One of the new female Labour MPs is Angela Smith, who previously occupied a senior position within the League Against Cruel Sports.

6. American Legislators and Animal Protection

1. Interestingly, there was not a particularly good correlation between the list of members based upon their scoring record and the membership of the Congressional Friends of Animals, a caucus set up in 1989. In the 102nd Congress, for instance, only nine of the 23 members of the caucus appear in the list of the 50 highest scorers. For the full membership see Rifkin and Rifkin, *Voting Green*, p. 212.
2. *The U.S. Congress Handbook 103rd Congress First Session* (Virginia: Barbara Pullen, 1993) pp. 210–17.
3. Rifkin and Grunewald Rifkin, *Voting Green*. See also C. Grunewald Rifkin, 'The Greening of Animal Rights', *The Animals' Agenda* (September–October 1992) pp. 36–41.
4. The eight categories were atmospheric protection, energy and transportation, defence, international development and foreign policy, agriculture, public lands, forests and wetlands, animal rights, and endangered species and biodiversity. It is difficult to make direct comparisons with the animal

protection scores in this present study and those provided by the Rifkins because their relevant category, called 'animal rights', focuses on laboratory animals whilst farm animal welfare is contained within a separate 'agriculture' section and wildlife issues are covered within at least two other sections.

5. Rifkin and Grunewald Rifkin, *Voting Green*, pp. 288–90.
6. Ibid., p. 290.
7. Calculated from the information provided in ibid., pp. 294–325.

7. The Politics of Farm Animal Welfare in the United States

1. Moyer and Josling, *Agricultural Policy Reform*, p. 106.
2. Goodman and Redclift, *Refashioning Nature*, pp. 116–19.
3. Ibid., p. 117.
4. See Smith, *Pressure, Power and Policy: State Autonomy and Policy Networks in Britain and the United States* (Hemel Hempstead: Harvester-Wheatsheaf, 1993) pp. 121–4.
5. Browne, *Private Interests.*
6. Ibid., p. 252.
7. Smith (*Pressure, Power and Policy*, pp. 125–7, 130–2) argues that the agricultural policy network in the US was always more open than its British counterpart.
8. Browne, *Private Interests*, p. 233.
9. *Hearing Before the Subcommittee on Livestock of the Committee on Agriculture on the Downed Animal Protection Act etc.*, House of Representatives, 103rd Congress, Second Session, 28 September 1994, p. 1.
10. Two members of the Committee, Charles Stenholm (Democrat–Texas) and John Boeehner (Republican–Ohio), have also been co-chairs of the Congressional Animal Welfare Caucus, an organization designed to oppose animal protection measures put before the House.
11. Rose, unlike Gunderson, who is a member of the Congressional Animal Welfare Caucus, has also been a member of the Congressional Friends of Animals.
12. Tweeten, 'Public Policy Decisions', p. 99.
13. Berry, *The Interest Group Society*, pp. 118–20.
14. Grant, *Dairy Industry*, p. 33.
15. This, and the following, data is compiled from L. Makinson and J. Goldstein, *Open Secrets: The Encyclopedia of Congressional Money and Politics* (Washington DC: Congressional Quarterly, 1994).
16. For a review of the literature, see J. Tierney, 'Organized Interests and the Nation's Capitol', in Petracca, *The Politics of Interests*, pp. 204–5.
17. Berry, *The Interest Group Society*, p. 128.
18. Those who doubt whether there is a close correlation between campaign contributions and Congressional behaviour include T. Eismeier and P Pollock III, 'Political Action Committees: Varieties of Organization and Strategy' in M. Malbin (ed.) *Money and Politics in the United States* (New Jersey: Chatham, 1984) pp. 122–41; M. Malbin, 'Looking Back at the

Future of Campaign Finance Reform: Interest Groups and American Elections', in Malbin (ed.) *Money and Politics*, pp. 232–76. For an alternative view see F.L. Davis, 'Balancing the Perspective on PAC Contributions: In search of an impact on roll calls', *American Politics Quarterly*, 21 (1993) pp. 205–22.

19. Moyer and Josling, *Agricultural Policy Reform*, p. 108.
20. One lobbyist told me (interview 8 April 1996) that USDA does not go out of its way to promote farmers as upholders of animal welfare. This can be contrasted with the way in which NIH promotes and defends the interests of animal research.
21. H.D. Guither, *The Food Lobbyists* (Massachusetts: Lexington, 1980) p. 78.
22. *Hearing Before the Committee on Labor and Human Resources on Poultry Safety*, United States Senate, 102nd Congress, First Session, 28 June 1991, p. 122.
23. Hausman, *Jack Spratt's Legacy*, pp. 19–20.
24. Moyer and Josling, *Agricultural Policy Reform*, p. 130.
25. Rifkin and Grunewald Rifkin, *Voting Green*, p. 160.
26. Hausman, *Jack Spratt's Legacy*, pp. 19–20, 235.
27. Grant, *The Dairy Industry*, p. 97.
28. M. Fox, *Returning to Eden: Animal Rights and Human Responsibilities* (Florida: Robert Krieger, 1986) p. 86.
29. See J. Robins' *Diet For a New America* (New Hampshire: Stillpoint, 1987) who provides an excellent account of agribusinesse's considerable efforts designed to show Americans that animals are humanely raised and slaughtered and that animal products have no negative health implications. See also Mason and Singer, *Animal Factories*.
30. Hausman, *Jack Spratt's Legacy*, pp. 196, 210.
31. Brown and Cigler, *US Agricultural Groups*, p. 142.
32. Robins, *Diet*, p. 129.
33. Interview with Steve Kopperud, 8 April 1996.
34. See H. Spira, 'Less Meat, Less Misery: Reforming Factory Farms', *Forum for Applied Research and Public Policy* (Spring 1996) pp. 39–44 and B. Feder, 'Pressuring Purdue', *New York Times Magazine*, 26 November 1989.
35. Spira, 'Less Meat, Less Misery', p. 43.
36. Interview with Steve Kopperud, 8 April 1996.

8. The Politics of Farm Animal Welfare in Britain

1. See Smith, *Politics of Agricultural Support in Britain*.
2. J. Bowers, 'British Agricultural Policy Since the Second World War', *The Agricultural History Review*, 33 (1986) pp. 66–74.
3. HMSO, *Food From Our Own Resources*, Cmnd. 6020 (April 1965); HMSO *Farming and the Nation*, Cmnd. 7458 (1979).
4. See Smith, *Politics of Agricultural Support*, ch. 2.
5. *Report of the Committee of Enquiry into the Export of Live Cattle to the Continent for Slaughter (the Balfour Report)*, Cmnd. 154 (1957).
6. Harrison, *Animal Machines*.
7. *Report of the Technical Committee to Enquire into the Welfare of Animals kept under Intensive Livestock Husbandry Systems (the Brambell Report)*, HMSO, Cmnd. 2836 (1965).

8. *Brambell,* pp. 10–11. The committee, following the Littlewood Committee (see Chapter 7) defined suffering in terms of discomfort, stress and pain. The committee was also heavily influenced by a paper 'The Assessment of Pain and Distress in Animals' by W.H. Thorpe, which was appended to the report, pp. 71–9.
9. *Brambell,* p. 13.
10. *Ibid.,* p. 20.
11. *Ibid.,* p. 60.
12. Radford, 'Animal Welfare and the Law', p. 72.
13. M. Mills, *The Politics of Dietary Change* (Aldershot: Dartmouth, 1992) p. 173.
14. *Animal Welfare in Poultry, Pig and Veal Calf Production,* p. 20.
15. *Hansard,* vol. 32, col. 545.
16. Thomas Torney, *Hansard,* vol. 32, col. 509.
17. P. Stevenson, *A Far Cry From Noah* (London: Green Print, 1994) pp. 6–9.
18. *Report of the Committee on the Export of Animals for Slaughter (O'Brien Report),* Cmnd. 5566 (1974).
19. Stevenson, *A Far Cry From Noah,* pp. 12–28.
20. *Animal Welfare in Poultry, Pig and Veal Calf Production,* vol. 2, p. 173. An FAWC report also referred to the 'apparent widespread ignorance' of the codes of practice. FAWC *Regulations Working Group Interim Statement,* p. 2 (n.d).
21. Stevenson, *A Far Cry From Noah,* pp. 59–60.
22. At the end of 1996, the EU Council of Agriculture Ministers agreed to a ten year phase-out of veal crates across the Union. See *Agscene* (Spring 1997) p. 5.
23. MAFF, *Animal Health, Report of the Chief Veterinary Officer* (1991) p. 67.
24. This is certainly the view of Barney Holbeche, the NFU's chief lobbyist. Personal interview, 3 May 1996.
25. FAWC, *The Welfare of Livestock when Slaughtered by Religious Methods* (July 1985).
26. *British Farmer* (5 March 1966).
27. Interview with Chris Ryder, 7 May 1996.
28. The head of the AWD secretariat for the FAWC, Bob Holdsworth, did indicate a great deal of sympathy for animal welfare and he suggested that other officials in the AWD did too. He recognized, though, that proposals which were too radical in the present climate would merely be rejected by MAFF. Interview, 7 May 1996.
29. On breaches to the transportation directive see Stevenson, *A Far Cry From Noah,* pp. 33–6.
30. MAFF, *Government Response to the Farm Animal Welfare Council's Report on the Welfare of Broiler Chickens* (April 1993).
31. I. Bowler, *Agriculture Under the Common Agricultural Policy,* (Manchester University Press, 1985) p. 39.
32. Harris, *Food and Farm Policies,* p. 18.
33. Bowler, *Agriculture Under the Common Agricultural Policy,* p. 39.
34. J. Peterson, 'Hormones, Heifers and High Politics: Biotechnology and the Common Agricultural Policy', *Public Administration,* 67 (1989) p. 446.
35. G. Barling, *'Welfare of Calves: Lawfulness of export restrictions* (London: S.J. Berwin & Co., 1995).

36. Stevenson, *A Far Cry From Noah*, pp. 47–50. *Agscene* (November–December 1990) pp. 2–4.
37. *O'Brien Report*, p. 24.
38. A European Court of Justice decision in May 1996, for instance, rejected the British Government's argument that it could refuse to grant export licenses to farmers intent on sending their animals to Spain simply because it suspected many Spanish slaughterhouses did not meet the standards set down by European directives.
39. *Daily Telegraph* (23 April 1996); *Guardian* (22 May 1996).
40. Gellately, *Silent Ark*, pp. 187–93.
41. Mills, *Politics of Dietary Change*, p. 108.
42. C. Walker and G. Cannon, *The Food Scandal* (London: Century, 1984).
43. M. Smith, 'From Policy Community to Issue Network: Salmonella in Eggs and the New Politics of Food', *Public Administration*, 69 (1991) pp. 235–52.
44. *Guardian* (10 April 1997).
45. *Animal Welfare in Poultry, Pig and Veal Calf Production*, vol. 2, p. 9.
46. *Ibid.*, vol. 2, p. 65.
47. See the RSPCA's evidence to the Agriculture Committee's enquiry, *Animal Welfare in Poultry, Pig and Veal Calf Production* vol. 2, p. 152.
48. *Animal Welfare in Poultry, Pig and Veal Calf Production*, vol. 1, p. 14.
49. *Ibid.*, vol. 1, p. 16.
50. MAFF, *The Government's Expenditure Plans 1994–5 to 1996–7*, Cmnd. 2503 (1994). See also MAFF, *Our Farming Future*, 1991 in which it is written (p. 29) that 'the Government is determined that the welfare of our farm animals should continue to be a high priority in shaping future policies, both here and elsewhere in the European Community'.
51. NFU, *Annual Report* (1979) p. 15.
52. *British Farmer* (October 1987).
53. *Ibid.* (November 1991).
54. *Caring for Livestock*, the Report of the Animal Welfare Working Group (June 1995) p. 2.
55. *Caring for Livestock*, p. 19.
56. *British Farmer* (July 1994, June 1995).
57. Interview with Chris Ryder, 7 May 1996.
58. See, for instance, *Hansard*, vol. 184, cols. 606, 609.
59. See one set of parliamentary questions asked about this issue in *Hansard*, vol. 97, col. 242.
60. *Hansard*, vol. 753, col. 1268.
61. *Hansard*, vol. 753 col. 1277. See also cols 1310–11, 1329–30.
62. Standing Committee, Official Report, Session 1967–68, vol. III, col. 42.
63. *British Farmer* (2 December 1967).
64. *Hansard*, vol. 759, cols. 459–60.
65. R. Harrison, 'Farm Animal Welfare, What, if any, Progress?', *Hume Memorial Lecture*, UFAW (1987) p. 5.
66. For the NFU's view, see *British Farmer* (August 1991 and November 1994), when the NFU was still calling for the regulation to be repealed or, at very least, reformed.
67. *British Farmer* (July–August 1995).

68. *Hansard,* vol. 184, col. 610.
69. *Hansard,* vol. 184, col. 615.
70. Interview, 17 August 1994.
71. *Animal Welfare in Poultry, Pig and Veal Calf Production,* vol. 2, p. 340.
72. The NFU 'rejected utterly the idea of giving the force of regulation to the standards which the [Brambell] report proposes'. *British Farmer* (5 March 1966).
73. See *British Farmer* (8 January 1966).
74. Stevenson, *A Far Cry From Noah,* pp. 97–8.
75. *Hansard,* vol. 163, col. 446.
76. Personal interview with Chris Ryder, head of the AWD, 7 May 1996,
77. Interview, 17 August 1994. The revolving door can benefit groups concerned with animal welfare too. For example, Howard Rees, former Chief Veterinary Officer in MAFF, is honorary Vice President of the BVA. Double standards operate here which underline the privileged position of industry groups. A MAFF official told me, for instance, that a woman who had previously worked for an animal advocacy group was refused a transfer to the AWD 'in the interests of balance'!
78. Interview with Peter Davies, 23 May 1996. The contrast between MAFF and the Home Office is confirmed by Chrissie Nicholls, Head of Veterinary Services of the BVA (interview 17 October 1994).
79. Interview with Peter Stevenson, 28 March 1994.
80. P. Lowe *et al.* (eds) *Countryside Conflicts: The Politics of Farming, Forestry and Conservation* (Aldershot: Gower, 1986).
81. Interview with Barry Mayes, 18 August 1994.
82. R. North and T. Gorman, *Chickengate: An Independent Analysis of the Salmonella in Eggs Scare* (London, Institute for Economic Affairs, 1990) p. 77.
83. M.J. Smith, 'From Policy Community to Issue Network', pp. 243–5.
84. Grant, *The Dairy Industry,* p. 107.
85. *Guardian* (30 and 31 January 1997).
86. *British Farmer* (April 1993).
87. R. Lacey, *Hard to Swallow: A Brief History of Food* (Cambridge University Press, 1994) *passim* but see pp. 171–5 in particular.
88. In fact, the evidence for the existence of serious public health problems from the intensive rearing of animals is substantial, see *Guardian* (6 January 1996) and J. Gray 'Nature Bites Back', *Guardian* (26 March 1996). In the salmonella outbreak, for instance, although the egg industry continually denied the link between salmonella and eggs, and blamed free-range producers for any problems that did exist, one cause identified – by the *Lancet* (24 September 1988) pp. 720–2 – was the recycling of infected slaughterhouse waste back to hens, a practice which occurs because it is cost-effective and because the integration of the poultry industry means that battery units and slaughtering facilities are owned by the same commercial operation. MAFF itself at least partly shared this interpretation of the outbreak and introduced the Processed Animal Protein Order in 1989 which sought to ban this practice. A similar practice, this time using recyled sheep protein in cattle feed, is widely thought to be responsible for the BSE outbreak. See C. Spencer, 'Food Chain's Deadly Floor', *Guardian* (12 May 1994). Finally, the use of excessive amounts of

antibiotics in intensive units could have human health implications. See *The Sunday Times* (19 November 1995).

89. A point emphasized by Fiddes, *Meat*, p. 224. This public perception was aided by considerable coverage in newspapers and quarterlies.
90. See 'Sainsburys roasts the food industry', *Guardian* (19 March 1997).
91. See report on divisions over the scheme in *The Sunday Times* (July 4 1993 and June 11 1995).
92. See the discussion in *Independent*, (9 April 1996).
93. An official of the BEIC described the United Kingdom Egg Producers' Association as 'cowboys'. Interview, 17 August 1994.
94. Grant, *Dairy Industry*, pp. 99–103.
95. See Stevenson, *Far Cry From Noah*, pp. 13–14, 22–3, 30–1.
96. Quoted in ibid., p. 82.

9. The Politics of Animal Research in Britain

1. See Rupke *Vivisection in Historical Perspective*.
2. Sperling, *Animal Liberators*, pp. 45–6.
3. *Ibid.*, pp. 46–7.
4. *Report of the Departmental Committee on Experiments on Animals (the Little-wood Report)*, HMSO, Cmnd. 2641 (April 1965) pp. 8–9.
5. *Littlewood Report*, pp. 7–8.
6. *Report of the Animal Procedures Committee for 1991*, p. 5.
7. *Littlewood Report*, p. 1.
8. *Hansard*, vol. 775, col. 561–3.
9. *Hansard*, vol. 814, cols 1634–46.
10. *Hansard*, vol. 818, col. 1396.
11. *Littlewood Report*, pp. 189–99.
12. *Littlewood Report*, pp. 73–6.
13. *Hansard*, vol. 818, cols 1397–8, 1399–401.
14. The full title of the paper was 'Experiments on Living Animals: a paper submitted to the Home Secretary by a group of members of the Animal Welfare Parliamentary Group, members of the Animal Experimentation Advisory Committee of the RSPCA and the Chairman of Animal Welfare Year.' The signatories, who later went on to form CRAE, were Lord (formerly Douglas) Houghton, the Labour peer, Lord Platt of Grindleford, a past president of the Royal College of Physicians, Clive Hollands, the director of the Scottish Society for the Prevention of Vivisection, Richard Ryder, a radical and leading member of the RSPCA Council (although he later resigned from CRAE in the run up to the 1986 Act on the grounds that the coalition was not bold enough), Bill Jordan, Kit Pedler and three MPs Freddie Burden, Janet Fookes and Ken Lomas.
15. R. Ryder, 'Putting Animals into Politics', in Garner, *Animal Rights*, p. 171.
16. The extent to which animal welfare had permeated the political process in the run up to the 1979 election can be seen in the lenghty Commons debate on the subject on 23 March 1979. *Hansard*, vol. 964, cols 1874–1966.
17. Ryder, 'Putting Animals Into Politics', pp. 170–4.

18. *Hansard,* vol. 923, col. 1807.
19. Interview with Clive Hollands, 8 May 1996.
20. In actual fact, some parts of the bill provided for weaker protection for animals than the administrative practices then in operation. In particular, the pain condition in the bill potentially allowed for the continuation of an experiment even if an animal was in severe pain and distress.
21. *Report of the Select Committee on the Laboratory Animals Protection Bill,* p. 132.
22. *Hansard* vol. 973, col. 1706. Fry's bill, despite having no chance of reaching the statute book, was discussed in a standing committee. Here, Tam Dalyell, the Labour backbencher, liaised with the research community as the key spokesman against the bill. Fry was given a very difficult ride. The proceedings degenerated into farce when Fry mistakenly referred to research on rabbits which had in fact used mice, leading Dalyell to illustrate the confusion by producing a rabbit in the committee room! See Standing Committee C Official Report, vol. IV, 1979–80.
23. *Hansard,* vol. 923, col. 1801.
24. Home Office, *Scientific Procedures on Living Animals, Supplementary White Paper,* HMSO, Cmnd. 9521 (May 1985).
25. Gamson, *Strategy of Social Protest,* p. 28.
26. Home Office, *Scientific Procedures on Living Animals,* p. 6. The Supplementary White Paper revealed that the CRAE Alliance was responsible for a 'large part' of the Government's proposals (p. 2).
27. Parliamentary Debates, House of Lords, vol. 468, col. 1004.
28. *Supplementary White Paper,* 1985, p. 2.
29. The government refused, however, to give way on its plans to charge fees to licence applicants, despite the criticism that this would be a 'burden on research'. *Supplementary White Paper,* 1985, p. 12.
30. Interview with Clive Hollands, 8 May 1996.
31. Parliamentary Debates, House of Commons, Official Report, Standing Committee A, 1985–6.
32. Interview with Clive Hollands, 8 May 1996.
33. *Hansard,* vol. 973, cols 1736–7.
34. *Hansard,* vol. 92, col. 130.
35. Parliamentary Debates, House of Lords, vol. 470, col. 919.
36. *Hansard,* vol. 92, col. 158.
37. Communication from Richard Ryder, 2 December 1993.
38. Ryder argues (communication, 2 December 1993) that the RSPCA should have taken a more rigorous lead in seeking improvements to the bill. Likewise, he resigned from CRAE on the grounds that it was 'capitulating' to, rather than negotiating with, the Home Office, by compromising 'far too early in the game'. My view is that there is some truth in what both Hollands and Ryder say about this. On the one hand, the RSPCA's particpation would have made it much more difficult for the Home Office to exclude, for instance, greater participation for animal welfare representatives on the APC or even a more critical attitude towards cosmetic testing. A BUAV senior staff member also revealed (interview, 26 June 1994) that subsequent to the passage of the legislation, his organization began to realize that they had 'missed the boat' and could have got more if they had been willing to engage in constructive

dialogue rather than resorting to the 'naive' tactics of attacking Mellor in his constituency during the 1983 general election campaign. There is no doubt, however, that some policy concessions did occur as a result of CRAE's participation in the formulation of the legislation.

39. Unlike most bills, this one started its parliamentary passage in the Lords before being considered by the Commons.
40. Parliamentary Debates, House of Lords, vol. 469, cols 1241–8.
41. Standing Committee A, sixth sitting, cols 187–204.
42. Standing Committee A, sixth sitting, col. 200.
43. The amendment was passed because the supporters of reform were divided on this issue. While the re-use of animals was something many would not contemplate, for others it was preferable if the consequence of prohibiting it was the use of more animals in the long run.
44. *Scientific Procedures on Living Animals*, p. 7.
45. *Supplementary White Paper*, 1985, p. 10.
46. *Supplementary White Paper*, 1985, p. 5. Mellor said in the Committee stage that 'I suspect that those of BVA, CRAE and FRAME who proposed this originally probably did not think that the Government would take such a step, and I suspect that it will bring a smile to the lips of one or two of them'. Standing Committee A, Fifth Sitting, clmn. 160.
47. *Littlewood Report*, p. 77.
48. *Report of the Select Committee on the Laboratory Animals Protection Bill*, p. 35.
49. See the RDS's submission to the Littlewood Committee, p. 65.
50. See R. Sharpe, *The Cruel Deception*, for a classic statement of this practical anti-vivisection position.
51. Elston, 'The Anti-vivisectionist Movement', pp. 160–80.
52. See NAVS, *The Campaigner* (January–March 1995) pp. 34–9 for a biting critique of this imbalance.
53. *Report of the Select Committee on the Laboratory Animals Protection Bill*, p. 271.
54. *Report of the Animal Procedures Committee for 1993*, p. 16; *Report of the Animal Procedures Committee for 1994*, p. 7.
55. *Report of the Animal Procedures Committee for 1992*, pp. 17, 35–9.
56. Parliamentary Debates Lords, vol. 410, col. 1343.
57. *Report of the Animal Procedures Committee for 1994*, p. 5.
58. This was the gist of the arguments of the small group of MPs who, backed by the anti-vivisection organizations, opposed the bill. A total of 28 MPs voted against the bill at second reading. These were David Alton, Paddy Ashdown, Tony Banks, Alan Beith, Tony Benn, Dale Campbell-Savours, Alex Carlile, Ann Clwyd, Harry Cohen, Edward Loyden, Mark Madden, Joan Maynard, Brian Sedgemore, Dennis Skinner, Thomas Cox, Terry Fields, Martin Flannery, Michael Hancock, Peter Hardy, Simon Hughes, Archy Kirkwood, James Lamond, Terry Lewis, Michael Meadowcroft, Dave Nellist, David Penhaligan, Clare Short, and James Wallace.
59. Parliamentary Debates, House of Lords, vol. 469, cols. 371, 389–94, 764–7.
60. Parliamentary Debates, House of Lords, vol. 470, col. 904.
61. W. Russell and R. Burch, *The Principles of Humane Experimental Technique* (London: Methuen, 1959).
62. C. Hollands, 'Achieving the Achievable: A Review of Animals in Politics, *ATLA*, 23 (1995) p. 36.

63. *Report of the Animal Procedures Committee for 1991*, p. 5.
64. *Report of the Animal Procedures Committee for 1992*, pp. 7–8.
65. *Report of the Animal Procedures Committee for 1994*, p. 7.
66. *FRAME News* (August 1996) p. 2.
67. *Report of the Select Committee on the Laboratory Animals Protection Bill*, p. 34. It should also be noted that this contradicts the Littlewood Report's own assessment of the Home Office inspectorate.
68. *Report of the Animal Procedures Committee for 1988*, pp. 4–5.
69. *Report of the Animal Procedures Committee for 1994*, pp. vi–vii.
70. *Report of the Animal Procedures Committee for 1988*, p. 7.
71. *Report of the Animal Procedures Committee for 1990*, pp. 9–10.
72. *FRAME News* (August 1996) p. 1.
73. See, for instance, NAVS, *The Campaigner* (January–March 1995) p. 34.
74. *Littlewood Report*, pp. 81, 151.
75. Reported in NAVS, *The Campaigner* (January–March 1991) pp. 6–7.
76. *Report of the Animal Procedures Committee for 1991*, p. 6.
77. *Ibid.*, p. 7.
78. *Report of the Animal Procedures Committee for 1993*, p. 3.
79. Interview with Mike Baker, 26 June 1994. See also BUAV *Campaign Report* (Autumn 1993) in which it was said that whilst the BUAV thought that stronger action should be taken against Wickham 'the company have been deeply wounded by the whole affair receiving widespread negative media coverage and losing business from a number of their client companies'.
80. See the article entitled 'Another smug Home Office retort' in the NAVS magazine *The Campaigner* (January–June 1997) pp. 4–5. For a more positive anti-vivisection response to an APC report see NAVS, *The Campaigner* (January–March 1993) p. 5.
81. *Report of the Animal Procedures Committee for 1992*, p. 15.

10 The Politics of Animal Research in the United States

1. The public interest generated is reflected in the media coverage.
2. Sperling, *Animal Liberators*, pp. 79–80.
3. Orlans, *In the Name of Science*, p. 50. See also Sperling, *Animal Liberators*, p. 81 and J. Reitman, *Stolen for Profit: How the Medical Establishment is Funding a National Pet-Theft Conspiracy* (New York: Pharos, 1992) pp. 55–67.
4. *Congressional Quarterly Almanac* (Washington DC, 1966), p. 366.
5. See *Hearing Before a Subcommittee of the Committee on Interstate and Foreign Commerce on the Humane Treatment of Animals Used in Research*, House of Representatives, 87th Congress, 28 and 29 September 1962.
6. This anecdote was relayed by Stevens to a later committee hearing. See *Hearing Before the Subcommittee on Department Operations, Research and Foreign Agriculture of the Committee on Agriculture on the Farm Animal and Research Facilities Protection Act*, House of Representatives, 101st Congress, Second Session, p. 75.
7. *Hearing Before the Subcommittee on Livestock and Feed Grains of the Committee on Agriculture on the Regulation of the Transportation, Sale and Handling of*

Dogs and Cats Used for Research and Experimentation, House of Representatives, 89th Congress, Second session, 7 and 8 March 1966, p. 47.

8. *Hearing Before the Committee on Commerce on Animal Dealer Regulation,* United States Senate, 89th Congress, Second Session, 25, 28 March and 25 May 1966, p. 112.

9. *Congressional Quarterly Almanac* (Washington DC, 1966) p. 365.

10. There is now an extensive literature on the Taub affair and its aftermath. See Blum, *The Monkey Wars'* pp. 105–9, 113, 121–3; Finsen *Animal Rights Movement,* pp. 62–7; Orlans, *In the Name of Science,* pp. 177–9. For the court case see H. Silverstein, 'Unleashing Rights', pp. 255–65 and for its role in the formation of the American ALF see Newkirk, *Free the Animals,* pp. 295–6, 331–2 and 359–60.

11. *Hearing before the Subcommittee on Science, Research and Technology of the Committee on Science and Technology on the Use of Animals in Medical Research and Testing,* House of Representatives, 97th Congress, First session, 13 and 14 October 1981.

12. As with the Taub case, there is a substantial literature on the Pennsylvania head-injury laboratory. For a general coverage see Blum, *The Monkey Wars,* pp. 117–21; Finsen and Finsen, *Animal Rights Movement,* pp. 67–71 and Orlans, *In the Name of Science,* pp. 179–82; on the legal issues, in particular, see Francione, *Animals, Property and the Law,* pp. 179–82; on the ALF raid and the aftermath see Newkirk, *Free the Animals,* pp. 179–205.

13. PETA initially intended to show the video at Congressional hearings on the issue but USDA and NIH personnel threatened to stay away so it was eventually shown in a church near to Capitol Hill.

14. Quoted in Blum, *The Monkey Wars,* p. 118. See also Francione, *Animals, Property and the Law,* pp. 179–82.

15. In addition to the two cases mentioned, publicity was also generated by an ALF raid on the City of Hope Medical Center in California in 1984 which resulted in a suspension of funding and a fine for violations of the Animal Welfare Act.

16. Interestingly, a number of research facilities now use footage from PETA's video for training purposes. The effect that this has on those planning to do animal research for the first time can only be guessed at, but one would have thought it would make them think very carefully about their ethical responsibilities towards animals.

17. A. Rowan and F. Loew, *The Animal Research Controversy: Protest, Process and Public Policy,* (Tufts University Center for Animals and Public Policy, 1995) p. 119; B. Rollin, *The Unheeded Cry: Animal Consciousness, Animal Pain and Science* (Oxford University Press, 1990) pp. 177–8. The first bill to incorporate these ideas was introduced by Representative Schroeder in 1980.

18. See *Hearing Before the Committee on Agriculture, Nutrition, and Forestry United States Senate on Improved Standards for Laboratory Animals,* Second Session, 98th Congress, 20 July 1983. The research community responded similarly to the bill introduced by Representative George Brown a year later. See *Hearings Before the Subcommittee on Department Operations, Research, and Foreign Agriculture of the Committee on Agriculture on Improved Standards for Laboratory Animals and Enforcement of the Animal Welfare Act by the Animal*

and Plant Health Inspection Service, House of Representatives, 98th Congress, Second Session, 19 September 1984.

19. See C. Stevens, 'Laboratory Animal Welfare' in AWI, *Animals and Their Legal Rights* (Washington DC: Animal Welfare Institute, 1990) pp. 79–82. Dole's commitment to reform can be seen in his participation in Congressional hearings. See *Hearing Before the Subcommittee on Health and the Environment of the Committee on Energy and Commerce on HR 6928*, 9 December 1982, p. 31; *Senate Hearing on Improved Standards for Laboratory Animals*, 20 July 1983; *House of Representatives Hearings on Improved Standards for Laboratory Animals Act*, 19 September 1984. In the latter, Dole (p. 273) wrote that:

> Some have questioned the need for legislation suggesting that abuses are infrequent. However, material obtained under the Freedom of Information Act shows that abuses are a commonplace problem even in some of our most prestigious institutions. I suggest that it is time to stop waving the banner entitled 'No legislation' and put action in place of words to assure the public that America has an adequate animal welfare system.

20. W. Oleszek, *Congressional Procedures and the Policy Process* 4th edn (Washington DC: Congressional Quarterly, 1996) pp. 104–5.
21. *Littlewood Report*, pp. 180–2.
22. Of the 1000 or so Class B dealers, only about 50 provide animals for research.
23. See Finsen and Finsen, *Animal Rights Movement*, pp. 142–6; Orlans, *In the Name of Science*, pp. 214–17.
24. See Reitman, *Stolen For Profit*.
25. Graphically described in Reitman, *Stolen For Profit*.
26. *See Hearings Before the Sub-Committee on Department Operations, Research and Foreign Agriculture of the Committee on Agriculture*, House of Representatives, 100th Congress, Second Session on S. 2353 Pet Theft Act of 1988, pp. 16–17, 21–4.
27. Information supplied by Adele Douglass, e-mail communication, 13 January 1997.
28. Food, Agriculture, Conservation and Trade Act of 1990, *Conference Report*, 22 October 1990, pp. 101–906, Title XXV.
29. Orlans, *In the Name of Science*, p. 58.
30. Food Security Act of 1985, p. 593.
31. Orlans, *In the Name of Science*, p. 78.
32. Quoted in L. Finsen, 'Institutional Animal Care and Use Committees: A New Set of Clothes for the Emperor', *The Journal of Medicine and Philosophy*, 13 (1988) p. 148.
33. Finsen, 'Animal Care and Use Committees', p. 151.
34. Rollin, *The Unheeded Cry*, p. 180.
35. Quoted in Orlans, *In the Name of Science*, pp. 84, 86.
36. Orlans, *In the Name of Science*, p. 103.
37. Finsen, 'Animal Care and Use Committees', p. 157. See also Francione, *Animals, Property and the Law*, pp. 203–5.

38. RSPCA, *Annual Report 1994*, p. 12. An informal meeting between scientists and moderate animal welfarists in 1995 also suggested this idea. See *The Times Higher Educational Supplement*, 28 April 1995.

39. Rollin, *The Unheeded Cry*, p. 185.

40. Finsen, 'Animal Care and Use Committees', p. 149.

41. Ibid.

42. Up to 1992, in at least six states, courts have been petitioned by animal advocates to allow the opening up of committee deliberations to public scrutiny. See Silverstein, 'Unleashing Rights', pp. 272–5.

43. Blum, *The Monkey Wars*, pp. 99–100; Silverstein, 'Unleashing Rights', p. 273.

44. Orlans, *In the Name of Science*, pp. 173–4, 257–60.

45. Ibid., p. 117.

46. Ibid., pp. 90–4, 103–13.

47. Ibid., pp. 94–8.

48. S. Sanders and J. Jasper, 'Civil Politics in the Animal Rights Conflict', *Science, Technology and Human Values*, 19 (1994).

49. Orlans, *In the Name of Science*, pp. 160–2.

50. *Hearing Before the Subcommittee on Science, Research and Technology of the Committee on Science and Technology, House of Representatives*, 99th Congress, Second Session, on Alternatives to Animal Use in Research and Testing, p. 146.

51. Francione, *Animals, Property and the Law*, p. 185.

52. *Hearing Before the Subcommittee on the Consumer of the Committee on Commerce, Science and Transportation*, United States Senate, 101st Congress, First Session on S. 891. Consumer Products Safe Testing Act, p. 13.

53. E. Marcus, 'Tackling the Titans', *Vegetarian Times* (September 1993).

54. *The Animals' Agenda* (September–October 1993) pp. 14–15.

55. R. Kaufman, 'Facing the Challenge', *AV Magazine* (March 1993) p. 22. See also A. Morrison, 'Improving the Image of Biomedical Research', *Lab Animal*, 23 (1994) pp. 36–9. Morrison also defended Edward Taub in the media and in court.

56. Orlans, *In the Name of Science*, pp. 47–8.

57. *New York Times*, 8 June 1990.

58. See W. Cloud, 'A View from within the DHSS', *AV Magazine* (October 1993) pp. 12–15.

59. Quoted in *AV Magazine* (May 1992) p. 5.

60. See Blum, *The Monkey Wars*, p. 5. There is some evidence that the two sides are more prepared to listen to each other now. For a conciliatory approach from the research side see F. Trull, 'The Research Movement', *Lab Animal*, 23 (1994) pp. 23–6. Trull, the President of NABR writes (p. 26) in this article:

> Let us cease the hectoring and start doing something harder but much more constructive – listening. Surely none of us is so naive as to believe that the world is divided into saints and sinners. The real world defies our attempts to pigeonhole issues or people. We need to ask ourselves if we aren't cultivating our own dislike of certain people rather than trying to build a consensus.

61. William F. Raub, speaking at the Senate Hearings on Improved Standards for Laboratory Animals, 20 July 1983, p. 7.
62. Blum, *The Monkey Wars*, pp. 123–6.
63. Ibid., p. 21.
64. Interview with Morley Cook, 8 April 1996.
65. *Hearing Before the Subcommittee on Department Operations, Research and Foreign Agriculture of the Committee on Agriculture on a Review of the US Department of Agriculture's Animal and Plant Health Inspection Service*, House of Representatives, 100th Congress, Second Session, 7 July 1988, p. 5.
66. The Farm Animal and Research Facilities Protection Act of 1990, *Report 101–953*, pp. 9–10.
67. *Senate Hearing on the Improved Standards for Laboratory Animals Act*, 20 July 1983, pp. 5–6; *House of Representatives Hearings on Improved Standards for Laboratory Animals Act*, 19 September 1984, pp. 22–7.
68. See Francione, *Animals, Property and the Law*, p. 230 who argues that the agency has been 'captured' by research interests.
69. Francione, *Animals, Property and the Law*, p. 79.
70. C. Kerwin, *Congressional Quarterly's Federal Regulatory Directory'*, 6th edn (Washington DC: Congressional Quarterly, 1990) pp. 19–27.
71. Blum, *The Monkey Wars*, p. 147; Orlans, *In the Name of Science*, p. 56.
72. Blum, *Monkey Wars*, pp. 184–7.
73. *Opinion of Charles R. Richey United States District Judge, Civil Action No. 91–1328*, 25 February 1993, p. 16. See also Francione, *Animals, Property and the Law*, pp. 80, 234–49.
74. Blum, *The Monkey Wars*, pp. 159–60.
75. Ibid., pp. 24–5.
76. Quoted in ibid., p. 191.
77. Rowan, *The Animal Research Controversy*, p. 9. Rowan's conclusion is supported by Orlans, *In the Name of Science*, pp. 57–8.
78. M.L. Stephens, 'A Current View of Vivisection: Animal research in America', *The Animals' Agenda* (October 1996) p. 21. There is some controversy over the claim that animal use has declined. See Rowan, *Animal Research Controversy*, pp. 15–20, who claims it has dropped substantially, as does Orlans, *In the Name of Science*, pp. 66–70. Their view is challenged by Francione, *Rain Without Thunder*, pp. 119–22.
79. The following account is based on G. Rubinstein. 'Creature Discomforts', *Government Information Insider* (Washington DC: OMB Watch, 1991).
80. To be more precise, USDA, HHS and OMB filed a 'protective' notice of appeal which allowed NABR to confirm its own right to appeal. When Judge Ritchie denied NABR's motion, NABR successfully appealed that denial to the U.S. Court of Appeals.
81. Quoted in Blum, *The Monkey Wars*, p. 147.
82. Wyngaarden was also responsible in 1990 for writing a strongly worded letter to the House Agriculture Committee attacking the animal rights movement and supporting the Farm Animal and Research Facilities Protection Bill. See The Farm Animal and Research Facilities Protection Act of 1990, *Report 101–953*, pp. 8–9.
83. Rollin, *The Unheeded Cry*, p. 176.

84. In 1986 and 1987, the administration wanted to remove all funding for the enforcement of the Animal Welfare Act!

85. *Animal and Plant Health Inspection Service Implementation of the Animal Welfare Act,* Washington DC, Audit Report no. 33002–0001, March 1992; *Animal and Plant Health Inspection Service Enforcement of the Animal Welfare Act,* Washington DC Audit Report no. 33600–1, January 1995.

86. Quoted in *Hearing Before the Subcommittee on Department Operations, Research, and Foreign Agriculture of the Committee on Agriculture,* House of Representatives, Review of US Department of Agriculture's Enforcement of the Animal Welfare Act, Specifically on Animals Used in Exhibitions, 8 July 1992, 102–75, pp. 2, 5.

87. Reitman, *Stolen For Profit.*

88. E-mail communication, 8 January 1997.

89. *Congressional Quarterly Almanac* (Washington DC, 1984) pp. 383–4; (1991) pp. 582; (1994) p. 478.

90. *Hearings Before the Subcommittee on Livestock and Grains of the Committee on Agriculture,* House of Representatives on HR 5808 and related bills, 94th Congress, First Session, 9 and 10 September 1975, p. 37.

91. Interview with Barbara Rich, 9 April 1996; interview with Louis Sibal, 4 April 1996.

92. *Hearings on USDA's Enforcement of the Animal Welfare Act,* 1992, pp. 93–4, 129.

93. See AWI, *Beyond the Laboratory Door* (Washington DC: Animal Welfare Institute, 1985).

94. Interview, 9 April 1996.

95. Interview with Morley Cook, 8 April 1996.

96. Interview with Morley Cook, 8 April 1996. Having said this, one NIH official I spoke to still thought that NIH, rather than REAC, should be responsible for enforcement because the latter does not have the necessary expertise (interview, 4 April 1996). Furthermore, Christine Stevens (interview 2 April 1996) argues that the creation of REAC has resulted in poorer quality inspections precisely because it has taken power away from the vets.

97. *House of Representative Hearing on the Use of Animals in Medical Research and Testing,* 13 and 14 October 1981, p. 248.

98. USDA Public Meeting, Animal Welfare Act Regulations, Washington DC, 10–12 April 1996.

99. *Animal Care Industry Report* (USDA, Spring 1997).

100. H. Kitschelt, 'Political Opportunity Structures and Political Protest: Anti-Nuclear Movements in Four Democracies', *British Journal of Political Science,* 16 (1986) pp. 57–85.

101. See Rollin, *The Unheeded Cry, passim* but particularly pp. 191–6.

Conclusion

1. G. Jordan and J. Richardson, 'The British Policy Style or the Logic of Negotiation', in J. Richardon (ed.) *Policy Styles in Western Europe* (London: Allen & Unwin, 1982) pp. 80–110.

2. See J. Francis, *The Politics of Regulation: A Comparative Perspective* (Oxford: Blackwell, 1993) p. 27 for a brief outline and M. Berstein, *Regulating Business by Independent Commission* (Princeton University Press, 1955) for the best known theory of regulatory capture.
3. See P. Sabatier, 'Social Movements and Regulatory Agencies: Toward a More Adequate – and Less Pessimistic – Theory of "Clientele Capture" ', *Policy Sciences*, 6 (1975) pp. 301–42.
4. See Berry, *The Interest Group Society*, p. 195.

Bibliography

The following individuals responded to a questionnaire and/or were interviewed in the course of this study:

Randy Sargent, Barbara Rich, Chrissie Nicholls, Nick May, Steve Kopperud, Grace Ellen Rice, Marci Brody, Kathleen Marquardt, Stuart Riley, Christine Corrica, Stephen McMillan, N. Lee Rucker, R. Allnot, S. Hughes, Christine Nelson, Jay Howell, Leslie Schultz, R. Griffith, Tom Cook, Diane Bateman, David Spangler, Jim Egenrieder, Joyce Hamilton, K. Renshaw, Mary Colville Hemsley, Joe O'Neil, D. Burrell, T.A. Wright, Susan Lamson, Mike Ring, Mark Matfield, P.J. Mobsby, John Thorley, P. Flanagan, R. McKeith, Ray Darlington, M.D. Stevens, Peter Lewis, John Martin, A.H. Buckenham, S. Stevens, R.W. Kershaw-Dalby, Maurice Hanssen, Michael Hurst, Robin Peel, Lynn Francis-Roberts, Jim Reed, Nick Herbert, Jamie Day, Keith Pulman, Paul Adams, J. Wade, Andrea Oakley, Richard Ryder, Kim Stallwood, Michael Fox, Robin Lohnes, Martha Cole Glenn, Alex Hershaft, Kathryn Cameron Porter, Adele Douglass, Henry Spira, J. Lorenz, Holly Hazard, Pamela Goddard, David Dexter, Scott Sutherland, Barney Holbeche, Louis Sibal, Morley Cook, Chris Ryder, Nat Williams, Mary Hanley, S. Ludicello, Rollin D. Sparrowe, Christine Stevens, Angela Smith, Michael Simmons, D. Brown, Julian Nassau-Kennedy, C.M. Baldwin, Les Ward, Tony Suckling, Clive Hollands, Tricia Holford, Kathy Liss, Peter Stevenson, Chris Stroud, Amanda Hillier, Barry Mayes, Andrea Fraser, Julia Fentem.

Official Documents

Animal and Plant Health Inspection Service Implementation of the Animal Welfare Act, Washington DC, Audit Report no. 33002–0001, March 1992.

Animal and Plant Health Inspection Service Enforcement of the Animal Welfare Act, Washington DC Audit Report no. 33600–1, January 1995.

Animal Care Industry Report (USDA, Spring 1997).

Animal Procedures Committee Reports, 1987–94.

M. Corn, 'The Steel Jaw Leghold Trap: Issues and Concerns', *CRS Report for Congress*, 29 March 1993.

'Early Day Motions, Factsheet', *Public Information Office*, House of Commons.

The Farm Animal and Research Facilities Protection Act of 1990, *Report 101–953*, pp. 9–10.

FAWC, *Report on the Welfare of Laying Hens in Colony Systems*

—, *Regulations Working Group Interim Statement*, p. 2, n. d

—, *The Welfare of Livestock when Slaughtered by Religious Methods*, July 1985.

Food, Agriculture, Conservation and Trade Act of 1990, *Conference Report*, 22 October 1990, 101–906, Title XXV.

Hearing Before a Subcommittee of the Committee on Interstate and Foreign Commerce on the Humane Treatment of Animals Used in Research, House of Representatives, 87th Congress, 28 and 29 September 1962.

Hearing Before the Subcommittee on Livestock and Feed Grains of the Committee on Agriculture on the Regulation of the Transportation, Sale and Handling of Dogs and Cats Used for Research and Experimentation, House of Representatives, 89th Congress, Second session, 7 and 8 March 1966.

Hearing Before the Committee on Commerce on Animal Dealer Regulation, United States Senate, 89th Congress, Second Session, 25, 28 March and 25 May 1966, p. 112.

Hearing before the Subcommittee on Science, Research and Technology of the Committee on Science and Technology on the Use of Animals in Medical Research and Testing, House of Representatives, 97th Congress, First session, 13 and 14 October 1981.

Hearing Before the Subcommittee on Health and the Environment of the Committee on Energy and Commerce on HR 6928, 9 December 1982.

Hearing Before the Committee on Agriculture, Nutrition, and Forestry United States Senate on Improved Standards for Laboratory Animals, Second Session, 98th Congress, 20 July 1983.

Hearings Before the Subcommittee on Department Operations, Research, and Foreign Agriculture of the Committee on Agriculture on Improved Standards for Laboratory Animals and Enforcement of the Animal Welfare Act by the Animal and Plant Health Inspection Service, House of Representatives, 98th Congress, Second Session, 19 September 1984.

Hearing Before the Subcommittee on Science, Research and Technology of the Committee on Science and Technology, House of Representatives, 99th Congress, Second Session, on Alternatives to Animal Use in Research and Testing.

Hearings Before the Sub-Committee on Department Operations, Research and Foreign Agriculture of the Committee on Agriculture, House of Representatives, 100th Congress, Second Session on S. 2353 Pet Theft Act of 1988.

Hearing Before the Subcommittee on Department Operations, Research and Foreign Agriculture of the Committee on Agriculture on a Review of the US Department of Agriculture's Animal and Plant Health Inspection Service, House of Representatives, 100th Congress, Second Session, 7 July 1988.

Hearing Before the Subcommittee on Department Operations, Research and Foreign Agriculture of the Committee on Agriculture on the Farm Animal and Research Facilities Protection Act, House of Representatives, 101st Congress, Second Session.

Hearing Before the Committee on Labour and Human Resources on Poultry Safety, United States Senate, 102nd Congress, First Session, 28 June 1991.

Hearing Before the Subcommittee on Department Operations, Research, and Foreign Agriculture of the Committee on Agriculture, House of Representatives, Review of US Department of Agriculture's Enforcement of the Animal Welfare Act, Specifically on Animals Used in Exhibitions, 8 July 1992.

Hearing Before the Research and Technology Subcommittee of the Committee on Armed Services on the Use of Animals in Research by the Department of Defense, House of Representatives, Second Session, 13 April 1994.

Hearing Before the Subcommittee on Livestock of the Committee on Agriculture on the Downed Animal Protection Act etc., House of Representatives, 103rd Congress, Second Session, 28 September 1994.

HMSO, *Sessional Information Digest.*

—, *Food From Our Own Resources,* Cmnd. 6020 (April 1965).

—, *Farming and the Nation,* Cmnd. 7458, (1979).

Home Office, *Statistics of Scientific Procedures on Living Animals,* 1987–94.

House of Commons, First Report from the Agriculture Committee. *Animal Welfare in Poultry, Pig and Veal Calf Production,* vol. 2.

House of Lords, *Report of the Select Committee on the Laboratory Animals Protection Bill,* vol. 1, 1980 (HMSO, 1980) 246–1.

MAFF, *Annual Review of Agriculture* (1988).

—, *Animal Health, Report of the Chief Veterinary Officer,* 1991.

—, *Government Response to the Farm Animal Welfare Council's Report on the Welfare of Broiler Chickens,* April 1993.

—, *The Government's Expenditure Plans 1994–5 to 1996–7,* Cmnd. 2503 (1994).

—, *Our Farming Future,* (1991).

Opinion of Charles R. Richey United States District Judge, Civil Action no. 91–1328, 25 February 1993.

Report of the Committee of Enquiry into the Export of Live Cattle to the Continent for Slaughter (the Balfour Report), Cmnd. 154 (1957).

Report of the Committee on the Export of Animals for Slaughter (O'Brien Report), Cmnd. 5566 (1974).

Report of the Departmental Committee on Experiments on Animals (the Littlewood Report), HMSO, Cmnd. 2641 (April 1965).

Report of the Technical Committee to Enquire into the Welfare of Animals kept under Intensive Livestock Husbandry Systems (the Brambell Report), HMSO, Cmnd. 2836, (1965).

Supplementary White Paper, HMSO, Cmnd. 9521 (May 1985).

The United States Government Manual, Office of the Federal Register, National Archives and Records Administration Washington DC, (1987) p. 316.

Pressure Group Literature

Agscene

The Animals' Agenda

Animal People

AV Magazine

The British Egg Information Service, *The British Egg Industry Council: Some Questions and Answers* (London, 1993).

British Farmer

British Veterinary Association, *Annual Review 1993–4*

BUAV, *Campaign Report*

Journal of the American Medical Association

NAVS, *The Campaigner*

NFU, *Annual Report and Accounts*

RDS Annual Report (November 1995).

RSPCA, *Annual Reports*

Wildlife Guardian

Books

J. Abrahams, *Science, Politics and the Pharmaceutical Industry: Controversy and Bias in Drug Regulation* (London: UCL, 1995).

C. Adams, *The Sexual Politics of Meat* (New York: Continuum, 1990).

—, *Neither Man Nor Beast: Feminism and the Defense of Animals* (New York: Continuum, 1995).

Animal Welfare Institute, *Animals and Their Legal Rights* (Washington DC, 1990).

Ball, A. and F. Millard, *Pressure Politics in Industrial Societies* (Basingstoke: Macmillan, 1986).

Ballance, R., J. Pogamy and H. Forstner, *The World's Pharmaceutical Industries: An International Perspective,* (Aldershot: Edward Elgar, 1992).

Barling, G., *Welfare of Calves: Lawfulness of Export Restrictions* (London: S.J. Berwin & Co., 1995).

Benton, T., *Natural Relations: Ecology, Animal Rights and Social Justice* (London: Verso, 1993).

Berry, J., *Lobbying for the People* (Princeton University Press, 1977).

—, *The Interest Group Society,* 2nd edn (London: HarperCollins, 1989).

Berstein, M., *Regulating Business by Independent Commission,* (Princeton University Press, 1955).

Body, R., *Agriculture: The Triumph and the Shame* (London: Temple Smith, 1982).

Bowler, I., *Agriculture Under the Common Agricultural Policy,* (Manchester University Press, 1985).

Browne, W., *Private Interests, Public Policy and American Agriculture* (Lawrence: University of Kansas Press, 1988).

— and A. Cigler, *US Agricultural Groups: Institutional Profiles,* (New York: Greenwood, 1990).

Cavalieri, P. and P. Singer, *The Great Ape Project* (London: Fourth Estate, 1993).

Clark, A., *Diaries* (London: Weidenfeld & Nicolson, 1993)

Close, A., *Washington Representatives* (Washington DC: Columbia), published annually.

Clunies-Ross, T. and N. Hildyard, *The Politics of Industrial Agriculture* (London: Earthscan, 1992).

Congressional Quarterly Almanac (Washington DC).

Dahl, R., *A Preface to Democratic Theory* (University of Chicago Press, 1956).

—, *Who Governs?* (New Haven: Yale University Press, 1961).

Dunleavy, P. and B. O'Leary, *Theories of the State* (London: Macmillan, 1987).

Fiddes, N., *Meat: A Natural Symbol* (London: Routledge, 1991).

Finsen, L. and S. Finsen, *The Animal Rights Movement in America: From Compassion to Respect* (New York: Twayne, 1994).

Ford, A., *John James Audubon: A Biography* (New York: Abbeville, 1988).

Foundation for Public Affairs, 'Public Interest Profiles 1992–3' (Washington, D.C.: Congressional Quarterly Inc., 1992).

Fox, M., *Returning to Eden: Animal Rights and Human Responsibilities* (Florida: Robert Krieger, 1986).

Francione, G., *Animals, Property and the Law* (Philadelphia: Temple University Press, 1995).

—, *Rain Without Thunder: The Ideology of the Animal Rights Movement* (Philadelphia: Temple University Press, 1996).

Francis, J., *The Politics of Regulation: A Comparative Perspective* (Oxford: Blackwell, 1993).

French, R., *Antivisection and Medical Science in Victorian Society* (Princeton University Press, 1975).

Gamson, W., *The Strategy of Social Protest* (Illinois: Dorsey Press, 1975).

Garner, R., *Animals, Politics and Morality* (Manchester University Press, 1993).

—, *Environmental Politics* (Hemel Hempstead: Harvester-Wheatsheaf, 1996).

—, (ed.) *Animal Rights: The Changing Debate* (London: Macmillan, 1996).

Gellately, J., *Silent Ark* (London: Thorsons, 1996).

Giannelli, M.A., 'What Do We Want? Animal Rights! When Do we Want it?: 'Til Ideology, Ego, or Whatever Do Us Part...' (unpublished document, 25 October 1996).

Goodman, D., B. Sorj and J. Wiljinson, *From Farming to Biotechnology: A Theory of Agro-Industrial Development* (Oxford: Basil Blackwell, 1987).

Goodman, D. and M. Redclift, *Refashioning Nature* (London: Routledge, 1991).

Gottlieb, R., *Forcing the Spring: The Transformation of the American Environmental Movement*, (London: Earthscan, 1994).

Grant, W., *The Dairy Industry: An International Comparison* (Aldershot: Dartmouth, 1991).

—, *Pressure Groups, Politics and Democracy in Britain*, 2nd edn (Hemel Hempstead: Harvester-Wheatsheaf, 1995).

Guither, H., *The Food Lobbyists*, (Massachusetts: Lexington, 1980).

Harris, S., A. Swinbank and G. Wilkinson, *The Food and Farm Policies of the European Community* (Chichester: John Wiley, 1983).

Harrison, R., *Animal Machines: The New Factory Farming Industry* (London: Vincent Stuart, 1964).

Hausman, P., *Jack Spratt's Legacy* (New York, Richard Mauk, 1981).

Heidenheimer, A., H. Heclo and C. Teich Adams, *Comparative Public Policy*, 3rd edn (New York: St Martin's Press, 1990).

Henshaw, D., *Animal Warfare: The Story of the Animal Liberation Front* (London: Fontana, 1989).

Hollands, C., *Compassion is the Bugler* (Edinburgh: McDonald, 1980).

Jasper, J. and D. Nelkin, *The Animal Rights Crusade* (New York: Free Press, 1992).

Johnson, A., *Factory Farming* (Oxford: Blackwell, 1991).

Jordan, G. and J. Richardson, *Government and Pressure Groups in Britain* (Oxford University Press, 1987).

Kerwin, C., *Congressional Quarterly's Federal Regulatory Directory*, 6th edn (Washington DC: Congressional Quarterly, 1990).

Lacey, R., *Hard to Swallow: A Brief History of Food* (Cambridge University Press, 1994).

Lowe, P., *et al.* (eds) *Countryside Conflicts: The Politics of Farming, Forestry and Conservation* (Aldershot: Gower, 1986).

Lowi, T., *The End of Liberalism*, 2nd edn (New York: Norton, 1979).

Lukes, S., *Power: A Radical View* (London: Macmillan, 1974).

Makinson, L. and J. Goldstein, *Open Secrets: The Encyclopedia of Congressional Money and Politics* (Washington DC: Congressional Quarterly, 1994).

Mansbridge, J., *Why We Lost the ERA* (University of Chicago Press, 1986).

Marsh, D. and R. Rhodes (eds) *Policy Networks in British Politics* (Oxford University Press, 1992).

Mason, J. and P. Singer, *Animal Factories* (New York: Crown, 1980).

Mighetto, L., *Wild Animals and American Environmental Ethics* (Arizona University Press, 1991).

Millard, P., *Trade Associations and Professional Bodies of the United Kingdom* (London: Gale Research International), published annually.

Mills, M., *The Politics of Dietary Change* (Aldershot: Dartmouth, 1992).

Moyer, H. and T. Josling, *Agricultural Policy Reform: Politics and Process in the EC and the USA* (Hemel Hempstead: Harvester-Wheatsheaf, 1990).

Newkirk, I., *Free the Animals* (Chicago: Noble Press, 1992).

New Labour Because Britain Deserves Better (London: Labour Party, 1997).

North, R. and T. Gorman, *Chickengate: An Independent Analysis of the Salmonella in Eggs Scare* (London: Institute for Economic Affairs, 1990).

Norton, P., *Does Parliament Matter?* (Hemel Hempstead: Harvester-Wheatsheaf, 1993).

Oleszek, W., *Congressional Procedures and the Policy Process* 4th edn (Washington DC: Congressional Quarterly, 1996).

Olson, M., *The Logic of Collective Action* (Cambridge Mass.: Harvard University Press, 1965).

Orlans, F., *In the Name of Science: Issues in Responsible Animal Experimentation* (New York: Oxford University Press, 1993).

Petracca, M. (ed.) *The Politics of Interests: Interest Groups Transformed* (Boulder: Westview, 1992).

Polsby, N., *Community Power and Political Theory* (New Haven: Yale University Press, 1963).

Reekie, W. and M. Weber, *Profits, Politics and Drugs,* (New York: Holmes & Meier, 1979).

Regan, T., *The Case for Animal Rights* (London: Routledge, 1984).

Reitman, J., *Stolen for Profit: How the Medical Establishment is Funding a National Pet-Theft Conspiracy* (New York: Pharos, 1992).

Rifkin, J., *Beyond Beef: The Rise and Fall of the Cattle Culture* (Harmondsworth: Penguin, 1992).

Rifkin, J. and C. Grunewald Rifkin, *Voting Green* (New York: Doubleday, 1992).

Ripley, R. and G. Franklin, *Congress, the Bureaucracy and Public Policy,* 5th edn (Pacific Grove: Brooks, 1991).

Robins, J., *Diet For a New America* (New Hampshire: Stillpoint, 1987).

Rollin, B., *Animal Rights and Human Morality* (New York: Prometheus, 1981).

—, *The Unheeded Cry: Animal Consciousness, Animal Pain and Science,* (Oxford University Press, 1990).

Rowan, A. and F. Loew *The Animal Research Controversy: Protest, Process and Public Policy,* (Tufts University Center for Animals and Public Policy, 1995).

Russell, W. and R. Burch, *The Principles of Humane Experimental Technique* (London: Methuen, 1959).

Ryder, R., *Victims of Science: The Use of Animals in Research* (London: Davis-Poynter, 1975).

—, *Animal Revolution: Changing Attitudes Towards Speciesism* (Oxford: Basil Blackwell, 1989).

Rydin, Y., *The British Planning System: An Introduction* (London: Macmillan, 1993).

Sharpe, R., *The Cruel Deception*, (London: Thorsons, 1988).

Silverstein, H., 'Unleashing Rights: Law and the Politics of the Animal Rights Movement', PhD thesis, University of Washington, 1992.

Singer, P., *Animal Liberation*, 2nd edn (London: Cape, 1990).

Smith, M., *The Politics of Agricultural Support in Britain: The Development of the Agricultural Policy Community* (Aldershot: Dartmouth, 1990).

—, *Pressure, Power and Policy: State Autonomy and Policy Networks in Britain and the United States* (Hemel Hempstead: Harvester-Wheatsheaf, 1993).

Sperling, S., *Animal Liberators: Research and Morality* (Berkeley: University of California Press, 1988).

Spiegel, M., *The Dreaded Comparison: Human and Animal Slavery* (Philadelphia: New Society, 1988).

Stevenson, P., *A Far Cry From Noah* (London: Green Print, 1994).

Tester, K., *Animals & Society: The Humanity of Animal Rights* (London: Routledge, 1991).

Thomas, R., *The Politics of Hunting* (Aldershot: Gower, 1983).

Truman, D., *The Governmental Process* (New York: Knopf, 1951).

The U.S. Congress Handbook 103rd Congress First Session, (Virginia: Barbara Pullen, 1993).

Walker, C. and G. Cannon, *The Food Scandal* (London: Century, 1984).

Wright Mills, C., *The Power Elite* (New York: Galaxy, 1959).

Articles

Bachrach, P. and M. Baratz, 'The Two Faces of Power', *American Political Science Review*, 56 (1962) pp. 947–52.

Benton, T. and R. Redfearn, 'The Politics of Animal Rights: Where is the Left', *New Left Review*, 215 (1996) pp. 43–58.

'Blood Sports, Lobby Groups and the Criminal Justice Bill: a survey of MPs' (London: Access Opinion Limited, 1994).

Bowers, J., 'British Agricultural Policy Since the Second World War', *The Agricultural History Review*, 33 (1986) pp. 66–76.

Burns, J., 'A Synoptic View of the Food Industry' in J. Burns, J. Mcinerney and A. Swinbank (eds) *The Food Industry: Economics and Politics'* (London: Heineman, 1983) pp. 3–10.

Charlton, A. and G. Francione, 'The American Left Should Support Animal Rights: A Manifesto', *The Animals' Agenda*, (January–February 1993) pp. 28–34.

Coleman, W. and W. Grant, 'Business Association and Public Policy: a Comparison of Organizational Development in Britain and Canada', *Journal of Public Policy*, 4 (1990) pp. 209–35.

Cowley, P. and N. Stace, 'The Wild Mammals (Protection) Bill: A Parliamentary White Elephant?', *The Journal of Legislative Studies*, 2 (1996) pp. 339–55.

Davis, F., 'Balancing the Perspective on PAC Contributions: In search of an impact on roll calls', *American Politics Quarterly*, 21 (1993) pp. 205–22.

Eismeier, T. and P. Pollock III, 'Political Action Committees: Varieties of Organization and Strategy' in M. Malbin (ed.) *Money and Politics in the United States* (New Jersey: Chatham, 1984) pp. 122–41.

Elston, M., 'The Anti-vivisectionist Movement and the Science of Medicine', in J. Gabe, D. Kelleher and G. Williams (eds) pp. 160–80. *Challenging Medicine* (London: Routledge,1993).

Feder, B., 'Pressuring Purdue', *New York Times Magazine* (26 November 1989).

Finsen, L., 'Institutional Animal Care and Use Committees: A New Set of Clothes for the Emperor', *The Journal of Medicine and Philosophy*, 13 (1988) pp. 145–58.

Gamson, W., 'The Social Psychology of Collective Action', in A. Morris and C. Mueller (eds.) *Frontiers in Social Movement Theory* (New Haven: Yale University Press, 1992).

Garner, R., 'Wildlife Conservation and the Moral Status of Animals', *Environmental Politics*, 3 (1994) pp. 114–29.

Goddard Svendsen, R., 'Animal Welfare and the European Union' in R. Garner (ed.) *Animal Rights: The Changing Debate* (London: Macmillan, 1996) pp. 143–65.

Gormley, W., 'Regulatory Issue Networks in a Federal System', *Polity*, 18 (1986) pp. 595–620.

Greanville, P. and D. Moss, 'The Emerging Face of the Movement', *The Animals' Agenda* 10–11 (March–April 1985) p. 36.

Greenwood, J. and K. Ronit, 'Established and Emergent Sectors: Organized Interests at the European Level in the Pharmaceutical Industry and the New Biotechnologies', in Greenwood (*et al.*) *Organized Interests and the European Union* (London: Sage, 1992).

Grunewald-Rifkin, C., 'The Greening of Animal Rights', *The Animals' Agenda* (September–October 1992) pp. 36–41.

Harrison, R., 'Farm Animal Welfare, What, if any, Progress?', *Hume Memorial Lecture*, (UFAW, 1987).

Heclo, H., 'Issue Networks and the Executive Establishment', in A. King (ed.) *The New American Political System* (Washington DC: American Enterprise Institute, 1978) pp. 87–124.

Herzog, H., ' "The Movement is My Life": The Psychology of Animal Rights Activism', *Journal of Social Issues*, 49 (1993) pp. 103–19.

Holbeche, B., 'Policy and Influence: MAFF and the NFU', *Public Policy and Administration*, 1 (1986) pp. 40–7.

Hollands, C., 'Achieving the Achievable: A Review of Animals in Politics', *ATLA*, 23 (1995).

Howard, J., 'The Politics of Animal Research', *The Animals' Agenda*, (January–February 1997) pp. 31–3.

Inglehart, R., 'Values, Ideology and Cognitive Mobilization in New Social Movements' in R. Dalton and M. Kuechler (eds) *Challenging the Political Order: New Social and Political Movements in Western Democracies* (Cambridge: Polity, 1990) pp. 43–66.

Jasper, J., 'Recruiting Intimates, Recruiting Strangers: Building the Contemporary Animal Rights Movement', unpublished manuscript, 1992.

— and J. Poulson, 'Fighting Back: Vulnerabilities, Blunders and Countermobilization by the Targets in Three Animal Rights Campaigns', *Sociological Forum*, 8 (1993) pp. 639–57.

— and J. Poulson, 'Animal Rights and Anti-Nuclear Protest: Political Networks and Moral Shocks in Recruitment', paper presented at the American Sociological Association annual meeting (San Francisco, 1989).

Jordan, G., 'Sub-Governments, Policy Communities and Networks: Refilling the Old Bottles?', *Journal of Theoretical Politics*, 2 (1990) pp. 319–38.

— and Richardson, J., 'Policy Communities: The British and European Policy Style', *Policy Studies Journal*, 11 (1983) pp. 603–15.

— and —, 'The British Policy Style or the Logic of Negotiation', in J. Richardson (ed.), *Policy Styles in Western Europe* (London: George Allen & Unwin, 1982) pp. 80–110.

Kaufman, M., 'Backlash: The Counter-Attack Against the Animal Rights Movement', *Animals' Agenda* (May–June 1993) pp. 14–19.

Kitschelt, H., 'Political Opportunity Structures and Political Protest: Anti-Nuclear Movements in Four Democracies', *British Journal of Political Science*, 16 (1986) pp. 57–85.

Klandermans, P., 'Linking the "Old" and the "New": Movement Networks in the Netherlands', in R. Dalton and M. Kuechler (eds), *Challenging the Political Order: New Social and Political Movements in Western Democracies* (Cambridge: Polity, 1990) pp. 122–36.

Lederer, S., 'The Controversy over Animal Experimentation in America, 1880–1914', in N. Rupke (ed.) *Vivisection in Historical Perspective* (London: Routledge, 1987) pp. 236–58.

Loew, F., 'Turning Plowshares into Volvos: Changing American Attitudes Toward Livestock', *Journal of Agricultural and Environmental Ethics*, 1 (1993) pp. 105–9.

Malbin, M., 'Looking Back at the Future of Campaign Finance Reform: Interest Groups and American Elections', in M. Malbin (ed.) *Money and Politics in the United States* (New Jersey: Chatham, 1984) pp. 232–76.

Malcolm, J., 'Food and Farming' in J. Burns, J. McInerny and A. Swinbank (eds), *The Food Industry*

Matlack, C., 'Animal Rights Furor', *The National Journal*, 23 (1991) pp. 2143–7.

McFarland, A., 'Interest Groups and Theories of Power in America', *British Journal of Political Science*, 17 (1987) pp. 129–47.

McInerney, J., 'A Synoptic View of Policy-making for the Food Sector', in J. Burns, J. McInerny and A. Swinbank (eds) *The Food Industry: Economics and Politics* (London: Heinemann, 1983).

MORI, 'Attitudes of Members of Parliament' (1993).

Morrison, A., 'Improving the Image of Biomedical Research', *Lab Animal*, 23 (1994) pp. 36–9.

Newby, H., 'Living From Hand to Mouth: the Farmworker, Food and Agribusiness' in A. Murcott (ed.) *The Sociology of Food and Eating: Essays on the Sociological Significance of Food* (Aldershot: Gower, 1983) pp. 31–44.

Peterson, J., 'Hormones, Heifers and High Politics: Biotechnology and the Common Agricultural Policy', *Public Administration*, 67 (1989) pp. 455–71.

Radford, M., 'Partial Protection: Animal Welfare and the Law', in R. Garner (ed.) *Animal Rights: The Changing Debate* (London: Macmillan, 1996) pp. 67–91.

Rhodes, R. and D. Marsh, 'The Concept of Policy Networks in British Political Science: Its Development and Utility', *Talking Politics*, 8 (1996) pp. 210–22.

Rowan, A., 'The Use of Animals in Experimentation: An Examination of the "Technical" Arguments Used to Criticize the Practice' in R. Garner (ed.) *Animal Rights: The Changing Debate* (London: Macmillan, 1996) pp. 104–22.

Rubinstein, G., 'Creature Discomforts', *Government Information Insider* (Washington DC: OMB Watch, 1991).

Rupke, N., 'Pro-vivisection in England in the Early 1880s: Arguments and Motives', in N. Rupke (ed.) *Vivisection in Historical Perspective*, pp. 188–208.

Ryder, R., 'Putting Animals into Politics', in R. Garner (ed.) *Animal Rights: The Changing Debate* (London: Macmillan, 1996) pp. 166–93.

Sabatier, P., 'Social Movements and Regulatory Agencies: Toward a More Adequate – and Less Pessimistic – Theory of "Clientele Capture"', *Policy Sciences*, 6 (1975) pp. 301–42.

—, 'Interest Group Membership and Organization: Multiple Theories', in M. Petracca (ed.) *The Politics of Interests: Interest Groups Transformed* (Boulder, Colo.: Westview, 1992).

Salisbury, R., 'An Exchange Theory of Interest Groups', *Midwest Journal of Political Science*, 13 (1969) pp. 1–32.

— *et al.*, 'Triangles, Networks, and Hollow Cores: The Complex Geometry of Washington Interest Representation', in M. Petracca (ed.) *The Politics of Interest: Interest Groups Transformed* (Boulder, Colo.: Westview, 1992).

Sanbonnatsu, J., 'Animal Liberation: Should the Left Care?', *Z Magazine* (October 1989) pp. 101–10.

Sanders, S. and J. Jasper, 'Civil Politics in the Animal Rights Conflict', *Science, Technology and Human Values*, 19 (1994).

Schlozman, K., 'What Accent the Heavenly Chorus? Political Equality and the American Pressure System', *Journal of Politics*, 46 (1984) pp. 1006–32.

Shapiro, K., 'Editorial', *Society & Animals*, 3 (1995) p. 2.

—, 'The Caring Sleuth: Portrait of an Animal Rights Activist', *Society and Animals*, 2 (1994) pp. 145–65.

Smith, M., 'From Policy Community to Issue Network: Salmonella in Eggs and the New Politics of Food', *Public Administration*, 69 (1991) pp. 235–52.

Spira, H., 'Fighting to Win', in P. Singer (ed.) *In Defense of Animals* (Oxford: Blackwell, 1985) pp. 194–208.

—, 'Animal Rights: The Frontiers of Compassion', *Peace and Democracy News*, Summer 1993) pp. 11–14.

—, 'Less Meat, Less Misery: Reforming Factory Farms', *Forum for Applied Research and Public Policy* (Spring 1996) pp. 39–44.

Stevens, C., 'Laboratory Animal Welfare', in AWI, *Animals and Their Legal Rights*, pp. 66–105.

Tierney, J., 'Organized Interests and the Nation's Capitol', in M. Petracca (ed.) *The Politics of Interests: Interest Groups Transformed* (Boulder, Colo.: Westview, 1992).

Trull, F.L., 'The Research Movement', *Lab Animal*, 23 (1994) pp. 23–6.

Tweeten, L., 'Public Policy Decisions for Farm Animal Welfare', *Journal of Agricultural and Environmental Ethics*, 1 (1993) pp. 87–103.

Twigg, J., 'Vegetarianism and the Meaning of Meat' in A. Murcott (ed.) *The Sociology of Food and Eating*, (Alderhot: Gower, 1983) pp. 18–30.

Walker, J., 'The Origins and Maintenance of Interest Groups in America', *American Political Science Review*, 77 (1983) pp. 390–406.

Wilson, G., 'American Interest Groups in Comparative Perspective', in M. Petracca (ed.) *The Politics of Interests: Interest Groups Transformed* (Boulder, Colo.: Westview, 1992) pp. 80–95.

Worcester, R., 'Scenting Dissent', *New Statesman and Society* (21 April 1995) pp. 22–3.

Index

AAMR, *see* Association for the Advancement of Medicine by Research
ABPI, *see* Association of the British Pharmaceutical Industry
Abrahams, John, 4, 8, 53
Advocates for Animals, 97, 107
AFBF, *see* American Farm Bureau Federation
AFIA, *see* American Feed Industry Association
Agricultural Adjustment Act (1933), 140
Agriculture Act (1947), 151
Agriculture (Miscellaneous Provisions) Act (1968), 23–4, 88, 111, 166
AHA, *see* American Humane Association
Alaska, 38
ALF, *see* Animal Liberation Front
AMA, *see* American Medical Association
American Association for Accreditation of Laboratory Animal Care, 205
American Farm Bureau Federation, 52, 57, 62, 63, 66, 70
American Feed Industry Association, 52, 57, 58–9, 62, 64, 65, 66
American Humane Association, 95, 96, 99, 100, 101, 106, 107, 108, 204, 224
American Meat Institute, 52, 59, 144, 146
American Medical Association, 53, 54, 55, 144, 205
Americans for Medical Progress, 53, 55
American Society for the Prevention of Cruelty to Animals, 75, 93, 96, 99, 101, 106, 209
American Veal Association, 52

American Veterinary Medicine Association, 52, 61
Amess, David, 117
Amory, Cleveland, 75
AMP, *see* Americans for Medical Progress
AMPI, *see* Associated Milk Producers Inc.
AMRIC, *see* Animals in Medicines Research Information Centre
Animal Aid, 75, 82, 94, 96, 104, 107
Animal and Plant Health Inspection Service, 34, 223–7, 231
Animal Health Act (1981), 23
Animal Health Institute, 52
Animal Legal Defense Fund, 219, 220
Animal Liberation Front, 96, 206
Animal Procedures Committee, 26, 182, 186, 188–91, 192, 193, 195, 196, 197, 198–9, 200, 201, 212, 232
Animals' Agenda, 78
Animals in Medicines Research Information Centre, 56
Animals (Scientific Procedures) Act (1986), 26, 27, 49, 56, 88, 97, 104, 114, 182–201, 234
Animal Welfare Act (1966), 9, 32–4, 36, 60, 62, 83, 90, 141, 202–7, 208, 218
Animal Welfare Division, 23, 24, 157–8, 165, 171, 173
Animal Welfare Institute, 41, 75, 94, 96, 101, 106
Animal Welfare Year, 103–4, 179
anti-cruelty statutes, 31–2, 35–6, 37, 87
APC, *see* Animal Procedures Committee
APHIS, *see* Animal and Plant Health Inspection Service
Arizona, 38

278

Ark Trust, 84
ASPCA, *see* American Society for the Prevention of Cruelty to Animals
ssociated Milk Producers Inc., 144
ssociation for the Advancement of Medicine by Research, 56, 177
sociation of the British Pharmaceutical Industry, 49, 52, 53, 56
dubon Society, 41, 42, 96, 99
'MA, *see* American Veterinary Medical Association
VD, *see* Animal Welfare Division
VI, *see* Animal Welfare Institute

esler, Scotty, 145
alfour Committee, 152, 154, 155
alls, Michael, 182, 183, 190
anks, Tony, 116, 117, 121
arlow, Tom, 145
attery hens, 13, 85, 86, 153, 157, 165, 168
EIC, *see* British Egg Industry Council
eilenson, Tony, 125, 135
ennett, Charles, 125, 147
nton, Ted, 86
gh, Henry, 75
nard, Claude, 176
ry, Jeffrey, 2, 76, 87
technology, 45
kemore, Colin, 217
m, Deborah, 212–13
A, *see* British Medical Association
y, Richard, 111, 114, 117, 119, 156–7, 165, 167, 235
somatotropin, 45, 174
spongiform encephalopathy, 160–1, 173, 174
Barbara, 214, 215
onald, 117
Andrew, 117
British Poultry Meat ration
Committee, 152–3, 154, 6, 157, 165
Margaret, 190, 191, 197
ssociation for the ncement of Science, 57

British Egg Industry Council, 52, 57, 70, 161, 174
British Field Sports Society, 111
British Meat Manufacturers' Association, 52, 57
British Medical Association, 57
British Organic Farmers, 52
British Pig Association, 52
British Poultry Meat Federation, 52, 57, 64, 161
British Union for the Abolition of Vivisection, 82, 94, 96, 98, 100, 101, 104, 200
British Veterinary Association, 103, 106, 183, 185
Broom, Donald, 165
Brower, David, 74
Brown, George, 125, 135
Browne, William, P., 140–1
BSE, *see* bovine spongiform encephalopathy
BST, *see* bovine somatotropin
BUAV, *see* British Union for the Abolition of Vivisection
Bureau of Land Management, 37
Burton, Sala, 124
Bush, George, 206
BVA, *see* British Veterinary Association

California, 32, 36, 124, 127, 128–9
Carlile, Alex, 117
Carlisle, Mark, 178, 179
Charles River Inc., 50, 55
CITES, *see* Convention on the International Trade in Endangered Species
CIWF, *see* Compassion in World Farming
Clark, Alan, 118
Clark, David, 117, 121
Class B dealers, 50, 209
Cohen, Harry, 117
Coleman, Donald, 117
Colorado, 38
Comité des Organizations Professionelles Agricoles, 66, 159–60

Committee for the Reform of Animal Experimentation, 85, 103, 104, 105, 179, 180, 181, 183, 184, 185, 186, 187
Compassion in World Farming, 75, 94, 95, 96, 97, 98, 100, 101, 103, 105, 111, 155, 160, 172
ConAgra, 46, 144
Congressional agriculture committees, 31, 62, 140, 141–6, 147, 149, 150, 203, 207, 209, 230, 231
Congressional Animal Welfare Caucus, 62
Congressional members' attitude towards animal protection, 122–38; by age, 133–5; by gender, 131–3; by geographical location, 127–9, 130, 132; by party, 130–1, 132
Conservative Party, 110, 112, 113, 117, 118, 119–21, 160
Convention on the International Trade in Endangered Species, 28
COPA, *see* Comité des Organizations Professionelles Agricoles
Corbett, Robin, 103, 117
Corbyn, Jeremy, 117
Cosmetic, Toiletry and Fragrance Association, 52, 53, 60, 61, 214
Countryside Movement, 112
CRAE, *see* Committee for the Reform of Animal Experimentation
Cruelty to Animals Act (1876), 26, 49, 176, 177, 182, 203
CTFA, *see* Cosmetic, Toiletry and Fragrance Association
Cunningham, Jack, 113
Currie, Edwina, 161, 172

Dairy Trade Federation, 52, 57
Dalyell, Tam, 117
Davies, Bryan, 75
Davies, Peter, 107, 171
Davies, Ron, 116, 117, 121
Defenders of Wildlife, 40, 42, 96, 99
Defense Department, 35
Dellums, Ronald, 125, 135

Democratic Party, 123, 124, 130–1, 136, 137, 234
Department for Education, 22, 27
Department of Health, 22, 27, 48, 172
Department of Health and Human Services, 32, 34, 35, 204, 206, 215, 216
Department of Health and Social Security, 48–9
Department of the Environment, 22, 28, 29
Department of the Interior, 37
Department of Transport, 22, 28, 215
DHSS, *see* Department of Health and Social Security
dietary policy, 10, 147, 148
dog registration scheme, 59, 110, 114
Dole, Robert, 207, 234
Donoughue, Lord, 113
Doris Day Animal League, 99, 100, 102, 106, 107
Dornan, Robert, 125, 135
Douglass, Adele, 100, 108, 224, 225
downed animals, 31, 32, 59, 142, 149
Dunn, Mike, 227
Dunnachie, James, 117

ECVAM, *see* European Centre for the Validation of Alternative Methods
early day motions, 16, 18, 115, 116
Elston, Mary Ann, 188
Endangered Species Act (1969), 9, 37, 40, 106
Ennals, David, 178
Environmental Defense Fund, 96, 99
Eurogroup for Animal Welfare, 105
European Centre for the Validation of Alternative Methods, 197
European Union, 8, 23, 25, 27, 28, 29, 44, 53, 65, 66, 110, 158–60, 168–9
EU, *see* European Union

FARM, *see* Farm Animal Reform Movement
Farm Animal and Research Facilities Act (1992), 63, 218

Farm Animal Reform Movement, 75, 94, 96, 106
Farm Animal Welfare Coalition, 62
Farm Animal Welfare Council, 23, 24, 156, 157, 159, 165, 171, 188, 189, 191, 232
Farm Sanctuary, 96, 149
FAWC, *see* Farm Animal Welfare Council
FDA, *see* Food and Drug Administration
Feldberg, Wilhelm, 198, 199–200
Field-Fisher, T., 182
Finsen, Lawrence, 85, 212
Finsen, Susan, 85
Fish and Wildlife service, 37, 43
Florida, 37
Flynn, Paul, 117
Foley, Tom, 207
Food and Drug Administration, 35, 148, 215
Fookes, Janet, 117, 184
Ford, Wendell, 209
Foreign Office, 22, 28
Fox, Michael, 148
FRAME, *see* Fund for the Replacement of Animals in Medical Experiments
Francione, Gary, 13, 81, 82–92, 236
Friends of Animals, 2, 75, 99
Friends of the Earth, 42, 74, 96, 101
Fry, Peter, 181, 184
Fund for Animals, 41, 75, 76, 96, 98, 99, 106
Fund for the Replacement of Animals in Medical Experiments, 94, 97, 103, 183, 185, 197–8

Gale, Roger, 117
Gamson, William, 14
GECCAP, *see* General Election Co-ordinating Committee for Animal Protection
General Election Co-ordinating Committee for Animal Protection, 104, 180
Gennerelli, Thomas, 206, 214, 223, 233
Gerard, Peter, 106

Gesell, Robert, 75
Giannelli, Michael, 80, 84
Glickman, Dan, 227
Glover, Mark, 42, 75
Godman, Norman, 117
Goodwin, Frederick, 216–17
Gormley, W., 79
Grant, Wyn, 148
Greanville, P. 77
Greece, 9
Green, Bill, 43
Greenpeace, 42, 96, 99
Greenway, Harry, 116, 117
Gunderson, Steve, 142

Halsbury, Lord, 114, 180–1, 188, 196
Hampson, Judith, 183
Hardy, Peter, 117
Harlow, Harry, 213
Harowitz, Michael, 222
Harrison, Ruth, 152, 165
Hazard, Holly, 100
Hazleton Laboratories, 49, 199
Health Research Extension Act (1985), 34, 206
Heckler, Margaret, 206
Herrington, Alice, 75
Hershaft, Alex, 75, 94
Herzog, H., 77
Hillsdown Holdings, 46
Hincliffe, David, 117
Hogg, Douglas, 154
Hollands, Clive, 97, 104, 165, 179, 182, 183, 184, 185, 189, 190, 193, 234
Home Office: and animal experimentation, 26, 114, 176–7, 180, 186, 187, 191–2, 193, 194, 195, 197, 198–200; and CRAE, 179, 183, 184; and domesticated and wild animals, 27; and RSPCA, 171–2; parliamentary questions, 22
Houghton, Douglas (Lord), 103, 105, 179, 181, 183, 185, 191, 192, 234
Houghton–Platt memorandum, 179, 180
HSUS, *see* Humane Society of the United States

Hughes, Roy, 117
Hughes, Simon, 117
Humane Slaughter Act (1958), 30
Humane Slaughter Association, 96
Humane Society of the United States,
    40, 74, 94, 95, 98, 99, 100, 101,
    102, 106, 107, 204, 221
hunting, 17, 29, 42, 59, 88, 91, 96,
    110, 111–13, 114
Huntingdon Research Centre, 49

IACUCs, *see* institutional animal
    care and use committees
IFAW, *see* International Fund for
    Animal Welfare
Improved Standards for Laboratory
    Animals Act (1985), 33, 35,
    205–7, 210–14, 230, 235
institutional animal care and use
    committees, 32, 33, 188, 207,
    210–13
intensive agriculture, 44–7, 140–1,
    146, 148–9, 151, 152, 155, 163
International Fund for Animal
    Welfare, 75, 96, 98, 99, 101,
    113
International Society for Animal
    Rights, 75, 204
Izaak Walton League of America,
    42

Jacobs, Andrew, 125, 135
Japan, 9
Jasper, James, 4, 77, 80, 213
Jenkins, Hugh, 181
Jenkins, Roy, 178
Jones, Helen, 75, 204
Josling, Timothy, 15

Kitschelt, H., 227
Knight, Greg, 117
Kopperud, Steve, 59, 62–3

Laboratory Animals Protection Bill
    (1979), 114, 180–1, 188
Labour Party, 88, 100, 112–13, 117,
    118, 119–21, 136, 138, 155, 234
LACS, *see* League Against Cruel
    Sports

Lacey, Richard, 173
Lantos, Tom, 125, 135
League Against Cruel Sports, 96, 97,
    98, 100, 101, 104, 105, 106, 113
Lewis, Terry, 117
Lipinski, Bill, 125, 135, 136
Littlewood Committee, 178, 179,
    182, 187, 196, 198, 208
live export of animals, 25, 86, 152,
    155, 156, 158–9, 160, 164, 168,
    174, 175, 230, 233, 235
Livestock Auctioneers' Association,
    52
local authorities, 28–9
Lyng, Richard, 146, 218
LYNX, 42, 75, 94

Maclean, David, 167, 169
MAFF, *see* Ministry of Agriculture,
    Fisheries and Food
Magendie, François, 176
Mallalieu, Baroness, 113
Mansbridge, Jane, 79
Manton, Tom, 125, 135
Marine Mammal Protection Act
    (1972), 37
Marquardt, Kathleen, 55
Massachusetts, 31, 32, 36, 38
Massachusetts Society for the
    Prevention of Cruelty to
    Animals, 96, 99
McNamara, Kevin, 113, 117
Meale, Alan, 117
Meat and Livestock Commission, 24
Medical Research Council, 52, 53,
    198, 199
Melcher, John, 207
Mellor, David, 104, 182, 183–4, 185,
    234
membership recruitment, 64, 68–81
Mid-American Dairymen, 144
Milburn, Cindy, 189
Mills, Michael, 154
Ministry of Agriculture, Fisheries and
    Food: and animal research, 26;
    and BSE, 160–1; and EU, 159,
    160, 168–9; and live exports,
    160, 230, 235; and wildlife, 28,
    29; attitudes to animal welfare,

111, 154, 155, 157, 160–1, 161–2, 163, 165–6, 167, 170; codes of practice, 156, 166–7; compared with USDA, 31, 146; dietary policy, 161, 172–3; enforcement, 161–2, 169; organization, 23, 24; parliamentary questions, 22; relationship with AWD, 158, 165; relationship with FAWC, 157; relationship with the NFU, 151, 171–3

Ministry of Defence, 22, 26–7
Monroney, Mike, 204
Morgan, Rhodri, 117
Morley, Elliot, 23, 116, 117, 118, 121, 234
Morrison, Adrian, 216
Mortimer, John, 113
Morton, David, 183
Moss, D., 77
Moyer, H., 15
MPs' attitudes towards animal protection, 97–8, 109–21; by age, 120; by constituency location, 118–19; by gender, 120–1; by party, 119–20
Mullin, Chris, 117

NABR, *see* National Association for Biomedical Research
Nader, Ralph, 74
Naish, David, 159, 164, 171
National Alliance for Animals, 105
National Antivivisection Society, 82, 104
National Association for Biomedical Research, 53, 54–5, 60, 61, 62, 64, 71, 220, 222–3, 225
National Broiler Council, 52, 59, 64, 66, 144, 148
National Cattle Breeders' Association, 52, 59
National Cattleman's Association, 52, 59, 66, 144
National Dairy Council, 148
National Farmers Union, 52; and animal welfare, 59, 163–4; and dog registration scheme, 110; and European Union, 158–9; and live export trade, 174; and salmonella, 161, 172–3; and sow stalls and tethers, 111, 156–7, 167; and veal crates, 167, 168; organization and resources, 47, 64, 65–6, 70, 151–2; relationship with MAFF, 151, 171, 172–3, 230, 235; relationship with other producer organizations, 57–8, 61–2; response to Brambell, 156, 157, 166, 168
National Federation of Badger Groups, 105
National Federation of Meat Traders, 52, 174
National Grange, 52, 62
National Institutes of Health, 32, 34–5, 203–4, 205–6, 210, 211–13, 216–17, 219, 223, 226, 231
National Livestock and Meat Board, 148
National Milk Producers' Federation, 52, 64, 144
National Parks Service, 37
National Pig Breeders Association, 167
National Pork Producers' Council, 52, 144, 148
National Rifle Association, 42, 102
National Sheep Association, 52
National Society for Medical Research, 54–5, 204, 205
National Wildlife Federation, 42, 95, 96, 99
Nature Conservancy, 40, 42, 96, 99
NAVS, *see* National Antivivisection Society
Nelkin, Dorothy, 80
New Jersey, 38
Newkirk, Ingrid, 75, 83, 99
New Welfarism, 81–92
New York, 31, 55, 94, 124, 127, 128–9
NFU, *see* National Farmers Union
Nicholls, Patrick, 185
Nicholson, Emma, 117
NIH, *see* National Institutes of Health

non-decision-making, 3, 142, 154
NRA, *see* National Rifle Association
NSMR, *see* National Society for Medical Research
NWF, *see* National Wildlife Federation

O'Brien Committee, 155, 160
Office of Management and Budget, 218, 219–20, 222
Olson, Mancur, 69–76
OMB, *see* Office of Management and Budget
Oregon, 38
Orlans, F., 89–90, 213

PAC, *see* Political Action Committees
Pacelle, Wayne, 98, 100
Pacheco, Alex, 75, 205–6
Packers and Stockyards Act (1921), 30–1
Paget, Stephen, 56
Pallone, Frank, 125, 134
parliamentary questions, 16, 17, 18, 21, 22, 24, 115, 116
Peart, Fred, 166
Pelosi, Nancy, 125, 132
People for the Ethical Treatment of Animals, 63, 75, 82, 83–4, 94, 95, 96, 97, 98–9, 101, 107, 206
PETA, *see* People for the Ethical Treatment of Animals
Peterson, J., 160
Pet Theft Act (1990), 33–4, 208–9
pharmaceutical industry, 4, 27, 35, 45, 48–9, 50, 51–3, 56
Pharmaceutical Manufacturers' Association, 53, 55, 60, 61
Pig Breeders' Association, 111
Pig Husbandry Bill, 110–11, 114, 156–7, 165, 167, 235
Pink, Jean, 75
pluralism, 5–7, 9, 12, 163, 165, 166, 176, 202, 235, 236
PMA, *see* Pharmaceutical Manufacturers' Association
policy network analysis, 6–8, 10, 13, 229–37

Political Action Committees, 65, 102, 143–4
Political Animal Lobby, 101
Portugal, 9
Poulson, Jane, 4, 77
pound-seizure, 55, 75, 84, 93–4, 208
private members' bills, 17, 105, 110, 111, 112, 114, 115
product testing, 27, 60–1, 85, 86, 178, 188, 189, 196, 214–15
Protection of Animals Act (1911), 23, 27, 28
Putting People First, 53, 55, 56, 61
Puttnam, David, 113

Radford, Mike, 153
Raison, Timothy, 181
Ravenel, Arthur, 125, 129, 135
Reagan, Ronald, 219, 222, 235
Redmond, Martin, 117
Reid, Harry, 214
Resnick, Joseph, 204
RDS, *see* Research Defence Society
Redfearn, R., 86
Rees, Merlyn, 178
Refuge Wildlife Protection Act (1988), 42
Regan, Tom, 77, 84
Republican Party, 130–1, 150, 228
Research Defence Society, 52, 53, 54, 56, 60, 61, 62, 64–5, 71, 180, 181, 183, 191–2
Research for Health Charities Group, 52, 57
Respect for Animals, 42, 75
Rhode Island, 37
Rifkin, Carol, 135–6, 137
Rifkin, Jeremy, 135–6, 137
Roberts, Peter, 75
Robins, John, 148–9
Rollin, Bernard, 212, 223, 228
Rose, Charles, 142
Rowan, Andrew, 100, 221
Royal Society for Nature Conservation, 96, 105
Royal Society for the Prevention of Cruelty to Animals, 4, 96, 115; and animal experimentation,

85–6, 181, 184, 187; and enforcement of the law, 27, 156, 162, 212; and EU, 158–9; attitude to FAWC, 157; dominance of, 95, 97, 98, 104–5; Freedom Food scheme, 173; organization, 80, 94, 100, 101, 103, 107; relationship with the Home Office, 171–2, 178; relationship with MAFF, 171–2

Royal Society for the Protection of Birds, 4, 42, 95–6, 97, 98, 101, 103, 171, 172

RSPB, *see* Royal Society for the Protection of Birds

RSPCA, *see* Royal Society for the Prevention of Cruelty to Animals

Ryder, Chris, 24

Ryder, Richard, 101, 179, 180, 184

Schroeder, Patty, 132–3

Scottish Office, 22

Seriously Ill for Medical Research, 57

Shackleton, Lord, 113

Shamrock Farms, 50, 199, 200

Shapiro, Ken, 76

Sierra Club, 41, 95, 96, 99, 106

Silver Spring monkeys, 36, 205–6, 217, 223, 226

Singer, Peter, 77

Smith, Robert, 125, 129

Society & Animals, 1

Soskie, Frank, 178

sow stalls and tethers, 23

Sperling, Susan, 77, 78

Spira, Henry, 83, 89, 94, 149, 214

Stamp Dawkings, Marian, 165

state initiatives, 38

State Veterinary Service, 24, 162, 169, 173

Steinberg, Geoffrey, 117

Stenholm, Charles, 142, 144

Stephens, Martin, 221

Stevens, Christine, 75, 203, 207, 223, 226, 234

Studds, Gerry, 124

Suckling, Tony, 107, 189, 190

Sullivan, Louis, 216

Summit for the Animals, 105–6

SVS, *see* State Veterinary Service

Taub, Edward, 36, 205–6, 214, 217, 226, 233

Taylor, Teddy, 117

Torricelli, Robert, 125, 134

Towns, Edolphus, 124, 135

Trull, Frankie, 63

Tucker Foreman, Carol, 146

Tuesday Group, 106

Tweeten, Luther, 143

UFAW, *see* Universities Federation for Animal Welfare

Unilever, 46

United Egg Producers, 52

United Kingdom Egg Producers' Association, 52, 59, 174

United States Department of Agriculture, 140; and dietary policy, 148, 161, 230; and animal experimentation, 32–6, 62, 204, 205, 210, 217–23; and enforcement, 223–7; and farm animal welfare, 30, 89, 140, 146–7, 149, 150; and wild animals, 37

Universities Federation for Animal Welfare, 107

USDA, *see* United States Department of Agriculture

US Surgical Corporation, 55

veal calves, 23, 32, 86, 88, 115, 147, 153, 155, 156, 166–7

Volkmer, Harold, 142

Wallace, James, 117

Washington, 38

Washington Animal Research Network, 62

Webster, John, 165

Welfare of Animals (Slaughter or Killing) Regulation (1995), 23

Welsh Office, 22

Wickham Research Laboratories, 199, 200

wildlife conservation, 9; and hunting, 112; bills on, 17, 18, 19, 20, 21, 115–16, 122–3; in Britain, 27–9, 112, 115–16; in the USA, 37–8, 122–3, 124–7; organizations, 96–7, 99, 101–2, 103, 106; political opponents of, 40–3; reasons for, 72–3
Wilderness Society, 42
Wildlife and Countryside Act (1981), 28
Wildlife Legislative Fund of America, 40, 42, 106
Wild Mammals (Protection) Act (1996), 28

Williams, Alan, 117
World Society for the Protection of Animals, 96, 99, 103, 189
World Trade Organization, 25, 29
World Wide Fund for Nature, 96, 103, 105
World Wildlife Fund, 41, 96, 99
WSPA, *see* World Society for the Protection of Animals
WWF, *see* World Wide Fund for Nature
Wyngaarden, James, 216, 223

Zoo Check, 94